Shed by

Part Six

Steam Locomotives
Allocated to Sheds
81A to 89D
1950 - 1968

Tony Walmsley

Western

Published by St Petroc InfoPublishing, Cork, Ireland

Email: shedbyshed@ymail.com

stpetroc@yahoo.com

Printed by Brennan Graphics Ltd., Wexford, Ireland

Typeset by JM Studios, Cork, Ireland

ISBN 978-0-9560615-2-2

Shed by Shed

Index

Introduction

This is the second of a series of six books showing the full shed allocations of BR steam locomotives from August 1950 until the end of steam in August 1968. The series is aimed at historians and modellers enabling a clear picture to be gained of the types of and specific locomotives allocated to each shed over the 18 years covered. The full set of books will be:

• Part 1 – London Midland Region, sheds 1A to 28B
• Part 2 – Eastern Region, sheds 30A to 41K
• Part 3 – North Eastern Region, sheds 50A to 56G
• Part 4 – Scottish Region, sheds 60A to 68E
• Part 5 – Southern Region, sheds 70A to 75G
• Part 6 – Western Region, sheds 81A to 89D

Within each book the sheds are listed alphabetically by their names (as they appeared in the books of the time). Within each shed all the steam locomotives allocated to that shed are listed in numerical order together with the dates that they were there for, even if it was only for one month. Thus this publication shows more than those which just have "snapshots" of allocations for specific dates. Using an alphabetical list gets around the problem that sheds changed code (and sometimes Region) over time. Where sheds moved from one region to another the full information for the 18 years is repeated in both relevant books – for example Exmouth Junction appears in both the Southern and Western books with allocations in full from 1950 to 1966. For cross reference purposes, a full list of BR codes and the sheds they applied to over which dates is included at the end of this book.

Format

Under each shed, the locomotives are listed numerically with simple class headings. Alongside each number are pairs of dates (sometimes multiple pairs), for example:

41XX
4101 3/63 6/64
4102 1/52 4/52
    5/52 5/55

At this particular shed, 51XX class 4101 was allocated there from March 1963 and was moved away in June 1964. 4102 was there from January 1952 until April 1952, but then came back to the same shed from May 1952 until May 1955. **It is important to note that any date of 8/50 (or 9/50 in the case of London Midland** sheds/locomotives) just means the loco was already there at the time.

Data Sources

The originating data for this book came from the Ian Allan Locoshed book for 1950 which included allocations for all locomotives in August 1950 (September 1950 in the case of the London Midland Region). This data was then updated from the monthly column in the Ian Allan magazines Trains Illustrated and Modern Railways. The resulting data was then cross-checked against the Railway Correspondence and Travel Society magazine Railway Observer and annual allocation lists such as locoshed books. This resulted in a numerical list for all steam locomotives with all their shed allocations and dates up to withdrawal. Using a data sorting technique, this data was then sorted in shed order giving the lists you find in this book.

This methodology can inevitably lead to some errors. The possible error points are original BR mistakes, transcribing mistakes by the magazine publishers and transcribing mistakes by me when collating the data (see the note below on dates). In publishing these books I must ultimately take responsibility for any errors within, but I am reasonably confident they are a good transcription of the original data sources.

Note on Dates

At the start of this exercise I chose to record dates at the accuracy level of months. This was in common with other similar texts, indeed the style was influenced by Roger Harris' series of diesel and electric allocation books. This posed some problems as the BR data was generally reported in four weekly periods (there being 13 such periods in a year). Each Region adopted differing levels of accuracy, the London Midland almost always reported allocation changes weekly (though not withdrawals), whereas, at times, the Southern and Western Regions lumped two or more periods together into one statement of "twelve weeks ending". To get to a recordable month in these circumstances was something of a challenge, so I applied a rule of the greater number of days within the reported period to get the month. For example the week ending 3rd June would be recorded as a May change and the four weeks ending 18th February would be recorded as a February change. This was not completely infallible but the results are here to see. Thus the exact months quoted may be out slightly, but some random cross-checking has shown that most of my dates agree. In some cases records have not been found so a footnote indicates the maximum range of date movement.

Acknowledgements

Many people have given me encouragement in this venture, but two must be singled out for praise. Firstly my wife, Caroline, for having the patience to put up with me spending hours with the computer and source books compiling the data and secondly Mike Silver for giving me the encouragement and professional partnership to convert my scrappy notes into the published article you see here.

Aberbeeg
86H 8/50   86F 1/61
Closed 12/64

	57XX			45XX				
3640	8/50	3/52	4514	8/50	1/53	5685	4/55	3/58
3647	3/56	12/63	4522	8/50	6/52		**57XX**	
3664	10/60	7/64		6/54	1/55	5706	3/60	8/61
3674	12/55	11/57	4533	9/51	1/52	5729	9/55	9/57
3676	6/60	5/61	4593	1/52	10/56	5731	1/60	5/60
3680	8/50	8/53	4597	8/50	9/51	5733	8/50	5/53
3683	8/50	11/50		**57XX**		5750	10/51	9/55
3686	1/62	8/64	4604	7/62	9/64	5759	11/57	3/58
3691	2/51	2/53	4627	1/59	11/62	5777	8/50	4/54
3700	11/57	2/58	4637	8/50	10/51	5785	4/53	11/58
3708	8/50	9/50	4643	4/53	4/57	5789	8/50	4/53
3711	8/50	1/59	4650	7/61	11/64	5790	10/57	1/58
3712	7/60	5/62	4652	8/50	2/61	5794	9/55	12/59
3716	8/50	4/56		3/61	11/62		**56XX**	
3747	10/53	10/59	4663	6/64	?/64 **[A]**	6620	3/53	4/53
3766	7/63	8/63	4682	8/50	1/58	6621	3/54	8/55
3776	8/50	2/51	4685	8/50	5/62		4/57	7/62
	51XX		4686	8/50	7/54	6629	9/58	5/61
4138	4/57	5/57	4693	1/62	12/62	6638	1/53	1/54
	42XX			**42XX**		6642	9/50	2/53
4200	2/56	3/58	5202	11/51	7/54	6644	3/58	5/61
4214	8/50	4/54	5206	12/55	10/63	6653	3/58	9/59
4215	12/52	3/56	5207	8/50	12/53	6663	11/51	3/55
4217	8/50	12/52	5214	3/63	10/63		8/55	4/61
4222	7/51	6/52		1/64	9/64	6672	2/53	8/53
4223	8/50	3/51	5218	9/61	9/64	6685	8/50	5/52
4227	7/51	2/56	5236	8/50	11/51	6692	5/52	6/52
4237	4/57	10/63	5241	12/53	1/59		**72XX**	
4238	8/50	1/58	5257	9/59	6/61	7212	1/63	10/63
4246	4/61	1/63	5260	11/62	3/63	7217	6/64	7/64
4247	4/61	6/62	5264	7/60	6/63	7245	1/63	2/64
4250	7/54	4/61		**45XX**			**57XX**	
4258	10/57	1/58	5516	4/57	10/60	7703	8/50	1/58
4259	2/56	4/57	5520	8/50	9/55	7721	8/50	9/51
4267	8/50	7/51	5532	8/52	12/53	7755	10/59	5/62
4269	4/54	4/57	5539	10/56	2/58	7774	4/54	2/58
4271	11/50	5/53	5544	3/55	7/60	7775	8/50	10/55
4276	4/57	1/58	5564	6/56	4/57	7778	8/50	11/51
4277	4/55	6/63	5568	5/58	10/60	7787	9/60	6/61
	3/64	5/64	5573	9/53	12/53		**94XX**	
4285	1/58	10/63	5574	12/55	6/56	8402	8/50	3/54
4287	3/51	1/61		**56XX**		8429	2/58	2/60
4290	8/50	10/50	5602	5/52	3/54	8436	5/53	6/53
4291	1/58	8/62	5645	7/53	1/58		7/53	5/62
			5657	10/57	11/57	8437	2/59	?/?? **[B]**
						8439	3/54	5/57

8440	4/61	6/62	8776	8/50	4/52	9459	3/52	7/54
8444	12/59	7/63	8786	12/52	11/57		11/57	8/59
8484	1/58	2/58		4/58	7/63	9460	4/52	2/62
8489	1/58	10/61	8794	8/50	1/53	9482	6/62	11/63
8493	1/53	8/55	8796	4/57	1/58	9494	9/61	11/64
	3/63	11/64		**94XX**			**57XX**	
8494	2/53	9/54	9425	8/63	11/63	9682	7/60	11/64
	10/54	9/59	9427	12/53	5/59	9796	8/50	11/52
8499	4/61	6/62	9444	8/61	3/63			
	57XX		9446	7/63	4/64	**[A]** Before 12/64		
8705	3/56	4/61	9450	12/53	11/57	**[B]** Before 11/64		
8724	8/50	10/53	9458	9/56	1/61			

Abercynon
88E 8/50
Closed 10/64

	TV 0-6-2T			**16XX**		5629	12/62	7/64
216	4/53	9/53	1610	10/50	12/59	5630	8/50	10/50
218	11/50	10/51	1612	10/59	11/64		1/58	5/58
219	8/50	6/51	1620	8/50	6/60		1/61	1/63
236	8/50	10/51	1641	1/60	11/64	5632	3/63	9/64
279	3/53	9/53	1663	4/61	11/61	5637	8/50	8/55
290	3/53	9/53		**1901**		5641	8/50	9/64
295	8/50	6/51	2008	8/50	10/50	5643	8/50	6/61
304	8/50	7/57		**57XX**		5644	8/50	9/53
307	3/55	4/55	3650	10/55	5/58		5/58	6/63
316	10/53	7/56	3695	10/62	7/64	5647	7/60	9/62
322	1/52	9/54	3707	8/55	11/63	5650	8/50	9/52
337	8/50	1/53	3730	7/57	11/64	5660	9/53	1/54
349	8/56	2/57	3734	7/57	4/64	5680	2/52	1/54
351	8/50	7/56	3783	7/57	8/62		2/54	9/62
356	8/50	12/54	4601	11/57	2/59	5682	8/50	5/62
365	8/55	9/57	4626	8/57	2/59	5685	7/62	2/64
368	2/56	9/56	4631	8/57	2/59	5686	8/50	11/64
370	3/53	7/57	4672	2/57	4/57	5688	4/63	11/64
373	9/56	7/57	4679	12/63	11/64	5691	2/63	11/64
375	6/51	12/51	4686	8/57	2/59		**64XX**	
377	1/56	2/56	4692	11/58	2/59	6401	8/50	8/56
379	9/53	1/56		**54XX**		6411	8/50	8/58
380	8/50	9/56	5421	8/50	10/52	6427	6/56	7/56
381	4/57	7/57		**56XX**		6435	11/57	7/62
383	4/57	7/57	5601	10/57	11/64	6436	11/55	12/55
385	2/53	5/54	5605	6/64	11/64	6438	8/50	12/60
386	8/50	3/56	5614	8/62	8/63		**56XX**	
390	7/56	1/57	5615	8/61	5/63	6603	6/63	3/64
	4/57	7/57	5617	1/54	8/62	6628	9/63	11/64
393	7/56	5/57	5618	8/50	9/59	6649	10/63	11/64
397	8/50	4/57	5619	8/50	10/50	6654	9/64	11/64
399	11/54	8/56	5623	10/50	10/60	6661	8/50	9/53
			5627	11/57	4/63	6685	3/64	9/64

	57XX			57XX				
7726	11/58	7/60	8717	1/62	7/64	9668	10/62	12/63
7733	11/56	5/60	8730	6/60	6/62	9723	6/62	6/62
7744	11/56	8/62	8735	11/58	1/62	9728	5/60	5/62
7751	1/58	5/58	9611	8/62	11/64	9759	7/62	9/62
	94XX		9622	11/58	11/64	9769	6/57	8/57
8420	8/51	3/53	9632	7/64	11/64	9776	6/57	8/57
8424	9/51	3/53	9642	12/56	5/58		3MT 2-6-2T	
8489	9/52	3/53	9667	4/64	11/64	82037	6/56	6/56

Aberdare
86J 8/50   88J 1/61
Closed 3/65

	RR 0-6-2T							
65	8/50	1/53	3610	8/50	6/62	4257	8/50	1/61
	TV 0-6-2T			7/64	3/65		7/61	9/62
204	8/50	11/53	3616	10/63	4/64		10/62	10/63
208	11/52	5/54	3627	2/60	2/63	4258	9/64	3/65
282	8/50	11/51	3634	12/63	7/64	4262	1/58	8/62
	2/53	5/54	3647	9/52	3/56	4263	3/55	10/55
284	8/50	10/52	3655	8/50	1/63	4264	8/50	9/55
357	11/51	1/53	3680	8/53	7/54	4266	5/52	5/53
362	8/50	1/53	3695	12/52	10/62	4268	11/64	2/65
371	6/52	11/52	3699	1/53	2/65		6/62	9/62
374	8/50	2/53	3716	4/56	11/62	4278	9/63	7/64
385	6/52	2/53		2/63	11/63	4279	11/62	1/64
	2021		3747	8/50	10/53	4289	8/61	9/62
2159	8/50	6/51	3753	8/50	1/65	4296	3/52	5/52
	28XX		3796	7/64	2/65	4297	8/50	11/52
2806	8/50	12/50		28XX			12/52	6/57
2808	8/50	5/54	3816	9/62	9/63		57XX	
2810	9/53	8/59	3822	9/62	11/62	4688	5/62	12/63
2813	11/58	10/60	3839	9/62	12/63		42XX	
2828	8/50	12/58	3843	9/62	9/63	5200	1/64	3/65
2831	8/50	2/60	3845	9/62	10/62	5210	2/64	9/64
2833	12/58	3/59	3847	9/62	6/63	5211	12/63	7/64
2836	8/50	12/58	3850	2/59	12/63	5223	9/64	3/65
2857	2/62	11/62	3853	8/62	9/63	5226	7/64	3/65
2862	8/52	10/52	3860	8/62	4/64	5230	6/64	7/64
2863	8/52	5/59	3866	4/59	4/64	5237	8/50	9/64
2870	8/50	5/59		51XX		5242	7/64	1/65
2873	9/59	11/62	4122	10/63	6/64	5245	8/50	10/58
2874	12/60	1/62	4124	10/63	12/63	5249	4/59	10/63
2876	6/53	8/63	4136	11/63	6/64	5252	10/63	3/65
2880	8/50	9/51		42XX		5256	1/64	3/65
2886	4/60	11/62	4225	8/61	9/62	5258	8/50	1/63
2895	12/63	1/64	4228	8/50	3/62	5263	8/50	12/63
	57XX		4236	1/62	8/62	5264	6/56	6/57
3603	10/58	4/64	4237	10/63	3/64		56XX	
3605	8/50	4/57	4252	10/62	1/63	5620	3/63	7/63
			4255	6/56	9/59	5624	6/55	10/63

5633	6/57	9/63
5638	5/51	5/52
5642	7/59	8/62
5644	9/53	5/58
5647	9/62	3/64
5649	8/50	3/63
5680	9/62	11/63
5698	9/53	8/62

57XX

5741	9/52	11/56
5770	8/50	9/53
5787	8/50	10/54
5796	8/50	8/53
5797	1/53	8/58

61XX

| 6144 | 12/63 | 7/64 |
| 6158 | 10/63 | 7/64 |

43XX

6361	6/56	5/64
6362	6/61	8/61
6386	6/61	8/61

64XX

6410	8/50	9/59
6413	8/50	7/59
6417	10/53	4/58
6431	7/56	4/58
	7/58	2/62
6437	8/50	5/60

56XX

6605	8/50	10/63
6622	8/50	4/64
6627	3/63	11/63
6628	8/50	9/63
6649	9/53	9/58
	7/63	10/63

6651	8/50	1/63
6652	8/50	7/62
6654	9/51	6/52
6661	9/53	4/64
6664	10/60	12/63
6673	3/62	2/63
6685	5/52	6/52
6687	5/53	5/62
6690	5/62	4/64
6692	8/50	5/52
	6/52	12/53
6693	8/50	3/52

57XX

| 6750 | 8/59 | 2/60 |

72XX

7203	11/59	3/62
7204	3/63	7/63
7205	1/65	3/65
7208	8/61	9/62
7209	11/62	6/64
7212	10/63	2/64
7213	8/50	11/60
7214	5/58	6/61
	11/62	12/63
7216	5/52	2/62
7221	8/50	9/62
7222	12/63	1/65
7224	11/59	6/61
7226	11/64	11/64
7234	11/62	10/63
7237	8/59	9/61
7242	8/50	2/51
7247	11/62	3/63
7251	9/63	1/64
7253	2/64	3/65

43XX

| 7322 | (ex 9300 | 4/57) |
| | 6/61 | 8/61 |

74XX

| 7423 | 8/50 | 7/64 |
| 7435 | 11/63 | 7/64 |

57XX

7720	8/50	5/62
7748	8/50	5/51
7773	8/50	12/59

94XX

| 8444 | 5/54 | 12/59 |
| 8445 | 7/54 | 6/62 |

57XX

8723	1/63	2/63
	4/63	7/64
8724	10/53	0/54
8786	8/50	10/50
9600	10/62	11/64
9607	8/50	3/64
9609	8/50	2/57
9615	1/65	3/65
9671	2/63	6/64
9678	3/64	4/64
9711	1/63	6/64
9712	8/50	8/62
9731	5/53	4/63
9747	12/62	1/63

WD 2-8-0

| 90323 | 11/52 | 3/53 |
| 90573 | 11/52 | 3/53 |

Abergavenny
86K 8/50
Closed 1/58

57XX

3700	2/58	6/60
3712	8/59	6/60
5790	3/58	3/59

43XX

| 6366 | 2/60 | 10/61 |

57XX

6734	5/52	1/59
7721	3/59	5/60
7736	8/59	6/60
7771	8/59	6/60

7774	2/58	3/58
7787	8/59	6/60
8711	7/59	6/60
9662	6/59	6/60

3MT 2-6-2T Stanier

40091	12/51	1/54
40097	12/51	5/55
40098	3/52	10/54
	3/55	3/60
40105	12/51	1/54
40141	12/51	6/54

| 40145 | 12/51 | 12/53 |
| 40171 | 12/51 | 7/60 |

2MT 2-6-2T

41201	8/50	5/52
	3/53	10/59
41202	8/50	3/55
41203	8/50	9/55
41204	8/50	11/59

G1 & G2a 0-8-0

| 48899 | 8/50 | 7/55 |
| 48921 | 8/50 | 3/58 |

49006	9/50	5/51	49243	8/50	11/54	58899	8/50	7/53
49028	9/50	11/54	49316	8/50	1/57	58902	8/50	11/54
49046	8/50	12/54	49345	8/50	11/54	58911	10/51	8/52
49051	8/50	11/54		**G2 0-8-0**		58912	8/50	12/50
49064	8/50	9/59	49403	8/50	11/54	58913	8/50	5/52
49082	4/57	5/57	49409	8/50	2/58	58915	8/50	3/54
49113	8/50	9/55		3/58	5/59	58916	8/50	9/50
49121	8/50	8/58	49422	8/50	11/54	58919	8/50	12/52
49146	8/50	11/54	49440	5/57	10/57	58921	10/51	6/53
49161	8/50	4/57	49448	6/51	11/54	58924	10/50	5/54
49168	8/50	11/54		**2F 0-6-2T**		58925	8/50	7/55
	1/55	9/55	58880	8/50	8/52	58926	5/54	9/55
	9/57	1/58	58888	8/50	5/54	58933	8/50	12/51
49174	8/50	9/55	58889	12/50	2/53	58935	8/50	9/51
	9/57	2/58	58891	8/50	7/55		**WD 2-8-0**	
49226	8/50	12/54	58895	8/50	9/51	90161	3/52	2/56

Banbury
84C 8/50   2D 9/63
Closed 10/66

	14XX		2816	8/50	1/58	2897	8/50	11/56
1401	8/50	1/52		9/58	9/59	2898	8/50	12/52
1411	8/50	9/50	2817	10/52	7/55	2899	8/50	5/52
1440	11/61	4/62	2819	10/52	3/53		**29XX**	
	5/62	3/63	2822	9/54	8/57	2981	8/50	3/51
1445	8/61	9/61	2823	9/52	8/58		**ROD**	
1453	11/61	7/62	2827	8/52	10/56	3017	5/52	10/52
1455	9/61	4/63	2834	10/52	4/55	3020	8/50	5/54
1458	8/50	12/50	2835	7/52	12/56	3024	11/52	9/53
	2251		2841	8/59	9/59	3026	6/51	9/53
2202	6/53	7/55	2845	6/62	7/63	3043	8/50	9/53
	9/55	3/56	2847	8/50	1/58		**2251**	
2209	9/53	7/55	2850	12/53	6/56	3216	8/50	5/53
	9/55	6/56	2851	6/62	3/63	3217	3/60	6/62
2210	11/64	6/65	2853	8/50	5/52	3218	8/50	5/53
2211	9/58	5/59		9/58	1/59		**57XX**	
2221	5/64	11/64	2855	7/62	1/63	3630	8/50	1/52
2230	9/58	7/59	2857	10/51	7/55	3646	10/55	3/61
2234	9/58	9/59	2858	4/54	11/54	3694	8/50	9/53
2246	5/53	1/58	2863	8/50	5/51		11/53	1/54
2247	5/53	6/57	2866	7/62	3/63		3/54	7/55
2256	8/50	7/55	2867	9/54	12/56		**28XX**	
	9/55	6/61	2869	8/50	12/50	3802	8/50	5/52
2259	9/53	12/58	2875	11/62	3/63	3806	6/62	12/63
2289	5/63	6/64	2882	5/58	8/58	3809	1/61	4/64
2295	8/50	10/51	2883	8/50	5/51	3816	6/59	4/60
2297	9/53	6/60	2886	8/50	4/58	3817	6/60	8/65
	28XX		2888	11/61	2/63	3819	8/50	8/58
2805	8/50	5/51	2889	1/61	5/62	3820	8/50	10/52
2812	9/52	8/58	2890	10/58	11/59		5/58	3/59

3821	12/61	7/64
3825	10/62	7/64
3828	11/62	9/64
3829	8/50	1/51
	9/54	10/57
3831	8/50	4/58
3835	9/54	12/56
3836	7/55	7/55
3839	8/52	10/52
3843	6/60	12/60
3845	10/62	6/64
3846	6/60	9/60
3849	8/50	5/51
	7/62	4/64
3850	12/63	10/64
3852	10/62	4/64
3855	1/61	10/64
3856	10/58	12/59
3857	10/62	3/64
3858	5/58	9/59
3859	9/52	2/58
3861	8/50	12/52
3863	8/50	5/52
	6/59	9/59
3865	8/50	5/51
4073		
4078	10/59	4/60
51XX		
4101	3/63	6/64
4102	1/52	4/52
	5/52	5/55
4105	9/62	2/64
4112	3/62	7/62
4149	8/50	2/63
4154	4/60	5/65
57XX		
4631	8/50	7/55
4646	8/50	6/51
49XX		
4900	10/51	8/52
4910	3/60	7/60
	9/60	11/60
4918	12/50	8/52
4923	3/60	6/60
4924	10/57	6/59
4942	9/55	6/60
4960	12/50	8/52
4964	10/57	6/62
4977	3/52	6/56
4980	12/50	12/55
4987	10/52	11/55
4990	8/59	10/59
4998	11/62	10/63

4073		
5057	11/59	4/60
51XX		
5137	6/51	10/51
5141	8/51	9/52
5152	9/55	9/61
5167	4/60	1/62
5170	5/53	12/59
43XX		
5306	10/55	9/58
5307	6/52	10/52
5317	8/50	4/56
5324	8/50	10/52
5332	8/50	10/58
5337	1/59	8/59
5351	5/59	8/59
5361	8/50	10/58
5369	7/51	11/51
5375	2/59	8/59
5379	8/56	5/58
5391	9/50	9/52
5399	12/52	9/55
54XX		
5404	8/50	11/57
5407	8/50	6/60
5417	8/50	5/51
5420	1/58	11/61
5424	8/50	4/59
57XX		
5724	8/50	9/53
	11/53	8/55
58XX		
5815	2/58	4/58
49XX		
5912	9/61	1/63
5921	1/58	6/60
5926	4/62	8/62
5930	8/50	4/60
5933	5/60	11/60
5945	7/54	9/54
5947	3/53	11/59
	4/60	6/62
5950	9/52	5/55
5954	1/52	6/56
5967	8/50	8/52
	11/52	1/55
5988	3/60	7/62
5989	10/57	11/60
5990	3/60	1/65
5994	1/51	1/52
61XX		
6129	8/62	1/65
43XX		
6311	11/58	2/50
6317	1/61	6/63

6331	11/55	4/59
6332	7/51	5/52
6335	2/60	7/60
6342	8/50	6/53
6354	9/50	12/50
6355	8/56	10/56
6362	4/55	4/57
6364	10/59	1/60
6367	1/61	10/63
6387	10/55	12/60
6390	8/50	10/52
6392	6/57	10/57
64XX		
6403	1/60	9/62
6418	8/50	7/51
6421	7/60	9/61
6429	5/59	9/61
56XX		
6625	4/52	10/52
6635	1/58	3/58
6671	6/65	9/65
6696	8/50	10/52
6697	6/65	10/65
68XX		
6803	8/50	7/51
6816	8/50	2/53
6819	8/50	7/53
6823	9/57	5/58
6833	1/52	7/52
6835	8/50	5/51
	6/51	7/52
6839	8/50	4/54
6848	3/58	5/58
6854	8/50	9/52
6856	5/52	9/52
6860	10/52	6/53
6879	5/52	9/52
49XX		
6901	12/50	1/52
6903	7/64	9/65
6904	9/61	1/65
6906	8/50	4/65
6907	6/64	2/65
6911	11/59	4/65
6915	7/64	2/65
6916	6/64	8/65
6917	1/65	9/65
6926	5/65	6/65
6929	8/50	8/52
	11/52	10/63
6930	5/65	10/65
6934	10/64	9/65
6949	9/58	1/60
6951	3/63	10/65

6952	5/60	9/62
	11/62	10/65

6959

6963	12/51	5/52
6964	5/65	9/65
6966	12/51	8/56
6976	12/51	9/65
6979	8/50	2/65
6980	10/64	9/65

4073

7011	10/59	4/60

72XX

7207	6/60	11/64
7208	11/60	8/61
7217	6/59	9/59
	11/60	2/61
7218	11/62	8/64
7221	12/63	11/64
7228	2/60	9/61
7236	6/60	11/63
7237	6/59	8/59
7244	2/60	8/61
7247	1/60	7/61

43XX

7305	5/58	11/60
7308	6/57	1/60
7315	10/52	12/60
7325	(ex 9303	5/58)
	9/56	10/61
7334	(ex 9312	12/58)
	9/56	6/60

57XX

7763	8/50	10/55

78XX

7800	12/50	7/51
	10/51	6/52
7805	8/50	9/50
7806	8/50	9/50
7811	8/50	7/52
7823	10/51	12/55

6959

7905	11/59	6/64
7912	4/62	9/65
7929	9/60	6/62

94XX

8400	8/50	7/55
8405	8/50	7/55
8407	8/50	5/55
8452	6/51	4/57
	6/57	5/60
8459	8/50	7/55
8498	11/59	5/60

57XX

8729	8/50	8/51
8787	8/50	7/55

43XX

9303	9/56	
	(renum 7325	5/58)
9312	9/56	
	(renum 7334	12/58)

94XX

9425	6/51	9/55
9426	9/50	5/55
9438	3/51	9/54
9449	6/51	6/60

57XX

9774	7/55	9/55
9782	8/50	7/51

5MT 4-6-0

44710	9/65	8/66
44840	12/65	9/66
44860	9/65	9/66
44869	9/65	5/66
44872	10/65	10/66
44914	12/65	10/66
44936	9/65	2/66
44942	9/65	9/66
45089	9/65	9/66
45114	9/65	2/66
45222	12/65	2/66
45288	9/65	2/66
45299	9/65	10/66
45308	9/65	10/66
45324	12/65	2/66
45331	9/65	8/66
45392	9/65	2/66
45418	9/65	2/66
45426	9/65	2/66
45454	9/65	2/66
45493	9/65	9/66

2MT 2-6-0

46522	3/66	3/66
	7/66	10/66
46526	3/62	9/62
46527	3/62	9/62

8F 2-8-0

48402	7/55	7/55
48412	7/55	5/58
48419	7/55	2/58
48471	7/55	5/58

7MT 4-6-2

70045	9/65	1/66
70046	9/65	1/66
70047	9/65	1/66
70050	9/65	1/66
70051	9/65	1/66
70052	9/65	1/66
70053	9/65	1/66
70054	9/65	1/66

5MT 4-6-0

73013	6/65	4/66
73014	6/65	4/66
73048	6/65	4/66

WD 2-8-0

90148	3/58	12/61
90192	12/51	7/52
90261	8/59	2/62
90268	6/59	12/61
90312	5/51	11/52
90313	12/51	4/54
	4/58	12/62
90315	6/60	8/62
90466	7/55	2/59
90483	8/59	12/62
90485	1/52	11/52
	10/61	12/62
90565	4/61	9/61
90572	6/52	7/52
	6/59	7/59
90579	5/51	7/55
90585	5/55	7/62
90693	1/61	9/61
90716	4/55	7/59

9F 2-10-0

92000	9/61	3/62
92002	7/64	11/64
92004	3/63	10/66
92013	6/65	9/66
92028	3/65	7/65
92030	6/65	10/66
92033	6/65	7/65
92067	6/65	10/66
92073	6/65	9/66
92074	6/65	12/65
92087	6/65	7/65
92107	11/63	9/64
92118	7/64	11/64
92128	7/64	9/66
92129	7/64	9/66
92132	6/65	8/65
	9/65	8/66
92203	3/63	9/66
92204	3/63	9/63
92212	9/59	6/61
92213	11/59	10/66
92214	11/59	11/61
92215	12/59	9/63
92217	3/63	9/63
92218	3/63	10/66
92221	5/58	6/59
	3/60	6/60
	9/60	10/60

92222	5/58	6/59	92226	5/58	7/60	92233	9/59	1/61
	3/60	6/60	92227	5/58	1/61	92234	9/59	9/61
92223	5/58	6/59		7/62	10/66		11/61	7/62
	3/60	6/60	92228	5/58	10/66		9/64	10/66
92224	5/58	6/59	92229	7/58	10/58	92247	7/62	9/66
	11/64	8/66	92230	7/58	10/58	92250	12/58	11/59
92225	5/58	6/59	92232	9/59	8/62			

Barnstaple
72E 8/50   83F 9/63
Closed 11/64

	57XX		30671	6/56	7/59	41214	1/63	8/64
4666	6/63	9/63		**T9**		41216	1/63	11/64
	M7		30717	8/52	9/52	41223	3/63	6/64
30023	9/60	10/61		**N**		41224	3/63	6/64
30033	5/59	12/62	31840	6/52	9/52	41230	3/63	9/63
30036	8/50	3/51	31841	6/52	9/52	41245	9/63	12/63
30042	8/50	5/51	31842	8/50	5/51	41248	12/63	11/64
30044	8/50	5/51		6/52	11/52	41249	12/63	11/64
30245	6/52	11/52		6/54	2/55	41276	3/63	12/63
30247	8/50	9/52		6/55	11/56	41283	3/63	9/64
	11/52	10/61	31843	11/52	11/56	41290	5/61	9/64
30250	8/50	9/57	31844	7/53	9/53	41294	5/57	3/63
30251	3/51	1/63	31845	7/53	9/53	41295	8/54	8/61
30252	3/51	2/59		**E1/R**		41296	11/56	3/57
30253	3/51	11/53	32095	8/50	9/53	41297	9/55	3/63
	1/54	10/61	32096	8/50	6/55	41298	7/53	3/63
30254	9/52	1/63	32608	8/50	5/57	41310	8/61	3/63
30255	5/51	9/60	32610	8/50	4/56	41312	1/60	3/63
30256	5/51	5/59	32696	8/50	1/56	41313	1/60	3/63
30321	8/50	3/51		**2MT 2-6-2T**		41314	5/57	3/63
30375	5/59	11/59	41208	12/63	11/64			
30670	8/50	3/51	41210	3/63	2/64			
	9/61	1/63	41213	3/63	12/63			

Barry
88C 8/50
Closed to Steam 10/64

	RR 0-6-2T		215	3/53	9/53	271	8/50	4/51
57	8/50	10/51	236	8/52	12/52	274	8/50	4/51
58	8/50	9/51		**BR 0-6-2T**		276	8/50	4/51
59	8/50	9/51	240	8/50	3/51		**TV 0-6-2T**	
	TV 0-6-2T		263	8/50	3/51	285	3/53	7/53
210	3/53	12/53	267	8/50	3/51	303	9/53	4/56
211	3/53	9/53	270	8/50	4/51	306	8/50	3/56

No.			No.			No.		
312	8/50	1/55	4616	11/58	2/59	6620	8/50	3/53
322	8/50	1/52	4618	12/58	2/63		4/53	9/53
349	12/54	8/56		4/63	10/63	6621	6/64	7/64
357	1/53	12/55	4632	11/58	4/59	6637	8/50	7/64
361	8/50	7/56	4634	11/58	2/59	6641	8/50	9/59
372	8/50	1/55	4667	12/58	4/64	6643	8/50	7/64
373	8/50	9/56	4675	4/64	9/64	6650	2/63	9/64
375	12/51	10/54	4690	8/50	12/50	6653	8/50	3/51
376	12/54	9/56	4692	8/50	11/58	6654	6/64	9/64
377	2/56	4/56	**51XX**			6655	3/60	7/63
379	8/50	2/52	5183	8/50	10/50	6656	5/62	8/62
382	8/50	3/56		7/53	8/56	6657	3/60	4/60
387	8/50	4/56	5195	8/50	8/53	6658	8/50	9/62
388	8/50	6/56	**45XX**			6664	2/51	5/51
389	8/50	3/55	5527	9/53	2/58	6668	8/50	9/53
390	11/53	7/56		5/58	5/58	6669	8/50	9/53
393	9/53	7/56	5529	9/53	2/58	6670	7/63	10/63
394	8/50	7/56	5534	9/53	10/53	6696	12/61	11/63
399	9/53	11/53		5/58	5/58	6697	4/60	7/64
16XX			5568	5/58	5/58	**57XX**		
1600	8/50	3/59	**56XX**			6712	8/50	10/57
1615	8/50	1/57	5609	8/50	10/60	6722	8/50	1/58
1901			5614	8/50	9/61	6723	8/50	6/57
1993	8/50	4/51	5615	11/58	4/59	6724	8/50	9/57
2008	10/50	9/53	5619	10/50	7/64	6733	8/50	5/58
94XX			5621	8/50	11/63	6736	8/50	2/54
3405	11/58	12/58	5622	1/58	4/59	6738	8/50	2/59
3406	11/58	12/58	5627	8/50	1/56	6740	8/50	1/58
57XX			5632	8/50	1/56	6745	8/50	7/58
3615	11/62	4/64	5634	5/60	9/61	6746	8/50	7/58
	6/64	9/64		11/61	9/62	6747	8/50	5/58
3663	8/62	1/63	5636	3/60	1/61	6748	8/50	1/58
3668	6/62	7/63	5639	7/60	5/62	750	8/50	4/58
3689	11/62	1/63	5643	6/61	7/63	6751	4/58	10/58
	10/63	7/64	5648	8/50	11/57	6752	8/50	7/60
3690	5/62	11/63	5653	6/62	1/63	6753	8/50	2/59
3710	8/60	5/63	5664	8/50	7/62	6754	8/50	5/60
3727	5/59	4/64	5665	8/50	9/55	6758	8/50	2/59
3748	8/62	1/63	5667	8/50	9/63	6765	2/58	7/60
3784	10/63	9/64	5668	6/61	9/64	6767	3/58	2/59
51XX			5679	12/62	1/63	6769	8/50	6/56
4160	8/50	9/53	5685	11/60	8/61		2/58	2/59
4161	8/50	9/53	5689	1/63	9/64	6770	8/57	2/59
4163	8/50	9/53	5699	8/50	11/64	6771	8/57	3/58
4177	10/50	9/55	**57XX**			6773	3/58	6/59
42XX			5769	6/57	3/58	6774	12/50	6/56
4224	8/53	4/55	**64XX**			6775	12/50	6/56
4267	5/52	1/56	6408	1/58	3/58		3/58	7/60
4273	4/64	9/64	**56XX**			**72XX**		
4283	4/64	9/64	6602	7/51	5/52	7202	9/62	7/64
45XX			6614	8/50	9/53	7208	9/62	4/64
4578	9/53	1/58	6615	8/50	8/59	7209	6/64	8/64
57XX			6619	8/50	8/56	7221	9/62	12/63
4601	8/50	11/57		9/56	2/63	7223	7/63	11/63
4610	1/57	2/59				7227	4/58	10/58

7228	9/62	7/63
7230	1/56	2/59
7231	9/62	6/63
7232	6/63	11/63
7238	6/63	4/64
7241	1/56	1/63
7252	3/55	8/59
57XX		
7717	12/58	3/60
7726	9/52	12/53
	7/58	11/58
7751	12/58	9/59
7766	12/58	10/60
7779	9/52	11/53
94XX		
8419	2/59	2/60
8425	8/62	9/62
8437	9/57	2/59
8446	9/56	9/64
8450	6/56	5/59
8451	8/50	9/53
8455	11/53	7/55
8457	6/56	9/56
8458	8/50	9/53
8459	6/56	1/59
8460	8/50	3/53
8461	8/50	9/53
8465	2/52	3/53
	9/56	12/58
8470	5/51	10/52

8478	6/52	7/52
8481	1/60	2/63
8484	7/52	8/52
8495	10/52	12/52
57XX		
8728	8/62	1/63
8735	8/50	11/58
8764	3/60	5/62
8776	8/62	1/63
8780	2/59	5/59
94XX		
9425	3/59	8/63
9426	10/63	9/64
9437	8/62	9/62
	10/63	12/63
9442	10/62	11/62
9453	9/56	1/59
9461	10/63	9/64
9470	11/53	3/55
9472	11/62	1/63
57XX		
9603	8/62	1/63
	10/63	12/63
9622	7/55	11/58
9631	8/50	10/58
9648	8/62	1/63
9676	8/50	11/58
9681	8/62	1/63
9713	8/62	1/63
9727	8/62	1/63

9775	8/62	1/63
9776	8/50	1/51
9780	7/61	1/63
9794	8/62	1/63
	10/63	9/64
9798	12/63	9/64
3MT 2-6-2T		
82000	7/53	9/53
82001	9/53	7/55
82002	9/53	7/55
82003	9/53	3/58
82004	9/53	4/55
82005	9/53	7/55
82006	9/53	7/55
82007	9/53	7/55
82008	9/53	8/55
82009	9/53	4/55
82030	12/54	5/55
82031	12/54	1/55
82032	1/55	7/55
82035	4/55	5/58
82036	4/55	3/58
82037	7/55	6/56
	6/56	4/58
82039	5/55	5/58
82040	5/55	5/58
82041	6/55	5/58
82042	7/55	7/58
82043	7/55	5/58
82044	7/55	5/58

Bath Green Park
71G 8/50   82F 2/58
Closed 3/66

	2251	
2283	8/63	10/63
57XX		
3677	6/65	9/65
3681	9/64	3/66
3742	1/59	1/65
3758	10/64	3/66
61XX		
6113	11/64	11/64
94XX		
8436	11/64	6/65
8486	3/65	6/65
57XX		
8745	11/63	9/64
8747	9/61	12/61
9770	7/63	11/63

	BB/WC	
34040	5/51	6/51
	6/52	10/54
34041	5/51	6/51
	11/51	10/54
34042	5/51	6/51
	11/51	10/54
34043	5/51	6/52
34044	5/51	11/51
2P 4-4-0		
40505	8/50	5/51
40509	6/55	7/57
40527	6/55	2/56
40568	8/50	9/53
	1/54	9/55
40569	8/50	9/53
	1/54	6/55

40601	8/50	9/53
	1/54	6/55
	9/55	12/59
40696	8/50	5/62
40697	8/50	2/62
40698	8/50	7/60
40700	8/50	7/62
2MT 2-6-2T		
41240	8/50	9/53
41241	8/50	5/58
	9/58	10/59
41242	8/50	5/62
41243	8/50	7/62
4MT 2-6-0		
43013	8/50	2/52
43017	8/50	6/53

43036	8/50	6/53	48471	9/61	12/61	73116	8/56	10/56
4F 0-6-0			48525	8/64	10/65		7/57	9/57
43853	1/63	6/63	48660	2/62	6/65		5/58	3/60
43875	8/50	1/52	48706	5/65	3/66	73164	9/63	11/63
44096	9/50	3/60	48707	7/64	9/64	**4MT 4-6-0**		
44102	10/63	9/64	48730	7/64	9/64	75004	5/62	10/62
44146	7/57	11/64	48737	12/61	5/65	75070	6/56	3/57
44235	8/50	1/52	48760	7/65	3/66	75071	6/56	11/62
44355	8/50	10/59	**0F 0-4-0T**			75072	6/56	10/62
44411	5/62	9/63	51202	8/50	11/52	75073	3/57	11/62
44422	8/50	4/60	**7F 2-8-0**			**4MT 2-6-4T**		
44523	8/50	6/60	53800	8/50	5/59	80037	1/65	3/65
44535	8/50	1/52	53801	8/50	6/61	80039	1/65	3/65
44557	8/50	7/57	53802	8/50	3/60	80059	6/65	12/65
44558	8/50	1/63	53803	8/50	2/62	**3MT 2-6-2T**		
44559	8/50	1/63	53804	8/50	2/62	82004	10/59	10/65
44560	8/50	4/60	53805	8/50	3/61	82037	5/58	1/59
44561	8/50	4/62	53806	8/50	1/64	82041	3/59	12/65
5MT 4-6-0			53807	8/50	9/64	**9F 2-10-0**		
44826	8/50	9/53	53808	8/50	3/64	92000	6/61	9/61
44830	8/50	9/53	53809	8/50	7/64	92001	6/61	10/61
44839	8/50	9/53	53810	8/50	11/63		6/62	9/62
44917	3/52	5/58	**5MT 4-6-0**			92006	6/61	9/61
44945	8/50	2/51	73001	3/65	12/65	92210	6/62	7/62
45440	8/50	5/58	73015	6/65	9/65	92212	6/61	6/62
Sentinel 0-4-0T			73019	5/58	7/60	92220	7/62	9/62
47190	8/52	3/61		9/60	4/62		8/63	10/63
47191	8/50	7/59	73023	6/64	9/64	92224	8/63	9/63
3F 0-6-0T			73028	5/58	7/60	92233	6/62	9/62
47275	8/50	3/62		9/60	5/61	92245	6/62	9/62
47276	3/64	3/66	73030	2/65	3/65			
47308	3/64	8/64	73031	11/61	4/62			
47316	8/50	1/63	73047	7/55	7/64			
47465	8/50	6/63	73049	7/55	4/60			
47496	8/50	11/63		6/62	9/64			
47506	11/63	3/66	73050	6/54	7/62			
47539	10/62	1/63		11/62	3/64			
47542	8/50	11/58	73051	6/54	9/65			
47544	3/62	12/65	73052	6/54	1/65			
47557	8/50	2/64	73054	4/61	9/65			
47623	11/63	3/64	73068	4/64	1/65			
8F 2-8-0				4/65	12/65			
48172	4/64	7/64	73073	4/55	7/55			
48307	6/64	9/64	73074	4/55	7/55			
48309	8/64	3/66	73087	8/56	10/56			
48347	12/61	9/64		7/57	9/57			
48409	8/64	4/65		5/58	9/58			
48431	1/64	7/64		5/59	3/60			
48436	9/61	12/61		6/60	8/61			
48438	6/64	9/64	73088	5/58	9/58			
48444	7/64	1/66	73092	7/64	4/65			
48463	3/64	7/64	73093	3/65	4/65			
48468	1/62	6/64						
48470	6/64	9/64						

Brecon
89B 8/50   88K 1/61
Closed 12/62

Cam R 0-6-0			2409	12/52	3/53		**57XX**	
844	1/53	4/53	2458	1/54	4/54	7794	8/59	10/59
873	1/53	3/53	2468	8/50	12/52		**94XX**	
896	12/52	3/53	2482	10/50	11/52	8438	9/55	11/57
	2251		2483	10/50	8/52		**2MT 2-6-0**	
2225	5/58	5/59	2513	11/54	7/55	46508	12/54	11/59
2235	7/54	9/58	2538	11/52	1/53	46516	7/53	10/59
2280	4/59	8/59		**57XX**		46517	7/53	6/57
2286	7/53	7/54	3634	7/55	8/55	46518	5/53	10/59
2287	8/50	12/59	3638	8/50	10/59	46521	3/53	10/59
	23XX		3706	8/50	10/59	46522	4/53	10/59
2343	8/50	1/53	3767	8/50	10/59	46523	4/53	1/55
2351	8/50	1/53	3770	8/50	9/59	46524	4/53	3/59
2354	10/52	3/53		**58XX**				
2401	8/50	12/52	5801	8/50	11/55			

Bristol Barrow Road
22A 9/50   82E 2/58
Closed 11/65

	2251		3758	3/64	10/64	4993	6/64	1/65
2205	11/58	12/58	3765	10/62	7/63		**42XX**	
2215	3/59	4/59	3795	7/61	11/61	5203	8/62	2/63
2217	11/62	12/63		1/62	5/63	5215	10/62	2/63
2221	6/62	5/64	3798	9/64	11/64		**43XX**	
2229	11/59	8/62		**28XX**		5393	11/58	12/58
2251	11/62	11/63	3802	9/64	7/65		4/59	9/59
2277	11/62	11/63	3836	12/64	10/65		**49XX**	
	28XX		3844	9/65	10/65	5932	4/65	10/65
2822	9/64	1/65	3863	9/64	10/65	5955	8/64	5/65
	2251			**51XX**		5971	7/65	12/65
3218	10/62	12/63	4103	10/62	9/64	5975	6/64	8/64
	57XX		4131	10/62	9/64		**61XX**	
3606	11/59	1/63		**57XX**		6141	10/65	12/65
3632	10/62	1/63	4619	10/62	9/64	6147	10/62	10/63
3643	10/62	1/65	4681	9/63	12/63	6148	3/63	6/64
3659	9/63	9/65	4684	7/63	7/65		**43XX**	
3675	10/62	1/65	4698	4/64	9/64	6323	10/59	7/60
3677	10/62	1/65		**49XX**		6346	12/58	9/62
3696	10/62	12/65	4920	6/64	12/65	6350	11/58	7/61
3702	10/62	4/64	4949	6/64	9/64	6376	12/58	5/62
3752	9/59	1/64	4992	6/64	1/65			
				4/65	4/65			

68XX

No.		
6804	6/64	8/64
6816	6/64	6/65
6821	6/64	9/64
6822	6/64	9/64
6829	6/64	6/65
6838	6/64	7/64
6846	6/64	9/64
6860	6/64	9/64

49XX

No.		
6900	6/64	11/64
6908	6/64	7/65
6918	11/64	9/65
6935	11/64	1/65

6959

No.		
6965	11/64	10/65
6973	4/65	9/65
6982	6/64	8/64
6984	4/65	12/65
6990	6/64	12/65
6997	6/64	11/64

57XX

No.		
7782	9/63	11/64

6959

No.		
7904	7/65	12/65
7907	6/64	12/65
7914	6/64	12/65
7924	6/64	12/65

81XX

No.		
8102	3/63	10/63

94XX

No.		
8403	1/65	6/65
8415	2/65	5/65
8471	1/65	6/65

57XX

No.		
8714	7/64	1/65
8725	1/59	9/62
8795	10/62	7/65

94XX

No.		
9405	3/65	6/65
9430	1/65	6/65

57XX

No.		
9601	12/63	1/65
9606	9/64	9/64
9620	9/63	10/63
9623	10/62	7/65
9626	10/62	9/65
9660	7/63	1/64
9672	8/64	12/65
9680	2/65	12/65
9711	3/65	7/65

3MT 2-6-2T Stanier

No.		
40098	3/60	12/60
40116	10/50	7/58
40120	11/53	2/54
40126	7/60	8/60
40161	7/60	10/60
40163	9/50	1/54
40164	9/50	7/54
40171	7/60	9/60
40174	9/50	8/54
40182	2/55	4/55

2P 4-4-0

No.		
40332	5/57	9/59
40409	5/53	6/53
40423	9/50	1/51
40426	10/51	11/57
40486	7/52	8/52
	5/53	2/57
40501	12/57	7/60
40537	2/59	8/61

3P 4-4-0

No.		
40741	11/50	9/51

4P 4-4-0

No.		
40935	9/50	10/51
41012	9/50	1/51
41028	9/50	2/52
	4/52	7/52
41030	9/50	8/51
41140	9/51	2/52
	4/52	7/52
41198	6/53	7/53

2MT 2-6-2T

No.		
41202	8/60	3/62
41203	8/60	7/61
	10/61	3/62
41207	6/56	7/63
41208	6/56	2/62
	10/62	12/63
41209	10/62	11/62
41240	9/53	3/60
	4/60	5/60
	8/60	9/62
41241	5/58	9/58
41245	10/62	9/63
41248	11/60	12/63
41249	8/60	12/63
41296	8/60	9/65
41304	8/60	7/63

1F 0-6-0T

No.		
41706	9/50	6/56
41879	3/55	3/60

4MT 2-6-0

No.		
43012	9/50	1/54
43036	7/53	9/53
43046	9/50	11/52
43047	9/50	6/53

3F 0-6-0

No.		
43344	9/54	3/60
43427	9/50	10/58
43436	9/50	11/52
43444	9/50	11/53
	9/54	11/60
43462	9/50	4/54
43464	9/50	7/58
43593	9/50	4/61
43712	9/50	1/59
43734	9/50	12/59

4F 0-6-0

No.		
43837	3/51	7/52
43847	9/50	9/50
43853	9/50	9/52
43887	7/64	9/64
43924	8/62	6/65
43926	9/50	6/59
43928	9/50	4/54
43932	9/53	4/54
43969	9/50	9/50
43972	3/51	4/52
44015	12/54	3/57
44135	9/50	11/52
	10/53	3/59
	8/59	5/65
44169	9/50	6/54
44209	6/62	6/63
44264	8/62	5/65
44266	9/50	10/56
44267	9/50	9/53
44269	9/50	5/65
44296	10/53	6/57
	6/63	1/64
44317	11/52	3/54
44335	9/50	12/50
44411	9/50	5/62
44422	4/60	11/60
	11/64	2/65
44424	9/50	10/59
44466	9/50	5/65
44523	6/60	7/63
44534	9/50	11/64
44536	9/50	10/59
44537	9/50	10/59
44553	9/50	8/62
44569	9/50	7/64

5MT 4-6-0

No.		
44743	9/50	5/57
44744	9/50	11/52
	5/55	5/57
44745	9/50	5/57
44746	9/50	11/52
	5/55	6/57
44747	9/50	7/57
44804	8/53	9/53
44855	9/50	11/52
	11/52	3/53

Number			Number			Number		
44966	11/56	4/57	47678	9/50	7/61	**4MT 2-6-4T**		
45040	11/56	4/57	**8F 2-8-0**			80035	9/64	1/65
45273	10/54	5/55	48110	11/62	6/63	80059	5/65	6/65
45274	10/54	5/55	48431	11/62	1/64	80064	5/65	9/65
45280	11/56	4/57	48474	6/62	9/62	**3MT 2-6-2T**		
6P 4-6-0 Patriot			**0F 0-4-0T**			82001	6/64	12/65
45504	11/58	3/62	51202	11/52	1/58	82003	4/61	2/62
45506	11/58	3/62	51212	9/50	8/57	82006	8/60	2/61
45519	11/58	3/62	51217	3/52	11/52	82007	8/60	2/61
6P 4-6-0 Jubilee				9/57	9/61		10/62	7/64
45561	9/50	1/57	51218	9/59	11/62	82009	8/60	9/60
45570	9/50	5/51	**5MT 4-6-0**			82030	8/60	10/61
45572	9/50	9/55	73001	1/64	2/65	82033	8/60	12/60
	10/55	9/61	73003	1/58	3/63	82035	8/60	2/62
45577	8/52	9/61		9/63	6/65		10/62	3/64
45585	11/52	1/53	73012	6/64	11/64	82036	10/62	7/65
45602	5/51	5/56	73015	5/57	4/59	82037	8/60	2/62
	6/56	9/56	73019	7/60	9/60		10/62	9/65
45651	1/53	9/61	73021	6/62	9/62	82038	10/62	7/65
45660	9/50	9/61	73024	6/62	9/62	82039	8/60	2/62
45662	9/50	9/61		6/64	9/64		10/62	3/64
45663	9/50	1/58	73028	7/60	9/60	82040	8/60	2/62
45679	2/52	9/52		5/61	11/63		10/62	10/63
45682	9/50	7/64	73030	9/64	2/65	82042	9/60	9/61
45685	9/50	3/64		3/65	6/65	82043	9/60	1/62
45690	9/50	3/64	73031	6/57	1/58		10/62	2/64
45699	9/50	9/61	73037	6/64	9/64	82044	8/60	9/61
2MT 2-6-0			73049	6/62	6/62	**9F 2-10-0**		
46400	2/54	6/56	73054	5/57	4/61	92000	11/62	3/65
46494	2/54	6/56	73068	5/57	9/62	92004	1/61	3/63
46506	10/62	1/62	73094	9/61	11/61	92007	12/60	3/65
46517	10/62	11/62	73164	11/63	9/64	92209	10/65	12/65
Sentinel 0-4-0T			**4MT 4-6-0**			92210	8/60	6/62
47190	9/50	8/52	75000	6/62	8/62	92221	10/60	9/63
3F 0-6-0T			75001	3/63	9/63	92224	9/63	10/63
47333	1/54	7/61	75002	6/62	9/62	92231	9/60	1/61
47544	9/50	3/62	75004	9/58	11/61	92235	10/65	12/65
47550	9/50	3/59	75021	9/58	10/60	92238	10/63	3/65
47552	1/53	10/59	75022	9/58	9/61	92243	10/65	12/65
	1/60	5/62		2/65	3/65	92248	8/60	2/65

Bristol Bath Road
82A 8/50
Closed to Steam 9/60

10XX						14XX		
1000	3/54	8/60	1011	8/50	8/60	1402	5/55	9/56
1002	8/50	3/53	1014	8/50	8/60	1409	4/57	6/59
1005	8/50	8/60	1024	5/58	8/60	1412	10/56	6/60
1007	8/50	12/54	1026	2/53	3/54	1415	8/50	5/55
1009	1/55	8/60	1027	11/59	8/60	1426	7/60	8/60
			1028	8/50	8/60			

No.		
1430	8/50	10/54
1433	1/57	2/57
1454	1/53	7/54
	7/54	7/59
1463	8/50	?/60 [C]
2021		
2072	8/50	10/53
2251		
2203	4/53	2/54
23XX		
2445	8/50	9/50
2449	8/50	12/52
2534	8/50	1/51
29XX		
2931	8/50	2/51
2939	8/50	12/50
2948	8/50	11/51
2950	8/50	8/52
57XX		
3604	9/59	8/60
3623	9/59	8/60
3650	10/53	12/53
3676	4/57	12/58
3677	10/58	8/60
3692	2/56	2/58
3720	2/57	6/57
3748	6/56	8/60
3759	6/54	10/57
	2/58	7/59
3764	9/58	10/58
	11/58	2/59
3784	9/54	1/55
	3/55	9/56
3795	6/54	10/56
	9/58	10/58
	11/58	2/59
40XX		
4020	8/50	3/51
4033	8/50	6/51
4034	8/50	12/50
4035	8/50	10/51
4041	8/50	4/51
4042	8/50	11/51
4043	8/50	1/52
4047	8/50	7/51
4056	8/50	9/57
4060	12/50	9/52
4073		
4073	8/50	10/52
	2/53	2/57
4075	12/50	10/52
	3/53	11/59
4077	2/60	9/60

No.		
4078	11/58	6/59
4079	6/57	?/60 [C]
4080	7/54	5/59
4081	12/50	4/58
	12/58	6/59
	7/59	?/60 [C]
4084	8/50	11/59
4091	8/50	12/55
4093	8/50	12/50
4094	12/52	7/54
4096	8/50	4/58
51XX		
4129	1/60	6/60
4139	2/53	4/57
4142	8/50	7/51
4143	8/50	11/51
4150	5/53	6/53
4151	8/50	5/51
4152	8/50	12/51
4155	8/50	2/51
4157	10/52	7/56
4159	10/52	6/56
4163	2/59	9/59
4166	11/53	6/54
45XX		
4511	9/53	10/53
4517	12/52	1/53
4521	1/51	10/52
4524	10/55	5/58
4532	9/53	1/55
4535	8/50	1/55
4536	8/50	12/50
4539	8/50	4/51
4544	5/51	8/52
4553	1/58	4/58
4558	11/53	3/55
4562	7/54	11/54
	12/54	1/55
4563	8/50	10/52
4567	4/57	3/58
4575	2/60	6/60
4577	8/50	1/58
4580	8/50	9/53
4582	9/53	4/58
4589	2/58	5/58
4592	8/51	9/55
4593	6/59	1/60
4595	8/50	8/58
4597	12/53	1/58
57XX		
4603	3/52	6/54
4619	4/57	8/60
4660	3/52	6/54
	2/57	9/58

No.		
49XX		
4909	11/53	1/56
4914	8/50	2/54
	9/54	6/56
4918	9/55	4/58
	5/58	3/59
4922	6/57	3/60
4924	9/55	6/57
4927	9/56	7/59
4930	4/52	6/52
4942	8/50	7/55
4947	2/56	3/56
	6/56	9/59
4949	10/58	11/58
4951	8/50	11/50
4954	8/50	2/51
4956	9/56	2/59
4958	5/54	10/54
	5/55	6/55
	6/56	6/57
4959	5/55	11/56
	1/58	9/58
4961	10/51	7/55
4972	11/53	1/54
4983	3/55	8/56
	11/56	5/58
4985	8/50	11/50
4988	11/58	7/59
4999	6/56	10/56
4073		
5000	8/50	11/55
5015	4/58	6/60
5018	8/50	11/50
5019	8/50	4/58
5025	8/50	3/51
	4/51	6/56
5027	6/54	4/58
5037	8/50	3/51
	4/51	6/54
5048	8/50	9/60
5049	5/60	8/60
5054	4/57	11/59
5057	6/54	11/59
5062	3/58	9/60
5063	6/54	5/58
5064	12/50	3/58
5067	8/50	2/59
5069	10/52	7/54
5073	4/58	?/60 [C]
5074	8/50	7/54
5076	8/50	5/51
	7/51	4/60
5077	7/54	7/56
5078	12/58	8/60
5082	8/50	11/52

Shed by Shed

5085	9/52	8/60
5090	4/58	9/60
5092	4/58	7/60
5094	8/50	6/51
	7/51	9/56
	7/60	8/60
5096	8/50	?/60 [C]
5097	6/59	9/60
5099	5/58	7/58
51XX		
5169	8/50	12/50
5182	12/52	9/55
5186	5/58	7/59
5188	7/57	3/58
	5/58	10/58
5197	5/53	6/59
43XX		
5306	10/54	5/55
5307	2/54	5/54
5311	8/50	4/53
	5/58	5/59
5325	8/50	11/51
5327	8/50	11/51
5351	3/54	12/54
54XX		
5403	1/57	4/57
45XX		
5506	8/50	9/55
5509	9/59	1/60
5511	8/50	9/53
	11/57	10/58
5512	8/50	10/52
	3/53	1/57
5514	8/50	1/55
5523	8/50	8/58
5525	9/53	5/58
	5/58	5/58
5527	8/50	9/53
	5/58	9/58
5528	8/50	11/58
5529	2/58	7/59
	9/59	7/60
5530	5/58	2/60
5532	12/53	11/58
5534	10/52	3/53
5535	8/50	6/57
5536	8/50	5/51
	8/58	12/59
5539	8/50	6/53
5546	8/50	9/58
5547	8/50	6/57
5548	8/50	3/56
5553	8/50	12/58
5555	8/50	9/53
5558	8/50	5/51

5559	8/50	9/58
5561	8/50	7/60
5564	8/50	7/51
5565	2/53	9/58
5572	8/50	9/53
5574	3/58	5/58
57XX		
5701	10/53	12/53
58XX		
5809	8/50	8/56
5813	8/50	4/57
49XX		
5904	1/52	5/54
	9/54	6/56
5908	1/62	7/63
5910	9/55	2/59
5919	6/52	6/56
	7/56	3/59
5934	11/53	2/54
	11/59	8/60
5940	6/59	8/60
5941	6/59	10/59
	12/59	8/60
5949	12/53	9/54
	6/56	11/57
	2/58	9/60
5950	9/55	6/59
5964	6/56	7/56
5975	7/60	8/60
5997	7/60	9/60
60XX		
6000	8/50	9/52
61XX		
6102	12/50	10/53
6107	12/50	10/53
	1/54	6/59
	7/59	8/59
6109	1/51	12/52
6114	7/51	10/53
6137	7/55	9/58
6153	1/51	7/51
6163	7/55	1/58
43XX		
6322	11/51	2/53
	3/54	6/54
6327	11/57	5/58
6351	8/50	3/54
6360	10/56	6/57
6363	2/56	6/56
	11/58	4/59
6374	11/51	2/53
6391	2/57	4/57
68XX		
6867	2/54	5/54

49XX		
6900	10/51	9/59
6908	6/54	10/54
	2/56	3/56
	6/56	9/59
6915	9/56	9/58
6919	1/58	8/60
6925	6/54	10/54
6936	5/54	2/58
	5/58	2/59
6951	9/55	5/58
6954	8/50	7/51
	5/54	12/59
6957	5/54	9/59
6958	8/50	2/53
	5/54	5/57
6959		
6965	8/50	2/51
6967	11/51	9/53
6972	8/50	3/55
	6/56	4/59
	5/59	8/60
6977	8/50	5/54
	3/55	7/56
	9/56	5/58
	9/59	4/60
6981	8/50	8/60
6982	4/51	5/54
	9/55	8/56
	5/57	8/60
6986	10/52	10/53
	7/55	5/58
6988	9/59	9/63
6996	3/58	9/58
6997	8/50	2/57
	4/57	6/64
4073		
7003	12/58	7/60
7011	8/50	7/59
7014	8/50	2/56
	3/56	9/60
7015	10/55	5/59
7018	7/56	8/60
7019	8/50	?/60 [C]
7034	8/50	8/60
7035	10/56	2/59
57XX		
7782	11/53	11/55
6959		
7900	12/51	2/52
7901	8/50	12/51
	10/53	8/60
7907	10/52	4/54
	9/55	2/60
7917	8/50	10/50

	94XX			9771	11/55	6/57		82030	4/59	5/59
8491	6/56	6/57			9/58	8/60			1/60	8/60
	57XX				2MT 2-6-2T			82032	5/58	7/58
8714	10/56	2/57		41202	3/55	8/60		82033	5/58	8/60
8741	6/57	8/60		41203	4/56	8/60		82034	5/58	7/58
8747	10/56	2/57		41240	5/60	8/60		82035	5/58	8/60
8795	6/56	9/58		41249	1/59	8/60		82036	5/58	7/58
	90XX			41304	7/60	8/60		82037	5/58	5/58
9008	1/53	10/53			2MT 2-6-0				1/60	8/60
9010	1/53	10/53		46507	12/54	6/56		82038	1/60	8/60
9016	1/53	7/54		46527	2/55	4/57		82039	5/58	1/59
9020	1/53	7/54			4MT 4-6-0			82040	5/58	8/60
9026	1/53	7/54		75004	9/51	10/51		82041	5/58	3/59
	94XX				3MT 2-6-2T			82042	7/58	9/60
9481	6/57	8/60		82001	3/58	7/58		82043	5/58	9/60
	57XX			82002	5/58	7/58		82044	5/58	8/60
9604	4/52	3/55		82003	3/58	7/58				
9610	10/53	2/57		82005	5/58	7/58		[C] Before 12/60		
9626	10/57	8/60		82006	1/60	8/60				
9729	6/56	9/59		82007	9/58	8/60				
9769	11/57	9/58		82009	1/60	8/60				

Bristol St Philips Marsh
82B 8/50
Closed to Steam 5/64

	10XX			2205	6/57	11/58			23XX	
1000	8/60	1/64			12/58	5/59		2322	8/50	6/51
1005	8/60	5/63		2213	8/56	10/60		2340	8/50	1/53
1009	8/60	1/63		2215	8/50	10/55		2411	2/53	3/54
1011	8/60	11/63			12/55	3/59		2426	9/50	1/53
1014	8/60	9/61			4/59	9/59		2445	9/50	2/53
1020	10/62	10/63			11/59	1/61		2462	8/50	12/52
1021	12/60	11/63		2220	8/50	5/53		2578	8/50	8/53
1024	8/60	10/63		2224	8/59	9/63			28XX	
1027	8/60	9/61		2225	8/50	5/53		2809	1/56	4/56
1028	8/60	10/63		2228	2/53	5/53		2818	8/50	8/52
	16XX			2232	2/61	1/62		2839	8/50	5/51
1649	6/51	6/58		2240	3/61	6/61		2844	8/50	5/51
1669	6/55	10/58		2250	10/52	10/59		2845	2/53	7/55
	2021			2251	8/50	11/57		2846	8/50	7/54
2031	8/50	12/52			2/58	3/58		2859	8/50	5/51
2053	2/53	3/54		2253	8/50	12/53		2868	11/54	7/55
2070	8/50	7/55		2258	9/50	12/53		2879	10/52	2/53
2072	10/53	10/54		2261	10/52	5/55			5/53	7/55
2135	8/50	12/52			7/56	6/61		2883	10/60	3/61
	2251			2265	8/50	6/60		2889	10/52	7/55
2201	3/54	5/58		2269	8/50	12/58		2898	12/52	6/56
2203	2/54	6/56		2277	2/59	6/60			ROD	
	9/59	6/60			6/61	10/61		3014	8/50	7/54
				2288	11/59	6/61		3017	10/52	9/55
				2293	8/50	12/55				

3022	4/56	6/56
3032	8/50	9/55
3034	8/50	1/53
3041	8/50	8/53
2251		
3215	8/50	6/60
3218	6/60	10/62
57XX		
3604	8/50	9/59
	8/60	12/63
3614	8/50	4/56
	9/60	10/60
3623	8/50	9/59
	8/60	8/62
3632	8/50	10/62
3643	8/50	7/55
	11/55	10/62
3650	5/58	10/61
3665	6/60	7/61
3675	10/61	10/62
3676	8/50	4/57
3677	9/58	10/58
	8/60	10/62
3692	2/58	10/60
3696	12/61	10/62
3702	12/61	10/62
3720	8/50	2/57
	6/57	9/59
3731	8/50	9/61
3746	8/50	5/51
3748	5/51	6/56
	8/60	8/61
3758	11/53	4/59
3759	8/50	6/54
	10/57	2/58
3763	8/50	3/56
3764	8/50	10/52
	11/52	9/58
	10/58	11/58
	2/59	7/61
3765	8/50	4/59
	10/59	10/62
3773	8/50	9/62
3776	3/58	11/61
3784	8/50	9/54
	1/55	3/55
	9/56	12/60
3795	8/50	6/54
	10/56	9/58
	10/58	11/58
	2/59	2/61
	4/61	7/61
28XX		
3800	10/60	3/61
3820	12/60	2/61

3823	6/54	7/55
3829	6/62	10/62
3842	8/50	5/51
	12/60	4/61
3854	10/52	6/56
	6/62	11/62
4073		
4073	10/52	2/53
4074	1/62	5/62
4075	10/52	3/53
4077	9/60	7/62
4079	1/61	7/62
	11/63	7/64
4087	3/63	10/63
4088	10/63	7/64
4093	2/63	6/64
51XX		
4103	9/62	10/62
4105	4/58	5/58
4129	9/59	1/60
4131	9/55	4/61
	7/61	10/62
42XX		
4248	11/61	2/62
4262	8/50	1/58
57XX		
4603	8/50	3/52
	6/54	9/61
4607	8/50	11/53
4612	8/62	10/62
4619	8/50	4/57
	8/60	10/62
4624	8/50	3/54
4626	8/50	6/54
4655	8/50	10/61
4660	8/50	3/52
	6/54	2/57
	9/58	7/62
4688	8/50	5/62
47XX		
4703	7/53	9/62
4705	6/61	9/62
4706	8/50	10/52
	9/53	9/62
49XX		
4905	4/61	10/63
4907	8/50	1/52
4909	8/50	5/51
	1/56	11/57
4912	12/50	8/51
4914	2/54	9/54
	6/56	11/63
4916	8/50	8/51
4917	5/51	5/53
4918	4/58	5/58

4922	12/55	6/57
	3/60	6/63
4930	6/52	10/53
4932	12/50	3/51
4933	11/62	6/63
4934	8/50	7/52
4942	11/60	7/62
4947	12/50	2/52
	6/52	2/56
	3/56	6/56
	9/59	9/61
	1/62	8/62
4948	8/50	10/50
4949	3/58	10/58
	11/58	6/62
	10/62	6/64
4953	7/60	7/62
4958	5/53	5/54
	10/54	5/55
	6/55	6/56
4960	9/59	8/62
4967	8/50	12/52
4968	10/59	6/62
4969	8/50	5/51
4980	12/55	6/63
4983	1/52	3/55
	8/56	11/56
	11/63	12/63
4986	8/50	3/53
4988	5/58	11/58
4990	8/50	3/52
4991	9/62	6/63
4992	9/62	6/63
	11/63	6/64
4993	9/62	6/63
	11/63	6/64
4999	8/50	2/52
	7/52	6/56
	10/56	6/57
	1/61	8/62
4073		
5002	11/63	3/64
5021	8/60	9/60
5023	4/58	5/58
5025	3/51	4/51
5037	10/63	3/64
5040	10/61	10/63
5048	9/60	11/60
5049	8/60	3/63
5050	8/61	8/63
5052	8/60	8/62
5071	2/62	10/63
5074	10/63	7/64
5075	6/62	8/62
5078	8/60	10/60

5085	8/60	7/62		**49XX**		6363	5/53	2/56
	2/63	2/64	5900	11/62	11/63		6/56	11/58
5090	9/60	10/60	5902	2/62	1/63		5/59	10/59
5094	8/60	8/62	5904	5/54	9/54	6364	10/60	9/62
	51XX			6/56	5/59	6370	8/52	9/54
5104	2/58	10/60		11/60	11/63	6374	2/53	9/60
5182	10/52	12/52	5919	8/50	6/52	6390	10/52	9/53
5188	3/58	5/58		6/56	7/56	6391	4/55	2/57
5197	1/60	7/60	5924	11/50	12/63		4/57	7/58
	42XX		5929	2/62	6/62		8/58	2/59
5202	10/63	12/63	5934	8/60	7/64		**56XX**	
5206	10/63	12/63	5935	5/58	5/59	6601	8/50	1/62
5215	4/59	3/60	5940	8/60	8/62	6630	7/55	2/62
	5/60	10/62	5941	10/59	12/59	6641	12/59	2/60
	43XX			8/60	6/62	6654	6/60	11/62
5306	10/52	10/54	5943	2/61	9/61	6656	8/50	6/59
	5/55	7/55	5949	8/50	12/53	6670	8/50	9/61
5307	10/52	2/54		9/54	6/56	6671	8/50	9/61
	5/54	10/56		11/57	2/58	6681	3/59	3/62
5311	1/58	5/58	5950	6/59	5/61		**57XX**	
	5/59	9/60	5953	2/61	9/62	6769	1/63	11/63
5315	1/58	5/58	5954	10/59	10/63		**68XX**	
	8/58	1/59	5958	12/53	1/54	6804	12/50	2/61
5323	7/54	5/58		2/62	3/64		11/63	6/64
5324	10/52	11/53	5960	5/51	1/52	6805	8/50	10/52
5325	5/52	9/54	5963	1/63	7/64	6809	2/58	9/62
5336	10/57	1/58	5969	5/58	12/59	6811	8/50	9/62
	9/58	2/59	5975	11/56	4/57	6814	6/62	12/63
5337	9/55	9/56		8/60	6/64	6816	9/60	6/64
5339	1/60	10/60	5978	2/63	10/63	6821	6/63	6/64
5345	1/55	7/58	5981	12/56	4/57	6825	4/64	7/64
	8/58	11/58	5982	8/50	4/57	6827	8/50	5/53
5350	5/51	7/55	5992	8/50	11/53		9/53	9/62
5351	8/50	3/54		**61XX**		6830	8/50	1/62
5356	11/57	9/59	6147	11/60	10/62	6831	5/58	1/62
5358	8/50	5/53	6148	2/63	3/63	6832	8/50	10/52
5360	5/55	5/58		**43XX**		6833	6/54	2/60
5361	12/58	3/59	6304	9/58	3/59	6834	9/56	9/62
5367	12/52	5/58	6306	7/54	8/58	6835	7/54	1/62
5369	10/60	9/61	6312	1/55	3/61		5/62	5/63
	8/62	9/62		6/61	8/62	6836	8/50	5/53
5376	1/60	6/62	6319	1/60	9/62	6837	8/50	12/50
5385	9/58	6/62	6322	2/53	3/54	6840	8/50	12/50
5393	12/58	4/59		6/54	9/54	6841	5/58	9/62
	56XX		6327	1/55	11/57	6842	8/50	1/62
5640	9/60	9/62		5/58	1/60		4/62	9/62
5642	10/55	7/59	6341	1/58	7/60	6845	12/50	9/55
5675	8/53	10/55	6345	5/51	8/53	6846	8/50	6/64
5697	3/60	5/60	6348	9/57	5/58	6849	8/50	12/50
	57XX		6351	3/54	10/60		10/60	1/62
5769	3/58	5/60	6356	5/55	10/62	6850	8/50	10/52
5771	12/59	3/61	6360	6/57	7/58	6852	8/50	1/62
5779	11/61	5/62		8/58	1/59	6854	10/60	11/60
5784	8/50	2/53		1/60	10/60	6859	5/58	2/59
	10/53	5/54				6860	5/62	6/64

6861	8/50	11/50
6863	8/50	4/58
6864	4/62	5/62
6865	11/59	5/62
6867	8/50	2/54
	5/54	1/58
6869	9/56	12/59
	4/62	9/62
6870	11/56	2/57
6873	5/62	7/64
6874	8/61	1/62
6875	2/64	3/64
6876	8/50	4/59
6878	5/58	3/64
49XX		
6900	9/59	11/62
	10/63	6/64
6908	11/50	6/54
	10/54	2/56
	3/56	6/56
	9/59	6/64
6909	8/50	4/51
6914	8/50	10/53
6919	1/54	2/54
	8/60	8/63
6922	8/50	10/53
6925	1/52	6/54
	10/54	1/55
6936	6/53	5/54
	2/58	5/58
6945	4/53	5/53
	2/57	4/57
6951	5/58	5/59
6954	8/51	5/54
	12/59	5/64
6957	8/50	5/54
	9/59	2/60
6958	2/53	5/54
	5/57	6/57
6959		
6972	3/55	6/56
	8/60	3/64
6977	5/54	3/55
	5/58	9/59
	4/60	6/62
6981	8/60	3/64
6982	5/54	9/55
	8/56	5/57
	8/60	6/64
6986	8/50	10/52
	10/53	7/55
	5/58	9/60
6990	10/63	6/64
6993	2/61	9/61
6997	2/57	4/57

4073		
7003	3/64	6/64
7014	9/60	8/61
7018	8/60	10/61
7034	8/60	12/61
72XX		
7201	9/51	1/55
7241	4/54	4/55
7250	9/52	9/57
43XX		
7301	6/57	8/62
7303	5/53	9/57
	1/58	2/59
7317	11/60	1/62
7323	(ex 9301 9/56)	
	9/55	11/58
	12/58	7/62
7332	(ex 9310 9/58)	
	9/57	9/62
7338	(ex 9316 3/58)	
	4/62	7/62
74XX		
7436	11/63	7/64
57XX		
7711	8/50	9/52
7718	8/50	3/54
7719	8/50	5/59
7726	8/50	4/52
	5/52	9/52
7728	8/50	9/57
	11/57	5/60
7729	8/50	6/62
7749	8/50	7/54
	10/54	8/62
7772	7/60	7/61
7779	8/50	9/52
7780	8/50	4/57
7782	8/50	11/53
	11/55	7/56
7783	8/50	8/62
7790	8/50	10/62
7793	8/50	1/59
7795	8/50	2/58
78XX		
7808	12/53	1/54
6959		
7900	8/50	12/51
7901	12/51	10/53
	8/60	3/64
7906	8/50	9/50
7907	8/50	10/52
	4/54	9/55
	2/60	9/61
	2/62	6/64
7908	8/50	7/55

7913	5/58	3/59
7914	3/64	6/64
7924	1/62	6/64
7929	7/55	1/60
81XX		
8105	8/50	12/51
94XX		
8413	8/50	1/57
8451	10/58	5/59
8479	11/61	10/62
8491	8/52	6/56
	6/57	5/59
8492	8/52	4/57
	6/57	5/59
57XX		
8702	8/50	2/56
8703	8/50	1/58
8713	8/50	1/56
8714	8/50	10/56
	2/57	7/61
	11/61	7/62
8722	8/50	6/54
8730	8/50	12/56
8737	8/50	3/59
	5/59	5/59
8741	8/50	6/57
	8/60	5/62
8746	8/50	10/62
8747	8/50	10/56
	2/57	9/61
	12/61	6/62
8766	8/50	1/54
8790	8/50	5/62
8795	8/50	6/56
	9/58	10/62
43XX		
9301	9/55	
(renum 7323 9/56)		
9310	9/57	
(renum 7332 9/58)		
9313	9/55	5/58
94XX		
9453	8/51	9/56
9466	1/61	6/62
9481	8/52	6/57
	8/60	1/61
9488	12/52	10/60
9495	9/54	11/61
9499	1/57	8/59
57XX		
9600	4/61	10/62
9601	4/57	12/63
9604	8/50	4/52
9605	8/50	4/56
9606	8/50	3/54

9610	2/57	10/58
9615	12/61	10/62
9620	8/50	11/50
9623	8/60	10/62
9626	8/50	4/57
	5/57	10/57
	8/60	10/62
9642	5/58	4/59
9651	4/59	9/62
9665	8/50	2/54
9668	2/62	10/62
9729	8/50	6/56
	9/59	11/63
9764	8/50	4/51
9769	9/58	9/60
9771	5/51	11/55
	6/57	9/58
	8/60	5/61

2MT 2-6-2T

41202	3/62	4/62
41203	3/62	4/62
41208	2/62	10/62
41209	6/62	10/62
41245	6/62	10/62

2MT 2-6-0

46506	12/56	10/59
	7/60	10/62
46517	6/57	10/62
46525	3/53	9/62
46526	4/53	12/56
46527	4/53	2/55
	4/57	1/58

8F 2-8-0

48330	8/61	9/61
48402	7/55	8/55
48404	6/56	6/61
	8/61	2/62
48408	4/57	3/58
48410	7/55	1/60
48412	5/59	1/60
48420	7/54	11/62
48430	4/56	3/58
48431	9/55	1/60
48434	7/55	9/60
48436	9/55	9/61
48444	7/60	2/62
48450	7/55	1/60
	2/60	9/61
48459	8/55	9/61
48461	4/56	2/58
48471	7/60	9/61
48475	7/54	5/59
	7/60	3/62

5MT 4-6-0

73019	9/53	5/58
73022	9/53	12/53
	1/54	7/54
73027	9/53	7/54
73028	9/53	5/58
73029	9/53	12/53
	1/54	9/57
73032	9/53	5/58
73039	9/53	5/58

3MT 2-6-2T

82003	2/62	3/62
82007	2/61	10/62
82009	9/60	2/61
82035	2/62	10/62
82036	6/62	10/62
82037	2/62	10/62
82038	8/60	10/62
82039	2/62	10/62
82040	2/62	10/62
82043	2/62	10/62

WD 2-8-0

90010	1/58	7/59
90176	8/50	10/55
	1/58	7/59
90207	8/50	7/51
90238	8/50	10/51
90251	5/52	6/56
90284	9/53	11/54
	3/55	6/56
90356	8/50	8/53
90563	10/54	7/59
90573	8/50	10/51
90693	9/51	8/52

9F 2-10-0

92203	4/59	10/60
92204	5/59	10/60
92205	5/59	9/60
92206	5/59	9/60
92207	5/59	2/60
92213	10/59	11/59
92217	1/60	3/63
92218	2/60	3/63

Bromsgrove
21C 9/50   85F 2/58
85D 1/61
Closed to Steam 9/64

42XX

5226	11/59	4/60

94XX

8400	11/56	9/64
8401	12/56	9/64
8402	7/56	9/64
8403	12/56	9/64
8404	11/56	10/61
8405	11/56	9/64
8406	1/57	1/61
8409	5/61	8/64

8418	7/63	8/64
8427	3/58	5/58
8480	8/61	9/61
8487	8/61	1/62
9401	11/62	7/63
9429	8/61	9/61
9430	6/61	9/64
9453	4/64	8/64
9455	2/58	5/58
9493	6/61	9/64

3F 0-6-0

43186	9/50	12/58
43462	4/54	4/56
43593	4/61	12/61
43667	9/50	4/54
43686	9/50	3/51
43762	4/56	3/61

3F 0-6-0T

47234	9/50	4/51
47257	11/53	12/53
47276	12/50	3/64

Shed by Shed

47301	12/50	12/56		**0F 0-4-0T**			**9F 2-10-0**	
47303	9/50	12/56	51217	5/55	9/55	92079	5/56	10/63
47305	9/50	12/56		**0F 0-4-0T**		92223	10/63	2/64
47308	9/50	3/64	56020	12/52 4/55		92230	1/64	8/64
47425	9/50	12/56		**0-10-0**		92234	9/61	11/61
47464	11/57	12/57	58100	9/50	5/56			
47502	3/51	9/57		**U1**				
47506	2/63	11/63	69999	8/50	11/50			
47565	9/50	8/57		7/55	10/55			
47635	5/53	6/53						

Cardiff Canton
86C 8/50   88A 1/61
Closed to Steam 9/62

	TV 0-6-2T		2834	12/58	10/61	3751	5/62	6/62
203	8/50	1/52	2835	5/52	7/52	3755	8/50	8/62
205	8/50	6/54	2837	8/50	1/59	3784	12/60	8/62
208	8/50	11/52	2847	3/58	12/58		**28XX**	
209	8/50	8/52	2859	2/57	4/57	3801	9/54	6/59
220	8/50	4/51		7/57	2/59	3803	5/52	8/58
282	11/51	2/53	2864	10/57	5/59	3804	2/61	8/62
335	8/50	11/53	2865	3/60	6/60	3809	8/50	1/61
349	5/51	7/54	2867	10/57	2/59	3810	9/54	8/62
357	8/50	11/51	2868	5/52	7/52	3812	8/50	3/55
371	1/52	6/52	2873	9/54	7/56	3814	8/50	7/55
	11/52	7/54	2874	3/56	12/60	3816	9/54	6/59
374	2/53	7/54	2877	8/50	2/60	3817	8/50	6/60
381	8/50	7/54	2887	1/62	8/62	3823	8/50	6/54
	BM 0-6-2T		2889	3/58	1/61	3824	8/50	9/54
425	8/50	3/51	2891	8/50	11/64	3835	4/57	6/60
	AD 2-6-2T		2892	12/50	2/59	3836	9/54	3/55
1205	5/51	12/55	2893	10/57	2/59		5/59	9/59
	15XX		2895	7/57	1/60	3842	5/51	5/59
1508	6/56	8/62	2896	9/54	3/55	3843	7/56	1/60
	2251			**29XX**		3845	1/57	10/61
2223	8/59	9/59	2906	8/50	8/52	3846	3/53	6/59
	23XX		2940	8/50	1/52	3849	5/59	5/62
2407	8/50	2/51	2943	8/50	1/51	3853	1/62	8/62
2537	8/50	12/52	2945	10/52	5/53	3854	1/57	6/57
	28XX			**ROD**		3855	3/58	1/61
2805	9/54	9/58	3024	9/53	9/54	3860	1/57	8/62
2806	12/50	5/54	3026	9/53	9/54	3862	6/62	8/62
2813	9/57	11/58	3036	8/50	5/52		**4073**	
2816	3/58	9/58	3043	9/53	9/54	4073	2/57	5/60
2818	8/59	9/59		**57XX**		4080	7/60	8/62
2820	8/50	4/54	3652	7/54	2/56	4081	4/58	5/58
2821	9/56	12/58	3663	12/61	8/62	4083	8/50	9/50
	10/59	8/60	3670	8/50	5/61		9/61	12/61
2826	5/52	7/52	3729	8/50	11/54	4084	1/60	9/60
	5/58	9/58	3748	8/61	8/62	4086	12/59	5/61

4094	8/50	12/52
	51XX	
4130	1/51	2/51
4145	8/50	12/51
	42XX	
4207	2/53	9/61
4222	8/50	7/51
4223	3/51	12/52
4224	8/50	8/53
4225	8/53	12/60
4226	5/53	3/59
4227	8/50	7/51
4230	6/59	6/60
4231	8/50	12/59
4242	12/61	8/62
4250	2/53	7/54
4254	12/54	2/62
4255	8/50	2/54
4266	8/50	5/52
	5/53	7/60
4267	7/51	5/52
4268	1/51	1/54
4270	8/50	8/62
4271	1/59	6/59
4275	8/50	3/51
4285	8/50	5/53
4287	8/50	3/51
4290	5/53	7/61
4297	6/57	8/59
4298	12/59	7/60
	43XX	
4303	11/51	10/52
4318	5/52	6/52
	57XX	
4622	8/50	10/59
4633	8/50	8/62
4662	7/54	6/56
4677	8/50	10/54
	49XX	
4901	8/50	6/54
	10/55	1/57
4913	8/50	1/57
4918	11/61	8/62
4928	10/59	6/62
4931	10/59	6/62
4934	5/54	2/58
4935	10/61	2/62
4936	5/62	8/62
4942	7/62	8/62
4946	6/53	1/60
4951	1/54	2/54
4952	8/50	2/52
	3/52	5/52
	5/59	8/62
4953	8/50	4/56
	7/62	8/62
4956	2/59	2/62
4963	12/50	12/53
4964	11/55	10/57
4968	12/50	2/52
	3/52	1/58
4971	9/60	7/62
4973	3/56	6/62
4974	8/50	5/58
4975	8/50	10/53
4977	5/61	5/62
4979	8/50	3/53
4982	4/58	11/58
4983	4/59	6/59
4984	6/62	8/62
4996	3/56	10/58
4999	6/57	1/61
	4073	
5001	8/50	1/57
5003	4/58	3/59
5004	9/57	4/58
5005	8/50	1/57
	5/59	6/59
5006	8/50	6/54
5007	8/50	4/57
5012	10/52	12/52
5018	10/52	12/52
5020	8/50	1/57
	4/57	11/57
	9/61	6/62
5021	9/59	8/60
	9/60	8/62
5030	8/50	7/58
5043	4/62	8/62
5044	7/60	6/61
	7/61	7/61
	10/61	4/62
5046	8/50	4/58
5048	11/60	7/61
	7/61	10/61
5049	8/50	2/56
	4/56	1/57
5052	8/50	1/57
5053	9/61	6/62
5054	8/50	4/57
5061	12/59	8/62
5072	12/55	2/56
	4/56	2/57
	9/60	10/60
5073	9/61	8/62
5074	7/54	7/55
	7/56	1/57
5075	1/62	6/62
5077	12/50	7/54
5078	5/58	12/58
5080	8/50	12/55
5081	8/60	8/62
5089	8/50	5/54
	6/54	7/54
5090	10/52	12/52
5091	9/61	8/62
5092	7/60	8/62
5095	2/57	5/58
	5/58	9/60
5096	9/61	8/62
5097	9/60	8/62
5099	8/50	1/57
	7/58	2/62
	42XX	
5202	7/54	9/55
5207	12/53	1/61
5218	2/54	9/61
5220	6/60	8/62
5224	3/62	8/62
5225	4/59	8/62
5226	8/50	7/52
5249	8/50	12/52
5260	5/58	9/61
5261	12/58	8/62
	43XX	
5307	8/50	10/50
5334	3/54	10/57
5337	5/58	1/59
5360	5/58	8/58
5362	8/55	9/56
5382	8/50	9/54
5388	8/50	9/55
	56XX	
5602	3/54	7/60
5620	1/54	9/55
5633	5/51	6/57
5679	8/50	2/59
5685	8/50	4/55
	3/58	11/60
	8/61	7/62
	57XX	
5727	10/57	11/57
	1/58	5/60
5749	8/50	8/62
5776	8/50	5/60
5786	8/50	4/58
5794	11/54	9/55
	49XX	
5903	5/60	6/62
5909	9/61	6/62
5910	8/50	5/55
	2/59	11/60
5911	12/50	3/51
	4/51	8/62

5913	7/52	6/53	6854	9/60	10/60	**43XX**		
5916	7/52	8/52	6858	4/60	5/60	7317	1/62	8/62
5923	7/54	3/58	6859	7/59	8/62	7322	(ex 9300 4/57)	
5925	3/51	10/58	6864	7/59	2/62		7/54	10/57
5929	3/51	5/51	**49XX**			**57XX**		
5935	11/61	5/62	6901	8/58	6/59	7775	10/55	10/60
5937	4/59	6/59	6909	7/60	8/62	**78XX**		
5946	8/50	1/60	6912	9/61	8/62	7805	9/58	8/62
5953	8/50	3/53	6918	9/61	8/62	7809	9/58	12/58
5958	8/50	5/53	6928	8/50	4/57	7814	9/58	2/59
5961	9/61	9/62		6/57	8/57	7815	9/58	12/58
5962	8/58	8/62	6932	8/53	8/62	7820	9/60	8/62
5969	3/56	4/56	6935	2/59	8/62	**6959**		
5970	8/50	6/59	6936	2/59	8/62	7913	3/59	8/62
5977	8/50	9/55	6939	8/50	8/62	7925	10/59	8/62
5984	9/60	9/62	6942	8/58	10/58	7927	9/60	8/62
5989	6/57	8/57	6943	8/50	2/62	**94XX**		
60XX			6944	9/60	8/62	8401	8/50	11/50
6010	9/61	6/62	6946	8/50	1/58	8402	3/54	7/56
6019	9/60	3/62	6948	8/50	3/58	8425	7/60	8/62
6024	9/61	6/62	6950	9/61	8/62	8429	1/58	2/58
43XX			6951	7/53	7/55	8439	5/53	3/54
6308	9/55	7/59	6957	10/61	8/62		5/57	10/59
6326	5/58	8/62	6958	6/57	6/59	8441	1/58	12/61
6333	8/51	11/59	**6959**			8445	6/62	8/62
6338	9/57	10/57	6963	8/58	10/59	8447	7/54	5/59
	8/58	9/58		11/59	12/60	8457	1/58	1/61
6345	7/60	8/62	6969	8/50	2/58	8464	1/58	11/59
6349	11/60	6/62	6995	9/61	8/62	8466	11/58	8/62
6352	7/54	10/60	6998	8/50	3/58	8471	3/62	8/62
6353	8/50	1/58	6999	8/50	11/60	8484	2/58	8/62
6362	4/57	10/57	**4073**			8497	6/60	1/63
6366	6/62	8/62	7000	5/57	7/57	**57XX**		
6370	5/52	8/52	7006	9/59	7/60	8722	6/60	4/61
56XX			7011	4/60	1/61	8723	8/50	6/62
6600	5/51	9/59	7016	8/50	9/56	8728	8/50	8/62
6602	5/51	7/51		9/61	8/62	8774	6/61	7/61
	5/52	9/55	7017	8/50	7/54	8776	4/52	8/62
6603	3/51	7/51	7020	8/50	1/57	**43XX**		
6607	3/51	8/51	7022	8/50	1/57	9300	7/54	
6621	11/51	3/54	7023	8/50	7/60		(renum 7322 4/57)	
	8/55	4/57	7037	5/59	6/59	9304	6/54	9/55
6630	2/62	8/62	**72XX**			9306	7/56	10/57
6644	2/56	3/58	7201	8/50	9/51	**94XX**		
6653	3/51	5/51		1/55	3/55	9426	6/56	8/62
6654	6/52	10/52	7208	10/52	12/52	9437	1/58	8/62
6663	3/55	8/55	7209	7/60	?/6? [D]	9443	1/58	5/59
6681	3/62	8/62	7210	9/50	5/52	9450	11/57	7/58
68XX			7216	5/51	5/52	9453	1/59	3/60
6822	1/60	8/62	7219	8/50	10/53	9459	1/52	3/52
6832	11/59	6/60	7227	10/58	11/58		7/54	3/56
6833	2/60	2/62		12/58	5/59		4/56	11/57
6837	12/50	10/52	7232	9/50	5/52	9460	1/52	4/52
6847	11/59	8/62	7243	6/61	6/61	9461	7/54	8/62
6849	9/60	10/60				9477	1/58	11/59

9493	7/54	6/61
9494	7/56	8/61
57XX		
9603	10/54	8/62
9629	8/50	6/53
9648	8/50	8/62
9681	12/60	8/62
9713	8/50	8/62
9723	8/50	3/54
	4/54	6/62
9727	4/61	8/62
9759	8/50	7/62
9775	1/60	8/62
9777	6/60	7/60
9794	6/60	8/62
8F 2-8-0		
48450	1/60	2/60
48460	9/59	2/60
48707	8/59	12/59
48737	8/59	10/59
48768	8/59	10/59
7MT 4-6-2		
70015	12/56	6/58
70016	12/56	9/61
70017	12/56	6/58
70018	12/56	9/61
70019	12/56	9/61
70020	12/56	9/61
70021	1/57	6/58
70022	12/56	9/61
70023	2/57	8/61
70024	12/56	9/61
70025	5/53	9/61
70026	9/52	9/61
70027	9/52	9/61
70028	9/52	9/61
70029	10/52	9/61
5MT 4-6-0		
73014	7/55	8/58

73017	6/56	6/56
73021	4/59	4/60
73023	4/59	5/60
73024	6/56	8/58
	4/59	4/60
73025	7/54	8/58
73026	7/54	8/58
4MT 4-6-0		
75004	7/55	9/58
75005	9/53	2/54
75006	9/53	12/53
75007	9/53	9/58
75008	10/53	10/58
75009	9/53	5/58
75021	11/53	9/58
75022	12/53	6/57
	7/57	9/58
WD 2-8-0		
90069	10/59	12/62
90125	10/54	8/62
90148	4/54	6/57
90149	10/59	9/62
90167	8/60	3/62
90188	3/51	6/51
	8/51	10/60
90192	7/52	9/54
90201	3/55	3/61
90238	10/51	7/59
90271	8/50	1/51
90312	9/56	3/60
90323	10/55	10/60
90355	10/55	6/56
90485	2/60	4/60
	6/60	10/61
90524	2/53	7/59
90565	5/52	11/59
90572	7/52	6/59
	7/59	9/62
90573	9/58	12/62

90579	7/55	9/62
90630	8/51	6/56
90685	9/58	11/59
90691	9/58	10/60
90693	9/54	1/61
90701	8/51	2/53
9F 2-10-0		
92001	10/61	6/62
92003	10/58	8/62
92004	9/59	2/60
92005	10/58	5/61
92166	8/59	9/59
92208	11/61	8/62
92209	8/59	5/61
92210	7/59	8/60
	7/62	8/62
92214	10/59	11/59
92216	12/59	8/62
92217	12/59	1/60
92219	2/60	8/62
92220	3/60	7/62
92227	1/61	7/62
92231	2/59	10/59
	2/60	9/60
92232	2/59	9/59
92233	2/59	9/59
	1/61	6/62
92234	2/59	9/59
92235	2/59	9/59
92236	11/58	8/62
92237	11/58	8/62
92241	10/60	8/62
92244	10/60	8/62
92245	10/60	6/62
92246	10/60	8/62
92247	2/62	7/62

[D] Before 10/62

Cardiff Cathays
88A 8/50
closed to Steam 12/57

RR 0-6-2T			43	8/50	8/55	66	1/51	10/52
31	8/50	3/51	44	8/50	8/55	73	2/51	7/52
35	8/50	5/51	56	8/50	10/52	79	6/54	7/55
38	8/50	9/51	57	10/51	4/52	80	11/53	1/54
40	8/50	9/51	58	9/51	10/52	**TV 0-6-2T**		
41	8/50	10/51	59	9/51	5/52	286	8/50	10/50
42	8/50	2/54	63	8/50	5/51	293	8/50	7/51

Shed by Shed

No.		
305	8/50	4/57
307	8/50	3/55
	4/55	2/56
312	9/55	6/56
343	8/50	9/55
344	8/50	10/52
345	8/50	8/55
346	8/50	9/55
347	8/50	11/56
348	8/50	4/56
360	8/50	1/55
361	7/56	12/56
362	1/53	4/56
364	8/50	2/57
367	8/50	2/56
371	8/50	1/52
376	8/50	11/53
	9/56	12/56
377	8/50	11/53
378	3/55	11/56
381	11/55	4/57
383	8/50	4/57
384	8/50	1/54
	9/55	1/56
385	3/56	4/57
387	4/56	10/56
388	6/56	9/56
390	8/50	11/53
	1/57	4/57
391	8/50	8/56
393	8/50	2/52
399	7/54	11/54
BM 0-6-2T		
433	8/50	2/51
434	8/50	8/53
14XX		
1420	8/50	8/53
1425	8/50	8/53
1461	8/50	8/53
16XX		
1629	9/50	11/50
	12/50	8/53
1901		
2008	9/53	10/53
2021		
2066	8/50	9/51
2140	8/50	1/52
57XX		
3672	11/50	12/57
3727	4/57	12/57
3734	8/50	6/54
51XX		
4101	9/55	7/56
	8/56	12/57
4105	11/55	8/56

No.		
4122	4/57	12/57
4123	4/57	12/57
4124	4/57	12/57
4126	4/57	12/57
4129	4/57	12/57
4177	9/55	12/57
42XX		
4224	4/55	10/55
45XX		
4553	6/57	8/57
4580	9/53	12/57
4581	8/53	7/56
4589	9/53	12/57
57XX		
4618	12/50	12/57
4634	10/55	12/57
4667	8/50	12/57
4672	4/57	12/57
4698	4/57	12/57
54XX		
5411	8/50	5/51
45XX		
5511	10/53	11/57
5534	10/53	12/57
5545	1/57	6/57
5568	11/53	12/57
5572	10/53	12/57
5574	6/56	12/57
56XX		
5600	11/54	7/55
5601	8/50	10/57
5608	11/54	7/55
5610	11/54	7/55
5617	1/52	5/52
5622	1/57	12/57
5623	8/50	9/50
5626	6/55	1/57
5627	1/56	11/57
5630	10/50	12/57
5636	8/50	3/56
	4/56	12/57
5637	8/55	12/57
5639	11/52	5/53
	6/53	9/53
5640	8/50	11/51
5650	9/52	10/55
5653	10/50	12/57
5654	10/50	11/57
5659	11/51	7/55
5663	10/53	12/57
5669	8/50	12/57
5670	8/50	12/57
5672	8/50	10/50
5677	2/54	10/56
5678	8/50	10/56

No.		
5680	1/54	2/54
5681	8/50	11/54
5683	10/50	12/57
5687	8/50	4/57
5692	10/50	12/57
5697	8/50	9/53
57XX		
5710	4/56	7/57
5724	3/56	7/57
5727	6/57	7/57
5793	7/54	12/57
64XX		
6402	8/50	12/57
6416	8/50	2/57
6423	8/50	3/56
6433	8/50	9/53
6434	5/57	9/57
	10/57	12/57
6435	8/50	9/53
	4/56	11/57
6436	8/50	9/53
56XX		
6603	8/50	3/51
	7/51	12/57
6606	10/56	12/57
6607	8/50	3/51
	8/51	12/57
6608	8/50	12/57
6612	8/50	12/57
6614	6/56	12/57
6618	8/50	12/57
6624	10/57	12/57
6626	8/50	12/57
6627	8/50	10/50
6634	8/50	5/51
6635	8/50	12/57
6638	11/54	12/57
6647	8/50	12/57
6648	10/56	12/57
6659	8/50	12/57
6660	8/50	12/57
6664	8/50	2/51
	5/51	9/53
6665	8/50	12/57
6682	8/50	12/57
6684	8/50	12/57
6689	8/55	12/57
72XX		
7202	8/50	12/57
7205	8/50	12/57
7242	2/51	12/57
7249	5/54	7/54
	11/54	4/55
7252	5/54	7/54
	11/5	3/55

	43XX			94XX				
7312	6/57	9/57	8420	5/51	8/51	8495	9/53	12/57
	74XX		8424	5/51	9/51		57XX	
7445	8/50	7/57	8455	12/52	11/53	8780	8/50	12/57
	57XX		8469	6/56	12/57		94XX	
7722	8/50	11/50	8470	10/52	12/57	9426	7/55	6/56
	11/57	12/57	8471	1/52	12/57	9470	5/52	12/52
7726	12/53	12/57	8478	10/52	12/57		9/53	11/53
7738	8/50	6/54	8481	5/52	12/57		57XX	
	8/57	12/57	8482	5/52	12/57	9679	11/57	12/57
7751	9/56	12/57	8484	8/52	12/57	9747	2/54	9/54
7772	7/55	12/57	8489	8/52	9/52	9769	8/57	9/57
7779	11/53	12/57		1/54	12/57	9776	8/57	12/57

Cardiff East Dock
88B 8/50   88L 1/61
88A 9/63
Closed 8/65

	RR 0-6-2T			91	8/50	5/54	378	11/53	5/54
33	8/50	2/51	92	8/50	5/54		11/54	3/55
35	5/51	10/56	93	8/50	4/54	381	7/54	9/54
36	8/50	9/57	94	8/50	4/54		7/55	11/55
37	8/50	8/56	95	8/50	8/53	385	5/54	9/54
38	9/51	9/57	96	8/50	3/54	389	3/55	12/55
39	8/50	7/55		Car R 0-6-2T		399	11/53	7/54
40	9/51	9/53	155	8/50	8/53		Car R 0-6-0T	
41	10/51	4/56		TV 0-6-2T		681	8/50	1/55
42	2/54	8/57	204	11/53	7/55	682	8/50	9/53
43	8/55	1/57	208	5/54	7/55	683	8/50	11/54
44	8/55	7/56	210	5/52	9/52	684	8/50	4/54
55	8/50	1/53		12/53	3/55		16XX	
56	10/52	8/53	211	3/52	9/52	1610	8/50	10/50
58	10/52	7/54		9/53	5/55		1854	
59	5/52	7/55	215	9/53	7/55	1705	8/50	11/50
63	5/51	8/52	216	9/53	12/54		2021	
65	1/53	1/54	279	9/53	4/54	2048	8/50	11/51
66	8/50	1/51	290	9/53	7/55	2086	8/50	9/51
	10/52	7/55	308	6/54	11/55	2123	8/50	9/52
67	8/50	8/52	312	1/55	9/55	2140	1/52	5/52
68	8/50	5/54	335	11/53	2/54	2141	8/50	10/50
72	8/50	2/52	349	7/54	12/54	2147	8/50	2/53
73	8/50	2/51	365	7/55	8/55		2721	
74	8/50	1/51	371	7/54	12/54	2754	8/50	10/50
78	11/54	7/55	374	7/54	8/55		28XX	
82	9/53	4/54	376	11/53	6/54	2859	8/64	9/64
83	9/53	5/55	377	11/53	9/54	2875	11/63	3/64
	RR 0-6-0T			4/55	1/56	2887	8/62	9/63
90	8/50	2/54				2895	3/63	12/63
							1/64	9/64

Shed by Shed

94XX		
3400	12/55	1/58
3401	1/56	1/58
3402	2/56	1/58
3403	2/56	1/58
3404	4/56	1/58
3405	6/56	1/58
3406	6/56	1/58
3407	7/56	1/58
3408	8/56	1/58
3409	10/56	1/58
57XX		
3650	12/53	10/55
3654	6/65	9/65
3672	8/50	11/50
3681	8/50	2/58
3689	1/63	10/63
3694	7/55	2/58
3707	8/50	8/55
3730	7/55	7/57
3734	6/54	7/57
3738	5/65	7/65
3748	1/63	7/64
3755	8/62	9/62
3783	8/50	7/57
3784	8/62	10/63
3790	9/64	6/65
28XX		
3804	8/62	7/64
3810	8/62	9/63
3818	7/64	9/64
3822	10/63	1/64
3837	4/64	9/64
3840	11/63	9/64
3862	8/62	9/63
4073		
4080	8/62	3/64
4090	9/62	5/63
42XX		
4242	8/62	3/64
4272	10/62	10/63
4285	9/64	11/64
4297	7/63	2/65
57XX		
4612	6/65	7/65
4616	8/50	5/52
4618	8/50	12/50
	2/63	4/63
4623	5/65	6/65
4626	6/54	8/57
4630	8/50	5/51
4631	7/55	8/57
4633	8/62	3/63
4639	5/65	6/65
4663	?/64 [E]	6/65

4686	7/54	8/57
4698	4/54	4/57
49XX		
4918	8/62	6/63
4936	8/62	1/64
4942	8/62	10/62
4953	8/62	4/63
4073		
5015	9/62	4/63
5029	11/62	12/63
5039	12/63	1/64
5042	12/63	3/64
5043	8/62	12/63
5056	7/63	3/64
5073	8/62	3/64
5074	9/62	10/63
5081	8/62	10/63
5091	8/62	3/64
5092	8/62	7/63
5096	8/62	3/64
5097	8/62	2/63
42XX		
5202	3/64	6/65
5206	12/63	11/64
5208	5/65	5/65
5220	8/62	12/63
5224	8/62	4/63
5225	8/62	8/63
5231	10/63	4/64
5261	8/62	3/65
56XX		
5642	1/54	7/55
5648	11/57	1/58
5687	4/57	1/58
57XX		
5710	8/50	4/56
5724	8/55	3/56
5749	8/62	7/63
49XX		
5932	3/64	4/64
5937	11/62	11/63
5952	11/63	7/64
5962	8/62	10/62
	11/62	10/63
5972	6/63	12/63
5984	4/63	1/65
43XX		
6326	8/62	12/63
6345	8/62	12/63
56XX		
6681	8/62	7/63
57XX		
6700	8/50	2/57
6701	8/50	5/58
6702	8/50	5/58

6703	8/50	1/58
6704	8/50	1/58
6705	8/50	1/58
6706	8/50	1/58
6707	8/50	1/58
6708	8/50	11/57
6709	8/50	1/58
6721	8/50	3/56
6736	2/54	3/58
6744	8/50	4/58
6751	8/50	4/58
6765	8/50	2/58
6767	8/50	3/58
6769	6/56	2/58
6770	11/50	8/57
6771	11/50	8/57
6773	11/50	3/58
6774	6/56	7/57
6775	6/56	3/58
6778	1/51	7/57
6779	1/51	6/56
68XX		
6808	9/62	2/63
6815	11/64	7/65
6820	6/64	7/65
6822	8/62	11/62
6826	4/64	5/65
6837	11/64	7/65
6838	11/64	7/65
6847	8/62	7/65
6859	8/62	7/65
6860	11/64	2/65
6863	4/64	11/64
6869	7/64	7/65
6872	11/64	7/65
6875	9/62	6/63
6876	3/65	7/65
49XX		
6909	8/62	10/62
6912	8/62	2/64
6914	11/63	3/64
6918	8/62	9/64
6931	9/62	9/65
6932	8/62	6/64
6935	8/62	6/63
	1/65	2/65
6936	8/62	6/63
	2/64	11/64
6939	8/62	10/63
6941	2/63	6/63
6944	8/62	9/65
6945	9/62	9/64
6950	8/62	7/64
6957	8/62	4/64

6958	6/64	9/64
6959		
6973	4/63	7/64
6984	11/63	9/64
6987	9/62	7/63
	11/63	9/64
6995	8/62	4/64
4073		
7016	8/62	1/63
72XX		
7249	4/63	5/65
43XX		
7303	11/62	11/63
7317	8/62	9/63
57XX		
7711	9/52	9/53
7722	3/52	11/57
	1/58	2/58
7738	6/54	8/57
7751	8/50	9/56
7772	5/55	7/55
78XX		
7804	3/65	7/65
7805	8/62	6/63
7811	3/65	7/65
7820	8/62	4/63
7826	3/65	5/65
6959		
7903	10/63	7/64
7913	8/62	7/64
7916	9/64	1/65
7923	2/65	5/65
7925	8/62	7/65
7927	8/62	7/65
94XX		
8400	7/55	11/56
8414	8/50	1/58

8416	8/50	1/58
8424	9/54	2/58
8425	9/62	11/63
8429	4/51	1/58
8437	8/55	9/57
8441	4/54	1/58
8446	10/55	9/56
8452	11/62	4/64
8455	8/50	12/52
8457	8/50	6/56
	9/56	1/58
8459	7/55	6/56
8464	5/51	1/58
8465	7/54	9/56
8466	8/62	1/63
8469	4/51	3/53
	7/54	6/56
8471	8/62	7/63
8478	7/52	10/52
8484	6/52	7/52
	8/62	11/64
8489	8/52	8/52
57XX		
8722	6/54	7/57
8728	1/63	7/63
8743	8/50	7/57
8787	7/55	7/57
94XX		
9426	8/62	10/63
9437	11/56	1/58
	9/62	10/63
	12/63	11/64
9443	10/56	1/58
9461	8/62	10/63
9470	3/55	4/56
9477	10/55	1/58
9494	9/54	7/56

57XX		
9603	1/63	10/63
9629	11/62	4/64
9648	1/63	3/63
9651	9/62	5/65
9671	6/64	3/65
9676	9/64	6/65
9677	8/50	8/57
9679	8/50	11/57
9681	1/63	7/65
9713	1/63	8/63
9769	2/54	6/57
	9/57	11/57
9776	1/51	6/57
9794	1/63	10/63
9F 2-10-0		
92007	6/65	7/65
92208	8/62	10/63
92209	9/63	5/65
	6/65	7/65
92210	8/62	12/63
92216	8/62	10/63
92219	8/62	9/65
92220	10/63	4/65
92224	10/63	11/64
92232	8/62	1/65
92236	8/62	11/64
92237	8/62	11/64
92241	8/62	11/63
92243	9/63	11/64
	2/65	7/65
92244	8/62	10/62
	11/62	7/65
92246	8/62	11/63
92248	2/65	5/65

[E] After 6/64

Cardiff Radyr
88A 12/57   88B 1/61
Closed to Steam 7/65

14XX		
1447	5/61	10/61
16XX		
1612	11/64	7/65
1613	11/64	3/65
1655	3/65	7/65
94XX		
3400	1/58	10/58
	5/62	11/64

3401	1/58	11/64
3402	1/58	11/64
3403	1/58	9/64
3404	1/58	6/62
3405	1/58	11/58
	12/58	11/64
3406	1/58	11/58
	12/58	11/64
3407	1/58	9/62

3408	1/58	8/62
3409	1/58	11/64
57XX		
3644	9/64	6/65
3672	12/57	1/64
3716	11/62	2/63
3717	5/65	5/65
3727	12/57	5/59
3728	11/64	4/65

3738	9/64	5/65
3784	9/64	5/65
51XX		
4101	12/57	2/58
4110	11/64	5/65
4122	12/57	3/58
4123	12/57	3/58
4124	12/57	8/58
4126	12/57	12/58
4129	12/57	2/59
4132	7/64	7/64
4143	5/58	11/60
	11/63	6/64
4152	5/58	8/58
4160	5/58	9/64
4163	5/58	2/59
	9/59	1/61
4164	5/58	9/58
4166	11/61	6/64
4169	7/64	5/65
4177	12/57	5/65
42XX		
4268	9/64	11/64
45XX		
4580	12/57	1/58
4589	12/57	1/58
57XX		
4616	5/58	11/58
4618	12/57	12/58
4620	9/64	5/65
4623	11/64	5/65
4634	12/57	11/58
4637	7/62	7/64
4650	11/64	7/65
4662	9/64	7/65
4667	12/57	12/58
4672	12/57	2/59
4674	9/64	11/64
4679	11/64	5/65
4698	12/57	2/59
45XX		
5527	2/58	5/58
5534	12/57	5/58
5568	12/57	5/58
5572	12/57	2/58
5574	12/57	3/58
56XX		
5602	7/64	9/64
5613	?/60 [F]	1/61
5615	9/58	11/58
	4/59	8/61
5618	9/59	7/60
5622	12/57	1/58
5623	12/63	3/64
5624	12/63	7/64

5625	11/62	10/63
5630	12/57	1/58
5633	9/63	5/65
5635	1/61	7/64
5636	12/57	1/59
5637	12/57	7/64
5640	1/59	9/60
5648	1/58	9/64
5651	11/62	5/63
5653	12/57	1/58
5660	9/64	11/64
5663	12/57	7/62
5669	12/57	9/58
	10/58	1/63
	6/64	9/64
5670	12/57	5/58
5672	11/62	9/63
5673	9/63	3/65
5675	1/59	9/59
5676	6/64	9/64
5683	12/57	3/64
5684	1/58	5/58
5687	1/58	5/58
5689	9/64	5/65
5691	11/64	6/65
5692	12/57	5/58
	12/58	9/60
	4/64	7/65
5694	3/64	11/64
5697	7/60	4/63
5699	11/64	11/64
57XX		
5793	12/57	2/58
61XX		
6108	9/60	9/64
6113	11/63	9/64
6116	4/63	6/65
6124	4/64	7/64
6169	4/64	6/64
64XX		
6402	12/57	8/58
6411	8/58	3/61
6416	4/58	7/58
6430	8/61	5/62
6433	8/50	9/53
6434	12/57	9/61
6438	9/61	5/62
56XX		
6603	12/57	6/63
6605	10/63	2/64
6606	12/57	1/65
6607	12/57	3/63
6608	12/57	7/63
6612	12/57	6/63
6614	12/57	5/65

6618	12/57	9/60
6621	7/62	6/63
	7/64	1/65
6624	12/57	7/64
6626	12/57	9/64
6635	12/57	1/58
	3/58	7/64
6638	12/57	7/64
6639	10/60	3/61
6647	12/57	8/62
6648	12/57	5/65
6650	9/64	5/65
6654	11/64	6/65
6656	8/62	7/63
6657	4/60	4/63
	4/64	6/65
6659	12/57	10/63
6660	12/57	7/64
6661	4/64	6/65
6665	12/57	9/64
6669	8/62	1/63
6672	12/63	7/65
6680	12/63	3/64
6681	6/64	9/64
6682	12/57	2/64
6684	12/57	1/65
6688	8/61	1/63
6689	12/57	5/65
6690	4/64	7/64
6695	10/63	7/64
6697	7/64	9/64
6699	5/58	12/63
57XX		
6704	1/58	3/58
6707	1/58	5/58
6744	4/58	5/58
6751	4/58	4/58
68XX		
6876	1/65	3/65
72XX		
7202	12/57	9/62
7205	12/57	1/65
7209	10/62	11/62
7217	6/63	7/63
7219	6/63	2/64
7231	6/63	7/63
7239	9/62	11/62
7242	12/57	7/63
7245	2/64	9/64
7250	7/62	9/64
7252	8/59	7/63
	9/64	1/65
57XX		
7717	10/58	12/58
7722	12/57	1/58

7726	12/57	7/58	8484	12/57	1/58	9488	7/64	5/65
7738	12/57	5/58		11/64	5/65	**57XX**		
7751	12/57	1/58	8489	12/57	1/58	9611	11/64	5/65
	5/58	12/58	8495	12/57	1/58	9615	3/65	7/65
7766	10/58	12/58		7/64	11/64	9622	11/64	7/65
7772	12/57	5/58	8497	1/63	7/64	9644	5/65	5/65
7779	12/57	9/58		**57XX**		9656	5/65	7/65
	81XX		8780	12/57	2/59	9667	11/64	5/65
8103	10/63	11/63		5/59	6/62	9675	5/65	7/65
	94XX			**94XX**		9679	12/57	10/58
8419	5/58	2/59	9425	5/58	3/59	9682	11/64	7/65
8420	5/58	6/62	9426	9/64	5/65	9711	5/62	1/63
8438	5/58	9/62	9430	9/64	11/64		6/64	9/64
8455	8/58	2/60	9437	11/64	5/65	9776	12/57	11/58
8460	5/58	9/59	9446	2/65	5/65	9778	9/64	11/64
8466	1/63	7/64	9456	7/63	3/64	9780	1/65	7/65
8469	12/57	11/64	9457	7/63	7/64		**3MT 2-6-2T**	
8470	12/57	1/62	9461	9/64	5/65	82032	3/58	5/58
8471	12/57	3/62	9464	2/65	5/65	82033	3/58	5/58
8475	7/64	9/64	9466	7/63	7/64	82034	3/58	5/58
8478	12/57	1/63	9472	1/63	4/64	82036	3/58	5/58
8479	10/62	9/64	9475	2/65	5/65	82037	4/58	5/58
8481	12/57	1/60	9480	10/62	4/64			
8482	12/57	1/58		7/64	5/65	**[F]** After 12/60		

Carmarthen
87G 8/50
Closed 4/64

	10XX		2248	8/60	11/63	3041	10/55	3/58
1006	6/54	10/54	2271	8/50	7/54		**2251**	
1020	9/56	10/56	2272	8/50	3/51	3216	1/54	6/55
	14XX			4/51	7/59		**57XX**	
1472	8/50	2/56	2273	10/52	1/59	3642	12/55	7/57
	16XX		2274	3/59	6/60	3693	6/61	6/62
1613	8/50	8/53	2284	8/50	8/53	3790	10/63	3/64
1648	1/60	8/60	2287	5/62	5/63		**4073**	
1659	3/55	4/57	2290	6/55	5/59	4000	9/56	10/56
1662	10/56	11/56		**2301**		4074	9/56	7/57
1669	2/62	11/62	2431	8/50	11/51	4081	?/60 [G]	6/61
	1901		2474	8/50	7/53		6/62	1/63
1903	8/50	6/52		**ROD**		4086	10/52	2/53
	2021		3010	8/50	2/56	4090	9/59	6/60
2056	8/50	3/51	3011	8/50	9/58	4094	9/61	3/62
2069	8/50	2/55	3014	7/54	9/55		**51XX**	
2111	8/50	2/53	3015	8/50	5/51	4106	8/61	9/61
	2251			1/53	9/58	4132	7/60	6/62
2216	8/50	1/62	3018	10/52	12/56	4134	1/52	6/56
2217	8/50	7/54	3024	11/56	9/58		7/56	6/60
2224	10/54	8/59	3025	10/52	6/54	4154	6/53	11/53
2236	8/50	3/53	3036	6/56	3/58	4178	8/50	2/53

Shed by Shed

42XX

4213	10/59	3/60

49XX

4901	6/57	9/57
4907	8/53	9/53
4910	8/50	3/60
4915	8/50	10/54
4916	6/59	12/59
4922	8/50	12/55
4923	6/60	7/60
4935	6/57	9/61
4937	8/50	10/54
	5/59	11/59
4958	6/57	11/59
4962	8/53	9/53
	4/60	5/62
4963	6/56	9/56
4981	8/50	6/53
4983	5/58	4/59
4984	8/50	9/56

4073

5002	8/56	10/56
5003	10/57	4/58
5006	4/58	7/60
	9/61	4/62
5027	7/61	6/62
5030	7/58	6/60
	9/60	8/62
5039	7/52	3/53
	5/53	2/56
	3/56	6/57
	9/60	1/63
5042	12/62	1/63
5043	6/52	2/53
	5/53	3/55
	4/55	2/56
5054	11/60	10/62
5055	12/62	7/63
5067	2/59	5/61
5080	9/56	1/57
5091	9/57	5/58
5098	7/62	1/63

51XX

5171	10/52	4/57
5180	12/59	1/62
5188	7/55	9/55
5192	7/54	9/54

43XX

5310	10/53	5/58
5330	6/59	9/59
5332	10/60	9/61
5339	8/50	10/52
5353	10/53	5/60
5360	12/51	10/52
5377	5/58	8/58

54XX

5400	5/52	2/57
5408	5/51	5/52

45XX

5558	6/56	7/56

57XX

5761	2/51	5/51
5775	10/52	3/56

58XX

5819	8/50	6/57

49XX

5902	6/60	2/62
5937	8/53	4/59
	6/59	11/62
5938	8/53	1/63
5953	6/59	11/60
5955	6/56	9/56
5958	6/56	9/56
5961	7/60	9/61
5963	8/50	2/56
5969	7/61	7/62
5972	8/50	3/51
5984	8/50	9/55
	6/60	9/60

61XX

6114	6/62	1/63
6118	6/62	1/63
6125	7/60	5/61
6151	6/62	4/63

43XX

6304	8/50	1/54
6305	8/58	8/59
6310	8/50	10/58
6316	3/60	6/62
6329	6/54	9/61
6331	8/50	2/53
6344	8/50	2/53
6347	5/60	6/61
	9/61	6/62
6357	1/62	6/62
6367	8/50	3/53
6375	6/63	9/63
6377	9/58	9/60
6393	10/58	9/59

56XX

6616	3/60	?/6? [H]

68XX

6800	10/53	12/53
6818	8/50	10/52
6836	10/53	12/53
6843	7/55	12/55
6865	7/55	10/55

49XX

6905	1/62	7/62
6912	6/57	9/57

6919	8/50	1/54
6927	8/53	9/53
6935	6/56	2/59
6950	6/61	9/61

6959

6965	9/62	1/63

4073

7002	10/56	5/58
7009	9/60	6/61
7012	9/59	11/60
7016	9/59	6/61
7021	8/50	12/50
	1/51	2/51
	9/57	6/59
7028	11/56	6/57

72XX

7203	3/62	6/62
7243	5/62	6/62

43XX

7306	11/61	12/63
7312	6/60	7/62
7320	11/61	6/62
7321	2/61	7/62
7332	6/63	9/63
7334	6/60	4/62
7340	9/62	11/62

74XX

7400	8/50	4/51
	5/51	6/60
7401	8/50	1/59
7402	3/55	6/62
7405	11/62	12/63
7407	8/50	11/63
7408	1/61	7/62
7419	8/50	7/60
7422	4/57	3/62
7425	8/50	6/62
7439	3/55	8/57
	1/60	3/64
7442	1/63	11/63
7444	8/50	2/64
7445	7/62	3/64
7448	8/60	1/63

57XX

7755	6/53	4/56

78XX

7804	6/54	6/62
7814	12/62	2/63
7815	11/62	3/64
7824	6/57	6/59
7825	2/53	10/61
7826	2/53	11/63
7829	3/53	3/64

81XX

8102	9/57	12/60

8103	10/52	10/59	9632	4/56	3/64	**WD 2-8-0**		
	11/59	6/62	9645	6/59	1/60	90167	3/58	6/60
57XX			9666	10/52	9/57	90169	3/58	6/62
8777	3/56	4/61	9787	7/57	9/63	90207	3/58	6/60
90XX			**8F 2-8-0**			90485	3/58	11/59
9008	10/53	7/54	48172	7/60	7/60	90529	3/58	6/60
9010	10/53	6/54	**5MT 4-6-0**					
93XX			73029	12/53	1/54	[G] After 1/60		
9310	6/54	9/57	**3MT 2-6-2T**			[H] Before 8/62		
57XX			82003	3/62	6/62			
9606	8/57	7/63						

Chester GW
84K 8/50   6E 2/58
Closed 4/60

10XX			3667	9/51	2/52	5033	8/50	5/58
1000	10/52	3/54	3676	12/58	4/60	5061	7/51	5/58
1008	10/52	5/58	3762	8/50	4/57	5075	8/50	6/56
1024	10/52	5/58	3786	8/50	4/60	5091	9/55	6/57
1026	3/54	9/55	**28XX**			**51XX**		
14XX			3811	1/57	2/57	5103	8/50	7/58
1434	8/50	3/55	3820	1/54	5/58	5129	8/50	7/51
2301			3829	1/51	7/52	5141	8/50	8/51
2513	8/50	11/54	3858	8/50	5/58	5160	8/56	7/58
28XX			3859	8/50	9/52	5174	8/50	5/60
2804	7/55	12/55	3860	8/50	7/51	5177	11/52	7/58
2807	9/57	5/58	**4073**			5179	8/50	7/58
2810	8/50	9/53	4000	10/54	12/54	5181	8/50	9/53
2812	8/50	9/52	4076	8/50	11/54	5184	8/50	2/53
2817	7/55	5/58	4078	1/58	5/58	5186	8/50	6/56
2822	1/51	8/52	**51XX**			**43XX**		
	3/53	4/54	4102	5/55	7/58	5311	4/53	1/58
2825	9/57	5/58	4115	6/53	7/58	5315	6/54	1/58
2833	9/57	5/58	4128	4/57	10/57	5319	7/55	10/55
2834	1/58	5/58	4165	10/52	7/58	5326	8/53	4/54
2848	12/56	5/58	**43XX**			5331	8/50	10/54
2855	9/57	5/58	4377	7/55	10/55	5334	4/53	5/53
2869	12/50	5/51	**57XX**			5344	8/50	6/56
2882	8/50	3/52	4602	8/52	4/60	5399	8/50	11/52
	12/56	5/58	4617	8/50	11/50		9/55	4/60
2890	8/50	9/55	**49XX**					
29XX			4905	8/50	10/53	**56XX**		
2915	8/50	10/50	4917	9/53	11/53	5647	8/50	12/56
2926	8/50	9/51		1/54	2/54	5690	8/50	10/54
2953	8/50	2/52	4918	8/50	12/50	**57XX**		
57XX			4976	8/50	10/53	5719	10/57	10/58
3619	8/50	9/51	4987	8/50	7/51	5723	8/50	10/57
3630	1/52	4/60	**4073**			5725	8/50	8/58
3646	8/50	10/55	5027	12/50	12/51	5739	11/54	8/58
3665	8/50	4/60	5031	11/54	3/55	5748	2/54	3/54

Shed by Shed

No.			No.			No.		
5791	8/50	6/57	7820	12/53	12/54	**5MT 4-6-0**		
49XX			7822	4/54	8/58	73013	7/55	4/59
5912	8/50	5/52	7823	1/51	10/51	73014	8/58	4/59
5923	8/50	2/51	7827	1/51	8/58	73020	9/53	9/54
5962	1/54	8/58	**6959**			73021	9/53	4/59
5966	8/50	2/51	7921	10/50	10/53	73023	9/53	4/59
5968	10/51	4/56		12/53	8/58	73024	9/53	9/54
5994	1/52	10/52	7922	10/50	3/51		8/58	4/59
43XX				5/51	8/58	73025	8/58	4/59
6308	8/50	12/52	**94XX**			73026	8/58	4/59
6331	2/53	11/55	8423	2/51	8/51	73033	5/58	9/59
6337	8/50	6/56	**57XX**			73038	9/53	4/60
6339	8/50	5/53	8709	9/58	4/60	73098	9/58	11/58
6344	2/53	1/58	8729	8/51	4/60	73099	9/58	11/58
6345	8/53	6/59	8730	12/56	4/60	**4MT 4-6-0**		
6362	1/52	12/52	**94XX**			75005	8/58	4/59
6367	3/53	6/54	9425	9/50	6/51	75006	8/58	4/59
	7/54	1/58	**57XX**			75020	8/58	4/59
6376	6/58	12/58	9719	8/52	9/52	75026	8/58	4/59
6380	8/50	4/60	9728	8/50	4/60	75028	8/58	6/59
6392	8/50	6/57	9740	2/56	3/56		9/59	4/60
6393	3/53	5/53	9774	8/50	6/53	75033	9/59	4/60
56XX			9794	8/50	4/60	**3MT 2-6-2T**		
6624	8/50	5/51	**Stanier 3MT 2-6-2T**			82001	7/58	4/60
6683	5/51	12/52	40106	10/58	4/60	82002	7/58	4/60
68XX			40116	7/58	6/59	82003	7/58	4/60
6806	9/54	7/55	**5MT 4-6-0**			82005	7/58	4/60
6817	9/54	5/58	45237	6/59	9/59	82032	7/58	4/60
6823	9/55	9/57	**Jubilee 6P 4-6-0**			82034	7/58	4/60
6833	7/52	6/54	45613	6/58	4/59	82036	7/58	4/60
6835	7/52	7/54	45624	9/58	4/59	**WD 2-8-0**		
6849	9/54	7/55	45632	6/58	4/59	90149	12/51	1/52
6857	9/55	9/57	**8F 2-8-0**			90214	8/50	4/60
49XX			48308	5/58	11/58	90466	11/51	7/53
6901	1/52	8/58	48344	5/58	4/59	90572	8/50	6/52
6941	8/50	6/56	48402	5/58	4/59	90685	12/50	2/51
6942	4/57	8/58	48408	5/58	4/59	90686	8/50	4/60
6959			48412	5/58	4/59			
6963	7/52	8/58	48415	5/58	4/59			
57XX			48417	5/58	4/59			
7762	9/58	4/60	48418	5/58	4/59			
78XX			48424	5/58	4/59			
7800	10/52	8/58	48430	5/58	4/59			
7801	9/53	8/58	48444	5/58	4/59			
7807	12/53	8/58	48471	5/58	4/59			

Croes Newydd
84J 8/50   89B 1/61
6C 9/63
Closed 6/67

14XX		
1410	7/51	3/54
1416	8/50	9/56
1426	9/51	12/51
1447	10/61	2/62
1457	8/50	4/53
1458	9/58	12/58
1465	11/56	1/57
	4/57	8/58
1473	8/50	11/53
16XX		
1618	1/60	5/62
1624	8/50	6/51
1628	10/62	10/64
	11/64	8/66
1632	6/62	4/65
1635	8/53	12/58
	1/59	9/59
1638	1/65	7/66
1646	2/53	2/57
1659	4/57	9/60
1660	3/55	2/66
1663	8/62	11/62
	5/63	1/65
2021		
2107	12/52	6/53
2181		
2184	8/50	11/50
2185	6/51	11/52
2186	6/51	4/55
2188	8/50	2/52
2190	8/50	4/51
2251		
2200	6/60	7/60
	7/60	9/60
2201	6/61	9/61
2202	7/55	9/55
2209	8/50	10/52
	5/53	9/53
	7/55	9/55
	6/56	9/57
2210	6/61	9/61
2211	5/58	9/58
2222	6/60	11/60

2230	5/58	9/58
2232	8/50	6/51
2236	6/61	9/61
2247	6/57	9/57
2256	7/55	9/55
2257	8/52	10/52
	6/62	11/62
2259	8/50	6/51
	8/51	9/51
	11/51	9/53
2262	8/50	10/51
2292	7/54	9/54
2294	6/59	10/59
2295	7/54	9/54
2296	6/56	9/57
2297	8/50	9/53
1501		
2716	8/50	9/50
2719	8/50	11/50
28XX		
2822	8/50	1/51
2840	8/50	5/59
2853	5/52	7/56
2855	1/59	7/62
2856	6/61	9/61
2871	8/50	2/61
2878	8/50	5/59
ROD		
3026	8/50	6/51
3028	8/50	6/51
3033	9/51	3/53
2251		
3201	6/59	8/62
3203	8/50	3/52
3204	2/60	3/60
3206	8/50	5/53
3207	6/60	9/60
3209	8/62	12/62
3210	7/60	10/60
57XX		
3665	5/60	6/60
3676	5/60	6/60
3689	1/59	11/62
3709	11/65	8/66

3749	1/60	10/65
3756	8/60	12/60
3760	1/60	8/62
3782	7/64	11/64
3786	6/60	7/60
3789	11/62	0/65
28XX		
3809	4/64	10/64
3813	3/63	6/65
3815	9/59	6/64
3825	8/50	10/51
3828	3/59	11/62
3829	3/63	3/64
3831	3/63	9/63
3846	9/60	11/63
3849	4/64	6/65
3850	1/65	8/65
3855	1/65	8/65
3862	9/63	2/65
3865	3/63	3/65
43XX		
4375	8/50	2/51
57XX		
4617	11/50	3/62
4645	10/50	10/65
4683	2/51	11/58
	1/60	9/65
43XX		
5315	8/50	3/51
	5/51	6/54
5319	8/50	3/55
	10/55	7/58
5328	9/53	11/53
5330	6/62	10/63
5334	8/50	4/53
5365	8/50	3/51
5378	4/59	8/59
5399	11/52	12/52
54XX		
5416	3/54	9/58
56XX		
5605	12/65	5/66
5606	1/60	10/60
5651	1/60	11/62

Number		
5659	9/65	11/65
5667	9/63	7/65
5676	9/64	10/65
5677	4/65	10/65
5679	4/62	12/62
	1/63	3/63
57XX		
5742	8/50	8/58
5774	8/50	9/62
58XX		
5810	8/50	12/58
5811	8/50	2/57
49XX		
5912	5/52	6/52
43XX		
6301	6/62	9/62
6303	8/50	10/58
6306	6/60	10/61
6307	4/59	7/60
6311	8/50	10/58
6316	8/50	3/60
6327	8/50	2/51
6338	9/54	7/56
6339	9/53	11/53
	9/54	6/62
6353	1/60	3/60
6357	4/59	1/62
6362	9/54	4/55
6374	9/60	10/60
6375	6/62	10/62
6380	5/60	6/61
64XX		
6404	8/50	11/54
	1/55	3/59
6405	8/50	5/59
6422	8/50	8/62
6429	12/58	5/59
56XX		
6604	8/62	9/65
6610	1/60	7/60
6611	6/51	10/65
6615	8/59	4/63
6617	6/51	8/62
6625	10/52	12/52
	11/62	7/65
6626	9/64	10/65
6632	1/52	9/63
6633	7/55	9/55
6651	5/63	9/65
6665	9/64	7/65
6668	11/65	11/65
6674	6/59	7/63
6683	9/65	10/65
6694	8/50	10/63
6696	10/52	9/60

Number		
6697	11/65	5/66
6698	8/50	12/52
	6/60	3/63
68XX		
6817	5/58	5/58
72XX		
7230	2/60	6/64
43XX		
7300	2/60	9/61
7305	8/50	3/55
7310	8/50	11/63
7313	8/50	6/62
7314	6/60	9/61
	8/62	10/62
7339	(ex 9317 9/56)	
	9/61	12/63
7341	(ex 9319 6/57)	
	11/59	7/60
	9/61	8/62
74XX		
7403	8/50	8/60
7409	8/50	7/61
7414	8/50	3/63
7418	2/62	3/63
7422	1/57	4/57
7428	12/58	9/60
7431	8/50	10/60
	2/61	8/64
7432	10/50	2/51
7433	8/50	2/61
7435	10/50	11/50
7440	8/50	9/62
7442	7/52	9/61
	2/62	3/62
	10/62	1/63
7443	8/50	3/63
7447	8/50	7/56
78XX		
7803	9/62	3/63
7811	9/61	12/62
7812	11/61	1/63
7817	8/50	9/58
	10/58	2/61
7821	9/61	3/63
7825	1/51	2/53
7826	1/51	2/53
7828	5/61	3/63
57XX		
8727	10/58	4/62
8730	5/60	6/60
8734	1/60	3/62
8767	7/66	7/66
8791	7/56	3/61
90XX		
9004	6/57	6/60

Number		
9014	6/57	9/60
9018	5/58	6/59
9028	6/53	8/57
57XX		
9608	10/62	11/64
9610	1/60	9/66
9621	12/58	12/59
9630	8/64	9/66
9639	8/64	9/65
9641	7/66	10/66
9669	8/50	5/62
9793	6/51	9/63
9794	5/60	6/60
3MT 2-6-2T Stanier		
40126	1/60	3/60
2MT 2-6-2T		
41201	1/64	6/64
41202	1/64	6/64
41204	7/64	6/65
41241	7/64	6/65
4MT 2-6-0		
43088	4/67	5/67
5MT 4-6-0		
44762	11/66	11/66
44776	11/66	5/67
44872	10/66	5/67
45045	11/65	8/66
45130	9/65	4/67
45198	9/65	3/67
45344	9/65	8/66
2MT 2-6-0		
46442	1/64	10/64
46507	1/63	2/65
	6/65	7/65
46508	1/63	2/65
	8/65	8/66
46509	1/63	2/65
8F 2-8-0		
48020	9/63	10/63
48122	8/65	2/67
48134	11/64	2/65
	5/65	1/66
48147	8/65	7/66
48252	8/65	6/67
48253	11/66	3/67
48255	12/65	12/65
48269	9/63	10/63
48287	12/65	2/66
	3/66	4/67
48325	11/64	3/67
48339	9/66	9/66
48353	12/64	1/65
48385	9/66	11/66
48411	11/65	2/66
48440	9/65	2/67

48479	11/64	12/64	75012	3/66	3/66	76040	9/66	4/67
48518	11/64	2/65	75013	3/67	5/67	76048	9/66	2/67
48554	12/65	12/65	75016	3/67	6/67	76086	9/66	9/66
48632	12/65	2/66	75020	3/63	1/65	**4MT 2-6-4T**		
	11/66	3/67	75021	3/63	3/66	80070	2/63	3/63
48659	6/63	7/63		7/66	4/67	80078	2/63	8/65
48665	11/64	3/67	75023	3/63	1/65	80079	7/62	8/65
48669	11/66	6/67	75024	3/63	6/65	80080	7/62	8/65
48697	11/65	2/66	75026	3/63	2/65	80096	11/62	3/63
	11/66	6/67	75027	3/63	2/65		9/63	4/65
48747	1/66	8/66	75029	3/63	6/65	80098	11/62	3/63
48762	9/63	10/63		3/67	6/67	80101	2/63	3/63
5MT 4-6-0			75033	5/66	1/67	80104	11/62	3/63
73004	6/65	4/66		3/67	4/67	80105	2/63	3/63
73032	5/65	8/65	75046	5/66	5/67	**2MT 2-6-2T**		
73040	7/65	4/66	75047	3/66	7/66	84000	1/65	10/65
73045	5/65	7/65		12/66	1/67	84003	3/64	6/64
73095	8/65	4/66		3/67	6/67	84004	1/65	10/65
73096	6/65	7/65	75048	5/66	5/67	84009	3/64	6/64
4MT 4-6-0			75052	12/66	6/67	**9F 2-10-0**		
75002	12/66	5/67	75055	3/67	5/67	92029	5/66	8/66
75006	3/63	11/64	75060	5/66	4/67	92074	5/66	12/66
	3/67	6/67	75071	7/64	6/67	92125	5/66	12/66
75009	3/63	2/66	**4MT 2-6-0**			92135	5/66	10/66
	3/67	5/67	76037	4/67	6/67	92137	8/66	12/66
75010	3/66	5/67	76039	4/67	6/67			

Danycraig
87C 8/50
Closed 3/64

	YTW 0-4-0T			SHT 0-6-0T			57XX	
1	8/50	1/54	1147	8/50	4/51	3633	8/56	11/59
	RR 0-6-2T			**PM 0-4-0T**		3679	8/56	11/59
60	8/50	3/51	1151	8/50	11/59	3781	8/50	11/59
	LMM 0-6-0T		1153	8/50	5/53		**42XX**	
359	8/50	1/54		1/54	2/54	4232	5/59	9/59
803	8/50	3/51		**16XX**		4299	8/50	11/59
	1101		1606	8/50	9/50		**57XX**	
1101	8/50	12/59	1634	3/51	2/60	4666	9/50	11/59
1102	8/50	2/60	1640	6/53	2/60	4681	9/59	3/63
1103	8/50	2/60	1643	5/51	7/53	4694	8/50	11/59
1104	8/50	2/60	1647	3/54	2/60		**42XX**	
1105	8/50	2/60	1648	3/54	1/60	5210	5/59	10/59
1106	8/50	2/60		**2021**		5211	5/59	10/59
	SHT 0-4-0T		2055	8/50	1/51	5232	5/59	10/59
1141	8/50	7/52	2082	8/50	1/51		**56XX**	
1142	8/50	6/57		3/51	3/52	5616	5/59	10/59
1143	8/50	12/59	2134	8/50	10/51	5628	5/59	10/59
1145	8/50	6/59	2146	8/51	2/53			
			2151	8/50	5/52			

57XX		
5703	11/51	9/54
	10/54	1/59
5704	8/56	1/60
5730	8/50	3/58
5731	9/56	1/60
5743	8/56	12/58
5775	8/50	10/52
43XX		
6337	10/59	11/59
6360	10/59	1/60
57XX		
6713	8/50	10/54
6714	4/54	4/55
6719	7/55	1/60
6734	8/50	5/52

6762	8/50	10/59
6763	8/50	5/55
	6/55	6/56
6766	8/50	10/52
	11/52	10/59
72XX		
7215	5/59	10/59
7225	5/59	10/59
7226	5/59	10/59
7248	5/59	10/59
74XX		
7439	8/57	1/60
57XX		
7793	1/59	1/60
94XX		
8408	8/50	8/56

8475	5/52	8/56
8476	4/52	8/56
8483	6/52	8/56
57XX		
8720	8/50	2/52
	3/52	12/59
8724	10/54	11/59
94XX		
9457	11/51	8/53
9485	10/52	9/56
9491	3/54	8/56
57XX		
9606	3/54	8/57
9645	1/58	6/59
9744	8/56	1/60

Didcot
81E 8/50
Closed 7/65

1854		
907	8/50	3/51
10XX		
1002	2/61	10/62
1007	3/61	9/62
1008	2/61	9/62
1015	8/61	10/62
MSWJ 2-4-0		
1334	8/50	8/52
15XX		
1502	12/50	1/61
16XX		
1636	6/62	7/64
1854		
1861	8/50	11/51
2251		
2200	1/60	6/60
2201	2/60	2/61
	2/62	1/64
2202	8/50	5/52
2214	10/54	5/60
2221	8/50	11/52
	10/54	12/60
	1/61	1/62
2222	8/50	12/52
2226	8/50	5/53
2230	3/60	1/62
2234	9/59	3/60
2240	8/50	3/61
2246	1/58	10/60

2252	8/50	12/59
2289	8/50	9/54
23XX		
2532	8/50	4/54
2579	8/50	5/51
28XX		
2802	5/58	11/58
2819	3/53	9/54
	11/58	1/61
2820	4/54	5/54
2821	5/59	10/59
2834	10/61	1/63
2836	8/59	10/63
2842	11/61	9/63
2844	5/59	3/60
2849	11/59	7/62
2852	11/62	10/63
2893	4/60	11/64
2898	5/61	5/63
	1/64	9/64
ROD		
3024	8/50	11/52
2251		
3206	1/54	8/60
3210	8/50	7/60
3211	8/50	1/61
3212	8/50	6/59
57XX		
3622	8/50	11/60
3653	9/53	12/60

3665	7/61	6/62
3697	3/62	5/62
3709	8/50	7/60
3721	8/50	12/60
3751	8/55	5/62
	6/62	1/65
3752	1/64	7/64
3763	5/62	4/63
28XX		
3814	7/55	10/55
	11/64	1/65
3819	9/61	1/65
3820	2/61	1/65
3835	11/64	1/65
3837	9/53	5/55
3838	6/64	9/64
3840	9/61	11/63
3845	5/53	5/55
3851	6/64	1/65
3859	6/64	9/64
4073		
4074	5/62	11/62
43XX		
4318	8/50	5/52
4326	8/50	4/53
57XX		
4606	4/62	4/63
4649	8/50	12/60
49XX		
4902	2/60	6/63

4905	10/63	11/63		**49XX**			**68XX**	
4908	7/62	10/63	5903	8/50	7/54	6824	9/62	10/63
4910	11/60	11/63	5915	5/58	8/58	6849	9/62	10/63
4913	11/59	12/59	5918	10/59	9/61	6868	9/62	10/63
4915	1/59	1/62	5935	8/50	5/58	6874	9/62	10/63
4928	1/57	2/57	5943	10/56	2/61		**49XX**	
4933	9/55	9/57	5953	1/61	2/61	6909	10/62	7/64
4935	8/50	6/57	5969	6/56	9/56	6910	9/50	9/62
	6/62	3/63	5987	11/59	4/63		1/65	6/65
4939	12/56	1/63		**61XX**		6915	9/58	2/61
4942	10/62	12/63	6105	11/59	3/60	6921	11/63	4/64
4945	9/53	6/56	6106	11/64	1/65		8/64	6/65
4950	9/60	7/63	6109	12/52	2/53	6923	8/50	11/50
	1/64	7/64		7/60	7/62	6928	3/65	6/65
4954	4/54	8/56	6112	8/50	3/51	6937	2/60	6/65
4959	9/58	1/65		2/62	12/64	6938	1/65	3/65
4962	6/64	6/65	6113	7/60	7/61	6952	8/50	4/60
4965	1/58	3/62	6116	9/51	10/53	6953	1/65	6/65
4969	2/59	11/61	6118	8/50	9/53	6957	2/60	5/61
4976	9/60	4/62	6120	10/60	4/62		**6959**	
4979	9/55	9/57	6124	11/59	1/62	6961	1/65	6/65
4994	4/53	3/63	6126	5/62	4/64	6963	1/65	6/65
4998	5/52	10/52	6130	5/61	1/64	6969	2/58	3/65
	43XX		6132	8/50	7/51	6983	9/53	6/65
5322	8/56	12/58	6134	8/50	9/53	6986	3/65	5/65
5326	10/57	3/62	6136	8/60	6/65	6991	1/65	6/65
5330	8/50	6/53	6139	3/60	1/64	6996	9/58	11/64
	7/55	2/58	6156	7/60	6/61		**43XX**	
	1/64	7/64		9/64	5/65	7308	6/63	7/64
5337	8/59	9/60	6159	7/60	6/65	7324	(ex 9302	2/57)
5351	8/59	6/61	6164	11/59	10/60		9/58	9/62
5361	12/59	2/60	6166	7/51	9/53	7327	(ex 9305	1/59)
5375	8/59	9/59	6167	8/50	6/64		9/58	11/64
5380	8/50	9/63		**43XX**		7340	(ex 9318	1/58)
5381	8/50	3/53	6302	12/59	3/62		11/62	7/64
5386	1/58	2/58	6304	1/54	5/58		**57XX**	
5390	1/58	7/58	6309	1/62	9/64	7705	10/57	7/59
5397	8/50	5/58	6313	5/53	10/56	7710	8/50	8/58
	56XX			10/59	10/61	7772	3/59	7/60
5626	11/53	12/53	6329	8/50	6/54		**78XX**	
5629	12/53	6/57	6333	2/60	6/60	7813	3/65	5/65
5639	9/53	7/60	6337	11/63	7/64	7814	5/65	6/65
5647	12/56	7/60	6340	8/50	4/57	7816	11/64	6/65
5675	10/55	5/58	6350	7/61	1/64	7829	11/64	6/65
5697	9/53	8/59	6359	8/50	11/53		**6959**	
	5/60	7/60	6363	9/60	6/64	7917	11/63	6/65
	57XX		6367	10/63	11/64		**94XX**	
5735	8/50	10/57	6378	8/63	7/64	8435	5/53	10/60
5737	2/53	9/59	6379	9/57	6/61	8458	1/56	10/60
5744	8/50	7/60		6/63	8/63	8494	12/60	1/62
5746	4/57	8/62	6385	10/63	11/63		**57XX**	
5752	8/50	1/57	6388	10/58	6/59	8720	12/59	9/64
5783	11/52	5/60		**56XX**			**90XX**	
5796	9/58	3/59	6654	10/53	1/54	9015	8/50	9/53
			6664	4/60	10/60			

Shed by Shed

43XX			9409	11/55	1/56	9791	2/62	1/64
9300	10/52	2/53	9413	8/50	11/55	**WD 2-8-0**		
9301	10/52	2/53	9417	8/50	11/55	90201	3/61	6/61
9302	10/52	6/53	9450	12/60	3/62	90312	3/61	5/61
9305	9/58		**57XX**			90327	8/50	9/50
(renum 7327 1/59)			9726	7/64	1/65	90565	3/61	4/61
94XX			9755	2/62	4/62			
9407	11/55	8/60	9781	2/61	5/61			

Duffryn Yard
87B 8/50
closed 3/64

RR 0-6-2T			42XX			5241	7/63	9/63
69	8/50	7/55	4207	10/52	2/53	5245	2/64	3/64
70	8/50	7/55	4212	8/50	3/59	5246	6/60	12/63
16XX			4213	3/60	10/62	5254	2/52	3/64
1601	8/50	11/50	4250	10/52	2/53	5257	8/50	9/56
1602	8/50	11/50		4/61	8/62		3/62	10/63
1606	9/50	11/50	4256	8/50	2/64	5264	6/57	7/60
1622	8/50	9/50	4265	8/50	5/60	**56XX**		
1643	7/53	10/53	4273	6/57	9/57	5604	5/58	8/61
1645	10/53	11/53	4278	11/58	9/63	5612	8/50	9/51
1901			4286	10/60	12/62	5626	12/53	6/55
1964	11/50	1/51	4288	9/60	10/60	5629	8/50	12/53
1996	11/50	12/50	4290	7/61	8/61	5639	8/50	12/51
2011	11/50	10/51	4292	8/50	10/59	5646	8/50	8/51
2021			4293	1/57	3/61	5670	12/59	12/63
2079	8/50	10/52	4296	5/52	10/63	**57XX**		
28XX			4299	11/59	8/62	5713	8/50	5/58
2800	12/50	4/55	**57XX**			5728	8/59	5/62
2813	1/51	9/54	4640	8/50	12/63	5731	8/50	6/53
2872	10/52	9/54	4651	5/62	9/63	5734	8/50	11/56
2894	6/53	4/55	4657	11/63	3/64	5738	5/57	8/59
57XX			4681	8/50	10/59	5761	8/50	2/51
3610	6/62	2/64	4684	8/50	6/52	5770	9/53	12/61
3613	7/55	3/64		7/52	1/55	5773	8/50	8/51
3626	1/62	8/63		3/55	3/63	5787	10/54	9/63
3642	4/61	3/64	4695	6/57	3/64	5789	9/53	1/57
3647	12/63	3/64	**49XX**			**56XX**		
3654	12/63	3/64	4928	1/63	11/63	6602	9/55	6/60
3682	8/62	3/64	4970	9/62	7/63		6/61	6/61
3688	1/61	8/62	4983	9/62	2/63	6616	8/50	3/60
3692	10/60	3/64	**42XX**			6620	9/56	11/63
3718	8/50	5/62	5202	12/63	3/64	6623	8/50	6/60
3762	4/57	11/63	5203	10/60	8/61		7/60	10/60
3791	8/50	8/63	5204	4/60	6/61		11/60	1/61
51XX			5216	8/50	4/63	6629	8/50	9/58
4101	10/52	9/53	5220	8/50	6/60	6644	8/50	8/51
4164	8/50	9/53	5221	1/58	4/61	6650	8/50	1/57
			5232	6/60	1/63	6680	6/61	2/63

6686	8/50	1/64	7240	10/52	8/53	8724	11/59	6/62
6691	8/50	1/64	7241	4/55	1/56	8746	10/62	1/63
57XX			7243	6/61	5/62	8772	8/60	7/61
6701	5/58	5/59		1/63	3/64	**94XX**		
6715	8/50	7/51	7244	1/52	2/60	9431	12/50	1/59
	8/51	5/58	7248	6/57	1/58	9437	2/51	11/56
6717	8/50	5/57	7249	4/55	11/64	9444	5/51	8/61
6718	8/50	6/57	7252	7/63	3/64	9447	6/51	4/59
6719	8/50	7/55	**43XX**			9454	9/51	1/62
6720	8/50	7/53	7312	2/63	3/63	9455	11/51	1/57
6725	5/59	9/59	7318	2/63	3/63	9456	11/51	7/63
6749	8/50	5/57	7320	2/63	3/63	9457	8/53	7/63
6760	10/62	11/62	**57XX**			9461	1/52	7/54
6761	8/50	6/53	7706	8/50	3/60	9464	10/61	3/64
	7/53	1/61	7715	1/62	1/63	9475	9/62	3/64
6766	10/59	7/60	7733	8/50	11/56	9483	9/52	7/63
6768	8/50	10/54	7744	8/50	11/56	9487	11/52	11/56
6776	1/51	4/57	7758	5/57	6/60	**57XX**		
6777	1/51	4/57	7790	10/62	1/63	9615	10/62	3/64
6778	7/57	8/57	**94XX**			9617	8/50	3/64
49XX			8405	7/55	11/56	9633	8/62	10/63
6909	10/52	11/52	8407	7/55	9/62	9634	8/50	3/64
6914	9/63	11/63	8410	8/51	2/60	9656	11/62	3/64
6920	9/62	11/63	8416	1/58	9/62	9669	5/62	1/66
6959			8418	8/51	6/59	9671	12/60	2/63
6987	7/63	11/63	8423	8/51	1/59	9715	6/61	8/63
72XX			8454	8/51	1/61	9735	8/50	3/61
7200	6/60	10/60	8464	11/50	5/51	9736	8/50	6/61
7204	7/63	3/64	8465	12/50	6/51	9737	8/50	12/60
7216	2/62	10/63	8466	1/51	11/56	9742	4/57	3/64
7218	8/52	12/52	8482	1/61	8/62	9760	9/63	12/63
7222	11/62	12/63	8490	8/52	8/52	9766	8/50	3/64
7229	2/62	3/64		9/52	9/62	9785	8/50	8/62
7235	1/60	10/60	**57XX**			9788	3/62	3/64
7238	2/53	6/53	8714	7/62	1/63	9799	8/50	9/63

Ebbw Junction
86A 8/50   86B 9/63
Closed to Steam 10/65

CMDP 0-6-0T			1430	10/54	11/55	**2021**		
28	10/52	10/53	1471	5/58	9/58	2035	9/52	3/55
BM 0-6-2T			**15XX**			2048	11/51	5/52
431	8/50	9/53	1506	9/59	5/62	2063	8/50	5/51
432	8/50	4/53	1509	8/50	7/59	2073	8/50	6/51
435	8/50	1/54	**16XX**			2090	9/51	3/55
436	8/50	1/54	1614	11/62	3/64	2122	8/50	10/52
14XX			1653	12/54	1/63	2136	7/52	9/52
1421	11/52	9/55	1656	1/55	7/64	**2251**		
	10/55	5/58	**1854**			2209	7/60	7/62
1422	10/55	9/56	1862	8/50	12/50	2218	8/50	11/63

No.		
2219	10/59	6/60
2223	9/59	?/?? [I]
2227	8/50	1/61
2236	10/59	6/61
2239	8/50	4/56
2240	9/61	6/62
2243	7/60	1/63
2247	3/60	1/63
2280	8/50	5/58
2298	7/62	12/63
28XX		
2800	4/55	4/58
2807	5/58	12/58
2814	6/56	7/58
2815	8/50	9/51
2817	8/50	10/52
2818	9/59	4/63
2819	8/50	10/52
2820	9/56	10/58
2821	8/50	9/51
2823	8/58	1/59
2834	8/50	10/52
2839	2/57	12/59
2842	8/50	2/60
2845	7/55	6/59
2851	8/50	6/56
2857	4/61	8/61
2858	5/52	7/52
	11/54	5/60
2861	8/50	12/58
2864	11/53	4/54
2865	8/50	7/52
2866	8/50	6/53
2867	11/62	7/63
2868	7/55	5/59
2873	2/54	9/54
2874	10/55	3/56
2876	8/50	6/53
	8/63	1/65
2879	8/50	10/52
2884	11/59	11/62
2885	9/62	5/63
2889	8/50	10/52
2890	9/63	2/64
	11/64	5/65
2893	10/59	3/60
2894	8/50	6/53
	4/55	8/63
2895	9/64	5/65
2896	8/50	9/54
2897	4/61	6/62
2898	1/58	5/61
29XX		
2936	8/50	4/51
2979	8/50	1/51

No.		
31XX		
3103	8/50	2/60
3150		
3170	11/54	7/58
2251		
3201	8/62	3/64
3211	1/61	8/62
57XX		
3621	7/63	11/64
3634	8/50	7/55
	8/55	12/63
3636	8/50	2/62
3638	10/59	1/61
3647	8/50	9/52
3661	6/61	10/62
3662	8/50	9/65
3667	1/61	5/61
3681	10/59	9/64
3691	2/53	4/65
3694	11/59	8/62
3700	8/50	11/54
	6/60	3/63
3705	6/63	3/65
3706	10/59	11/63
3708	5/65	7/65
3712	8/50	8/59
	6/60	7/60
3713	1/60	6/60
3714	8/50	12/63
3722	7/60	5/62
3726	8/50	1/62
3729	11/62	12/62
3747	10/59	3/65
3756	12/60	2/61
3764	7/61	1/63
3767	10/59	10/65
3772	2/57	6/65
3796	8/50	8/53
3798	8/50	7/62
28XX		
3800	8/50	9/59
	3/61	8/64
3801	8/50	9/54
3804	8/50	6/59
3805	8/50	9/64
3806	5/54	7/54
3807	8/50	2/65
3808	5/54	7/54
	9/56	7/65
3810	8/50	9/54
3812	7/63	3/65
3816	8/50	9/54
3818	5/61	4/64
	9/64	3/65

No.		
3824	9/54	6/56
	11/59	7/64
3827	10/55	1/63
3830	8/50	5/65
3832	2/57	4/63
3833	8/50	7/63
3836	8/50	9/54
3837	4/59	4/64
	9/64	7/65
3840	9/64	7/65
3853	3/59	1/62
3861	8/64	7/65
3864	1/65	7/65
51XX		
4119	6/56	1/58
4130	12/50	1/51
	7/55	2/58
4137	8/50	11/53
	6/62	8/62
4145	12/51	11/53
4146	1/60	6/62
4148	8/50	11/54
4151	6/62	8/62
4156	8/50	11/53
4168	8/50	1/58
42XX		
4200	3/58	3/59
4203	8/50	1/61
4206	8/50	12/52
4211	12/54	3/55
	2/58	7/59
4214	4/64	7/64
4225	8/50	8/53
	12/60	8/61
4227	2/56	10/63
	12/63	3/65
4229	10/58	10/59
	7/60	3/61
4230	8/50	5/54
	6/60	7/61
4233	6/63	11/63
	4/64	11/64
4235	11/60	7/62
4238	6/63	12/63
4241	3/64	4/64
4242	8/50	11/55
	3/56	6/56
4246	12/53	4/61
4247	8/50	12/52
	1/58	4/61
4248	8/50	7/61
4252	10/61	10/62
4254	12/64	4/65
4255	2/54	6/56
	3/64	4/64

No.		
4257	3/61	7/61
4258	10/60	4/63
	6/63	10/63
4259	9/54	2/56
	6/63	3/64
4263	8/50	9/50
4265	5/60	6/63
4266	7/60	7/62
4267	1/56	12/59
4268	8/50	1/51
	2/65	9/65
4271	6/63	12/63
4275	3/51	4/51
4277	7/53	4/55
4283	9/54	4/63
4286	2/54	5/59
4289	8/50	7/53
4290	8/61	1/63
4293	3/61	7/62
4294	8/50	9/57
4297	1/60	7/63
4298	12/52	2/53
4299	8/62	12/63

57XX

No.		
4611	9/51	3/63
4620	5/65	7/65
4627	11/62	9/64
4643	6/63	4/65
4657	12/60	11/63
4662	7/65	9/65
4671	8/50	9/64
4679	4/62	12/63

49XX

No.		
4916	10/53	6/59
4941	8/50	5/52
4951	10/53	1/54
	2/54	2/57
4957	11/53	1/58
4982	10/53	4/58
4983	3/51	4/51

51XX

No.		
5173	10/52	11/59
	6/61	9/61
5188	10/58	6/62

42XX

No.		
5200	6/63	11/63
	3/65	4/65
5201	8/50	1/51
	12/53	10/61
5203	2/63	4/63
5205	7/56	1/62
5206	8/50	12/55
5208	8/50	11/53
5209	4/64	7/65
5212	8/50	11/53

No.		
5213	9/60	4/63
5214	10/63	11/63
5217	8/50	5/63
5218	8/50	2/54
5222	8/50	6/56
5223	3/65	3/65
5224	8/50	2/54
5227	9/54	1/63
5228	12/53	6/63
5229	8/50	5/63
5233	8/50	8/63
5234	8/50	6/63
5235	12/62	11/63
	11/64	9/65
5236	11/53	7/55
	6/61	10/63
5238	8/50	4/63
5241	6/64	6/65
5243	8/50	7/55
5244	6/63	7/64
5250	6/63	12/63
5251	8/50	12/62
5252	3/65	5/65
5255	8/50	5/63
5256	8/50	10/59
	6/63	9/63
	3/65	3/65
5257	6/61	3/62
5259	8/50	3/64
5260	5/52	7/56
5261	10/57	11/57
5264	8/50	6/56

43XX

No.		
5306	10/61	1/63
5318	8/51	6/52
	10/54	6/57
5330	10/61	6/62
5364	8/50	7/51
5382	9/54	6/57

54XX

No.		
5414	9/54	8/57

45XX

No.		
5545	8/50	11/51
5550	8/50	10/52

56XX

No.		
5602	8/50	10/51
5657	12/55	10/57
	11/57	6/62

57XX

No.		
5709	8/50	3/60
5732	8/50	1/58
5741	8/50	9/52
5772	1/56	5/58
5790	1/58	3/58

49XX

No.		
5906	8/50	5/52
5911	8/50	12/50
	3/51	4/51
5916	12/56	2/57
5921	11/53	1/58
5938	1/63	5/63
5939	2/63	11/64
5961	3/65	9/65
5992	6/65	9/65

61XX

No.		
6102	11/53	1/58
6107	11/53	1/54
6114	11/53	6/56
	7/56	1/58

43XX

No.		
6318	10/54	6/57
6348	5/58	12/60
6361	3/56	6/56
6366	10/61	6/62
6370	9/54	8/60
6386	9/51	10/52

64XX

No.		
6401	8/56	12/58
	5/60	6/60
6408	6/60	8/60
6409	8/50	10/50
6412	7/56	7/63
6415	8/50	3/58
6417	4/58	5/59
6425	7/56	1/61
6426	8/50	4/57
	9/57	3/61
6428	8/50	1/58
6430	9/54	3/59
6431	4/58	7/58
6434	9/61	7/63
6439	8/50	8/52
	7/54	5/60

56XX

No.		
6639	7/55	11/55
6642	2/53	11/55
6654	8/50	9/51
6656	6/59	5/62
6672	8/50	2/53

57XX

No.		
6754	10/60	10/62

68XX

No.		
6805	9/60	3/61
6812	10/52	3/56
6813	9/60	6/64
6818	2/64	3/64
6819	6/61	8/61
6820	8/50	6/56
	6/61	6/64

Shed by Shed

6821	8/50	5/52	**7233**	6/57	6/63		**57XX**	
	6/61	8/61	**7234**	6/57	11/62	**8702**	1/62	3/63
6823	10/52	11/52	**7237**	9/61	11/62	**8710**	8/50	5/59
	12/52	2/53	**7238**	1/62	6/63	**8711**	8/50	7/59
6829	9/60	3/63	**7240**	5/58	6/63		6/60	9/60
6834	8/50	5/52	**7241**	8/50	4/54	**8751**	4/60	1/63
6838	9/56	10/61	**7243**	11/52	6/61	**8766**	1/54	7/63
6847	10/52	11/59	**7245**	8/50	1/63	**8778**	8/50	7/60
	7/65	10/65	**7246**	6/56	2/58	**8781**	8/62	1/63
6849	8/56	6/57	**7247**	8/50	3/55	**8794**	1/53	7/56
	1/62	9/62	**7249**	8/50	4/54		**94XX**	
6850	10/59	3/63		7/54	11/54	**9424**	8/60	1/63
6852	1/62	2/64		11/64	4/65	**9458**	1/52	9/56
6865	9/56	11/59	**7250**	5/58	2/62	**9459**	3/56	4/56
6870	8/50	6/56	**7251**	4/56	10/57	**9468**	11/56	7/60
6874	8/50	5/52	**7252**	8/50	4/54	**9482**	9/52	6/62
6876	4/59	10/61		7/54	11/54	**9488**	10/60	10/63
	7/65	10/65	**7253**	8/50	6/63	**9490**	2/54	12/59
6878	4/64	6/64		3/65	4/65	**9494**	8/61	9/61
	49XX			**43XX**		**9499**	7/55	1/57
6918	9/64	11/64	**7319**	2/53	12/58		**57XX**	
6927	8/50	5/52	**7325**	(ex 9303 5/58)		**9600**	5/65	9/65
6932	9/51	5/52		10/61	8/62	**9616**	8/50	9/64
6935	6/63	11/64		**57XX**		**9632**	8/50	4/56
6958	9/64	11/64	**7736**	8/50	8/59	**9637**	8/50	3/56
	6959			6/60	5/62	**9644**	8/50	11/63
6965	1/63	11/64	**7738**	5/58	1/59	**9649**	11/64	7/65
6978	3/65	6/65	**7753**	8/50	8/53	**9662**	8/50	6/59
	72XX		**7755**	4/56	10/59		6/60	9/65
7201	7/64	9/64	**7768**	8/50	12/59	**9664**	8/50	1/63
7203	8/50	3/55	**7771**	8/50	8/59		6/63	7/64
	1/63	9/63		6/60	9/60	**9666**	3/65	9/65
7204	12/59	6/61	**7774**	3/58	12/59	**9667**	8/50	4/64
7206	4/64	7/64	**7781**	8/50	7/60	**9674**	8/53	10/62
7208	12/52	2/53	**7787**	4/56	8/59	**9678**	11/63	3/64
7210	5/52	2/58		6/60	9/60	**9731**	8/50	5/53
7211	8/59	10/60	**7794**	10/59	9/60	**9745**	3/59	6/61
7212	6/56	9/60		**6959**			**8F 2-8-0**	
7214	8/50	5/58	**7925**	7/65	10/65	**48475**	7/54	7/54
	6/61	1/62	**7927**	7/65	10/65		**WD 2-8-0**	
7215	8/50	8/53		**94XX**		**90069**	12/54	10/59
	10/57	11/57	**8406**	8/50	1/57	**90125**	10/51	10/54
7217	8/50	7/52	**8440**	3/54	12/59	**90149**	11/51	12/51
	12/59	11/60	**8450**	8/50	9/50		1/52	5/53
	12/62	6/63	**8453**	8/50	8/59		9/58	10/59
7218	12/52	1/60	**8493**	8/52	1/53	**90167**	8/50	1/51
7219	10/53	6/63		8/55	7/59	**90174**	11/51	6/52
7222	11/55	11/62	**8494**	8/52	2/53	**90179**	12/54	6/57
7223	10/61	7/63		9/54	10/54	**90188**	6/51	8/51
7224	11/61	1/63	**8495**	1/58	6/59		12/60	11/62
7227	11/52	4/58	**8497**	12/52	1/53	**90201**	6/61	5/62
7229	3/54	2/62	**8498**	12/52	1/53	**90225**	6/51	6/60
	6/64	8/64	**8499**	12/52	1/53		8/60	11/62
7231	8/50	9/62		9/53	12/59	**90261**	8/50	10/53
7232	5/52	1/59						

90312	8/56	9/56	92005	2/54	10/58	92231	10/59	2/60
	5/61	9/61		5/61	9/63	92233	9/62	10/63
90323	12/51	11/52	92006	2/54	6/61	92235	9/59	10/65
	11/60	5/62		9/61	9/63	92236	9/58	11/58
90356	8/53	10/53	92007	2/54	12/60	92237	9/58	11/58
90529	6/62	11/62	92012	9/61	7/63		3/65	10/65
90544	12/51	12/62	92166	9/59	2/60	92238	9/58	12/58
90565	8/50	5/52	92207	11/64	1/65		12/61	10/63
	7/60	11/60	92209	5/61	9/63	92239	9/58	12/58
90573	10/51	5/52	92210	6/64	11/64	92240	9/58	11/58
90585	10/51	5/55	92214	11/61	7/64	92241	10/58	11/58
90630	6/51	8/51	92222	10/60	11/63	92242	10/58	10/64
90676	12/51	11/52	92223	3/61	10/63	92243	10/58	11/62
	5/54	9/61	92225	3/60	10/63		7/65	10/65
90685	6/51	3/53		6/64	6/65	92244	10/58	11/58
	6/60	10/60	92226	10/60	10/61		7/65	10/65
90701	6/51	8/51		10/62	7/64	92248	12/58	9/59
	9F 2-10-0			10/64	6/65	92249	12/58	6/60
92000	1/54	6/61	92229	1/60	11/63		9/60	10/63
92001	1/54	6/61		6/64	11/64	92250	11/59	11/63
92002	1/54	4/63	92230	1/60	9/62		6/64	7/64
92003	1/54	10/58		10/62	1/64			
92004	1/54	9/59		8/64	10/65	[I] Before 5/62		
	10/60	1/61						

Exeter St Davids
83C 8/50
Closed 10/63

	10XX		1469	8/50	8/58		28XX	
1007	9/59	3/61	1470	5/61	9/62	3834	8/50	9/50
1023	9/59	3/61	1471	9/58	10/63		4073	
	14XX			16XX		4037	6/62	8/62
1405	8/50	8/58	1608	2/60	2/62	4081	5/58	12/58
1409	5/53	6/53	1650	7/60	10/61	4083	9/60	9/61
1420	?/?? [J]	2/62		2021			51XX	
1421	10/62	10/63	2088	8/50	9/52	4105	5/60	9/60
1429	8/50	3/59		2251		4117	5/57	6/57
1434	?/?? [K]	6/62	2211	9/54	5/58		9/57	9/58
1435	8/50	5/58	2230	8/50	6/57		3/59	9/60
1439	7/55	9/55		28XX		4129	6/60	9/60
1440	8/50	5/61	2873	8/50	9/50	4133	3/55	4/55
1442	11/62	10/63		57XX		4145	5/60	10/60
1449	8/50	9/58	3603	8/50	10/58	4150	5/60	7/61
1450	6/62	10/63	3606	8/50	11/59	4165	2/61	6/62
1451	8/50	9/63	3659	3/62	9/63	4174	7/56	9/57
1452	7/59	6/60	3677	8/50	9/58	4176	8/50	7/54
1462	3/59	8/62	3709	3/62	6/62		5/60	11/60
1466	4/61	10/63	3746	1/58		4178	5/60	9/60
1468	8/50	12/60	3794	8/50	10/63			
	7/61	1/62						

44XX

4401	2/52	1/53
4410	8/50	4/53

45XX

4540	8/50	3/59
4548	9/57	10/57
4553	4/58	5/58
	5/58	7/58
4589	9/58	6/60

57XX

4673	6/62	10/63

49XX

4909	10/61	3/62
4917	12/53	1/54
	2/54	4/54
4924	5/60	9/60
	10/60	6/62
4930	5/60	9/60
	10/60	6/62
4932	3/51	10/52
4942	7/55	9/55
	6/60	11/60
4944	10/58	6/62
4948	1/53	9/61
4954	3/51	6/53
4955	7/55	9/57
4960	2/59	9/59
4967	6/57	9/57
	3/61	6/62
4970	6/61	6/62
4984	6/61	6/62
4988	7/55	9/55
4992	5/58	9/60
4993	6/61	6/62
4996	7/61	6/62

4073

5003	4/51	12/56
	2/57	4/57
5020	6/60	9/61
5021	10/52	4/57
5059	8/50	5/53
5062	8/50	3/51
5075	6/59	7/61
5091	6/57	9/57

51XX

5174	5/60	9/60
5175	10/60	12/60
5190	6/62	8/62

43XX

5321	8/50	9/53
5339	2/58	5/59
5344	6/56	9/56
5362	1/55	8/55

54XX

5412	10/54	4/62
5422	7/56	8/56

45XX

5508	10/60	11/61
5522	7/53	8/53
5524	9/58	2/59
	4/59	6/60
5525	8/50	9/53
5530	1/58	5/58
5536	6/57	8/58
5546	9/58	6/59
5555	9/61	7/63
5560	9/61	4/62

57XX

5760	8/50	10/54
5796	1/55	3/55
	7/56	9/56

49XX

5902	8/50	7/52
5913	6/61	5/62
5917	6/62	6/62
5946	3/60	6/62
5959	12/56	4/57
	6/57	9/59
5976	8/50	1/59
	?/60 [L]	?/61 [M]
5992	7/54	9/54
5994	7/61	11/62

61XX

6103	3/55	4/55
6146	7/60	5/62

43XX

6301	8/50	9/55
6318	6/53	10/54
6319	12/59	1/60
6322	12/54	2/58
6337	6/56	9/56
6346	9/62	5/63
6365	2/54	7/54
6371	11/58	1/59
6385	6/54	11/59
6394	6/57	9/57
6397	8/50	10/52

64XX

6407	7/55	9/55

68XX

6813	5/60	9/60
6814	10/60	2/61
6820	6/56	9/57
6829	5/60	9/60
6868	10/60	2/61
6870	6/56	11/56

49XX

6938	5/54	1/56

6959

6965	3/58	9/62
6994	8/50	4/54
	10/61	2/62

72XX

7224	6/61	11/61

43XX

7311	5/58	8/62
7316	8/50	8/62
7326	(ex 9304 5/58)	
	5/58	7/58

57XX

7711	9/53	12/54
7716	8/50	12/59
7761	8/50	1/61

94XX

8421	8/50	5/59
8456	8/50	11/58
9439	3/51	5/59
9474	2/57	7/60
9480	2/60	10/62
9487	7/60	6/62
9497	12/54	5/62

57XX

9629	6/53	5/60
9633	1/62	8/62
9635	3/62	3/63
9647	8/50	5/51
9668	7/55	8/55
9765	4/53	12/61

[J] After 7/59
[K] After 5/55
[L] After 1/60
[M] Before 12/61

Exmouth Junction
72A 8/50   83D 9/63
Closed 6/65

Class/No.	From	To
14XX		
1442	2/65	5/65
2251		
2214	8/63	5/65
2241	7/63	8/63
2277	11/63	12/63
3205	12/63	5/65
57XX		
3633	12/59	4/60
3679	12/59	2/63
3759	8/63	3/65
4610	8/63	11/64
4616	8/63	2/64
4655	2/63	6/65
4666	11/59	12/59
	1/63	6/63
	9/63	6/65
4673	10/63	11/63
4692	7/63	9/64
4694	11/59	12/59
	1/63	6/65
64XX		
6400	3/63	11/63
6412	7/63	11/63
6430	3/63	11/63
57XX		
9647	9/64	5/65
9756	11/59	4/60
M7		
30021	3/51	9/61
30023	3/51	3/53
	7/53	9/60
30024	8/50	11/62
30025	8/50	11/56
30027	2/59	11/59
30030	8/50	3/52
30034	8/50	3/51
30039	8/50	3/51
30040	6/51	9/52
30041	4/51	6/54
30042	5/51	6/54
30044	5/51	9/61
30045	9/51	12/62
30046	8/50	2/59
30048	8/59	4/63
30049	8/50	4/51
30055	8/50	6/51
30105	8/50	6/51
T9		
30120	3/61	10/61
M7		
30124	8/50	3/52
30125	9/60	12/62
30133	8/50	9/52
O2		
30182	9/58	1/60
30183	6/56	7/57
30192	8/50	9/51
30193	8/50	12/53
	1/54	5/57
30199	8/50	5/57
	7/57	10/61
30224	8/50	8/53
30230	8/50	9/51
30232	8/50	10/59
M7		
30245	8/50	6/52
30252	8/50	3/51
30253	8/50	3/51
30255	8/50	5/51
30256	8/50	5/51
T9		
30283	8/50	1/51
30313	8/59	8/61
700		
30315	11/54	3/58
30317	3/58	8/61
M7		
30320	8/50	9/52
30321	3/51	9/52
30323	8/50	12/59
700		
30327	2/59	5/61
T9		
30338	5/59	4/61
M7		
30356	3/51	7/53
30357	6/51	7/53
30374	8/50	1/51
	3/51	11/53
	1/54	11/56
	5/57	10/59
30375	3/51	7/53
30376	8/50	9/52
30377	8/50	9/52
L11		
30408	8/50	3/51
30409	8/50	6/51
N15		
30455	8/50	11/50
	3/51	4/51
30457	8/50	11/50
	3/51	4/51
Q		
30530	12/62	7/63
30531	12/62	7/63
0395		
30564	8/50	5/58
30575	11/52	11/54
30580	1/51	11/54
30581	8/50	3/53
0415		
30582	8/50	8/61
30583	8/50	8/61
30584	8/50	1/61
M7		
30667	5/51	11/53
	1/54	4/63
30668	8/50	9/61
30669	8/50	8/61
30670	3/51	9/61
30671	8/50	6/56
30676	3/52	8/61
700		
30689	9/61	11/62
30691	11/54	8/61
30697	9/61	11/62
30700	9/61	11/62
T9		
30702	8/50	6/52
	2/59	10/59
30703	8/50	9/51
30704	1/51	9/51
30705	1/51	11/51
30706	8/50	11/51
30707	8/50	11/51
	9/52	1/53
30708	1/51	11/51
	9/52	12/57

Part		
30709	5/51	8/61
30710	5/51	2/59
30711	1/51	10/59
30712	1/51	2/59
30714	9/50	4/51
30715	8/50	8/61
30716	8/50	9/51
30717	8/50	8/52
	9/52	8/61
30718	5/59	4/61
30719	5/59	4/61
30723	8/50	5/51
30726	5/58	10/59
30727	7/53	2/55
30729	4/60	4/61
S15		
30823	8/50	6/51
30824	8/50	6/51
30825	8/50	6/51
30841	8/50	8/63
30842	8/50	8/63
30843	8/50	8/63
30844	8/50	8/63
30845	8/50	7/63
30846	8/50	6/51
	9/53	1/63
30847	8/50	6/51
Z		
30950	4/56	11/62
30951	5/59	12/62
30952	5/59	12/62
30953	2/59	12/62
30954	8/50	12/56
	5/59	12/62
30955	9/58	12/62
30956	4/56	12/62
30957	4/59	11/62
N		
31406	2/62	9/64
31407	8/50	1/51
31408	8/50	1/51
31409	10/61	11/62
U		
31626	9/58	2/59
31634	1/51	6/51
31635	1/51	6/51
	6/56	1/57
31636	1/51	6/51
31790	9/58	5/59
31791	9/58	5/59
31804	6/56	1/57
N		
31812	8/63	7/64
31818	1/62	9/63
31821	8/63	7/64

Part		
31828	10/50	6/51
31829	8/50	6/51
31830	8/50	10/62
31831	8/50	10/62
31832	8/50	10/62
31833	8/50	10/62
31834	8/50	9/64
31835	8/50	9/64
31836	10/50	1/64
31837	8/50	11/52
	1/53	9/64
31838	8/50	2/64
31839	8/50	12/63
31840	8/50	6/52
	9/52	9/64
31841	8/50	6/52
	9/52	3/64
31842	5/51	6/52
	11/52	6/54
	2/55	6/55
	11/56	7/64
31843	1/51	11/52
	11/56	9/64
31844	1/51	8/52
	9/53	12/63
31845	8/50	7/53
	9/53	9/64
31846	10/50	9/64
31847	8/50	9/63
31848	4/51	10/55
	10/61	2/64
31849	4/51	7/64
31850	5/59	1/64
31851	4/51	9/51
	7/53	1/55
	5/59	11/59
31852	4/51	9/51
	5/59	11/59
31853	8/50	9/51
	5/59	9/64
31854	8/63	7/64
31855	8/50	9/51
	1/61	9/64
31856	8/50	9/51
	1/61	7/64
31857	1/61	10/62
31859	8/63	9/64
31860	5/59	10/63
31866	10/50	4/51
31867	10/50	4/51
31869	8/50	4/51
31874	8/50	11/50
	1/61	3/64
31875	8/50	11/50
	1/61	8/64

Part		
U1		
31901	5/61	9/61
31902	5/61	9/61
31903	5/61	9/61
31904	5/61	9/61
W		
31911	11/62	9/63
31912	11/62	9/63
31913	11/62	1/63
31914	11/62	9/63
31915	11/62	9/63
31916	11/62	7/63
31917	12/62	1/63
31924	11/62	9/63
E1/R		
32124	8/50	2/59
32135	8/50	4/59
32695	8/50	3/57
32697	8/50	12/59
BB/WC		
34001	8/50	9/57
34002	8/50	8/64
34003	8/50	9/57
34004	8/50	2/58
34005	8/50	4/51
34006	8/50	4/51
34007	8/50	4/51
34008	8/50	4/51
34009	8/50	4/51
34010	8/50	4/51
34011	2/59	11/63
34012	11/50	1/51
	3/51	4/51
34013	5/51	9/57
34014	8/50	2/58
34015	8/50	1/51
	3/51	8/64
34016	8/50	2/58
34017	8/50	3/54
34018	8/50	4/51
34019	8/50	4/51
34020	8/50	4/51
	5/62	9/64
34021	11/50	12/57
34022	5/51	12/57
34023	5/51	8/64
34024	8/50	10/63
34025	8/50	9/57
34026	8/50	2/58
34027	8/50	9/57
34028	8/50	1/51
	3/51	2/59
34029	8/50	2/59
34030	8/50	9/64

34031	8/50	11/50	34097	11/60	5/62	41315	6/52	1/53
	5/51	2/59	34098	11/60	5/62		9/63	2/64
34032	5/51	10/63	34104	2/58	10/61	41316	9/63	7/64
34033	5/51	9/51	34106	2/58	9/64	41317	9/63	12/64
	11/51	8/64	34107	5/59	9/64	41318	5/57	9/63
34034	9/50	11/50	34108	2/58	10/63	41320	9/61	7/64
	3/52	10/61	34109	2/58	9/64	41321	9/61	7/65
34035	12/57	5/63	34110	2/59	11/63	41322	9/61	7/64
34036	12/57	10/63		**MN**		41323	9/61	7/64
34037	12/57	2/58	35001	8/50	1/57		**4MT 2-6-4T Fairburn**	
34038	12/57	11/60	35002	8/50	4/54	42099	9/51	1/52
34044	8/50	5/51		6/54	5/58	42102	11/51	1/52
34045	8/50	5/51	35003	8/50	6/64	42103	9/51	1/52
34046	8/50	5/51	35004	8/50	3/57	42105	9/51	1/52
34047	8/50	5/51	35005	5/51	3/54		**5MT 4-6-0**	
34048	8/50	1/51	35008	8/54	2/60	73030	10/63	9/64
34049	4/51	5/51	35009	3/57	9/64	73044	10/63	1/65
34050	4/51	6/51	35010	2/60	8/64	73161	9/63	1/65
34051	4/51	6/51	35011	5/57	2/60	73162	9/63	1/65
34052	4/51	6/51	35013	3/54	8/64	73166	10/63	9/64
34053	4/51	6/51	35014	4/54	8/54		**4MT 4-6-0**	
34054	4/51	6/52	35021	8/50	5/51	75005	3/64	5/65
	10/63	9/64	35022	8/50	6/52	75008	9/64	5/65
34055	4/51	6/52		2/60	2/64	75022	4/64	2/65
34056	4/51	10/54	35023	8/50	2/60		3/65	5/65
	11/54	10/63	35024	8/50	4/59	75025	3/64	5/65
34057	4/51	5/51	35025	3/52	6/54	75070	9/55	6/56
	6/52	10/54		2/60	9/64	75071	9/55	6/56
	11/54	11/60	35026	1/57	5/57	75072	9/55	6/56
34058	4/51	10/63		4/59	2/64	75073	9/55	6/56
34059	4/51	9/55		**2MT 2-6-2T**		75074	9/55	6/56
34060	5/51	10/63	41206	1/63	5/65	75075	9/55	6/56
34061	6/51	11/60	41208	11/64	11/64	75076	9/55	6/56
	10/63	7/64	41210	2/64	2/64	75077	9/55	6/56
34062	6/51	7/64	41216	11/64	5/65	75078	9/55	6/56
34063	2/59	5/63	41223	6/64	5/65	75079	9/55	6/56
34064	5/59	5/62	41224	6/64	9/64		**4MT 2-6-4T**	
34065	5/59	3/64	41238	6/61	5/64	80035	5/62	9/64
34066	1/61	8/64	41249	11/64	5/65		1/65	2/65
34069	3/54	11/63	41270	6/61	5/64	80036	5/62	11/64
34070	10/61	8/64	41272	6/61	7/63	80037	6/62	1/65
34072	2/58	7/64	41284	6/61	9/64		3/65	5/65
34074	2/58	5/63	41291	3/63	5/65	80038	6/62	7/63
34075	9/57	3/64	41292	1/61	9/63		9/63	9/64
34076	9/57	8/64	41296	8/54	2/55	80039	6/62	1/65
34078	1/61	9/64	41297	6/55	9/55		3/65	5/65
34079	2/58	8/64	41299	1/61	3/63	80040	6/62	7/64
34080	12/57	9/64	41302	9/63	10/63	80041	6/62	5/65
34081	9/57	7/64	41306	6/55	12/63	80042	6/62	2/65
34083	10/61	7/64	41307	6/55	5/65	80043	6/62	9/64
34084	11/60	5/63	41308	1/60	2/65	80059	6/62	9/64
	10/63	8/64	41309	1/60	12/63	80064	6/62	5/65
34086	9/57	2/58	41313	6/52	2/55	80067	5/62	9/64
	5/61	8/64	41314	6/52	2/55			
34096	12/57	9/64						

3MT 2-6-2T

82001	4/63	12/63	82017	8/52	9/62	82035	3/64	9/64
82002	4/63	2/64	82018	9/52	9/62	82039	3/64	5/65
82010	6/52	9/62	82019	9/52	9/62	82040	10/63	5/65
82011	8/52	9/62	82020	8/54	9/54	82042	6/64	5/65
82012	8/52	1/53	82021	8/54	9/54	82044	6/64	5/65
82013	8/52	9/62	82022	10/54	9/62	**2MT 2-6-2T**		
82014	8/52	8/52	82023	10/54	9/62	84020	5/61	9/61
82015	8/52	10/52	82024	8/54	9/62	84021	5/61	9/61
82016	8/52	10/52	82025	8/54	9/62	84022	5/61	9/61
			82030	6/64	5/65	84023	5/61	9/61

Gloucester Barnwood
22B 9/50   85E 2/58
85C 1/61
Closed to Steam 4/64

14XX			40933	12/57	4/58	**2P 0-4-4T**		
1409	4/63	10/63	40934	11/52	3/57	41900	2/57	4/57
1421	10/63	12/63	40935	10/51	8/52		7/57	3/62
1426	4/61	10/61	41001	9/50	10/51	**3F 0-6-0**		
1445	12/63	4/64	41025	9/50	1/53	43213	9/50	1/58
1474	8/63	4/64	41028	2/52	4/52	43258	9/50	1/58
57XX				7/52	9/52	43337	9/50	2/60
4614	7/61	6/62	41047	9/50	2/54	43344	9/50	1/54
54XX			41049	5/56	5/58	43373	9/50	10/59
5420	7/63	8/63	41058	8/50	6/53	43427	3/60	6/60
	9/63	10/63	41069	3/54	11/55	43506	9/50	1/58
64XX			41074	9/50	12/51	43520	11/55	10/59
6424	4/62	11/62	41078	9/50	5/55	43593	12/61	1/63
74XX			41093	12/57	5/58	43645	9/50	1/63
7432	3/62	4/62	41095	5/57	2/58	43682	2/55	11/56
57XX			41097	9/50	8/52	43754	9/50	1/63
7723	11/59	7/60	41117	2/54	5/55	**4F 0-6-0**		
7756	11/59	6/61	41123	5/57	12/59	43837	7/52	9/54
3MT 2-6-2T Fowler			41140	2/52	4/52	43846	9/50	2/55
40040	9/50	1/53		7/52	6/53	43853	9/52	1/63
3MT 2-6-2T Stanier			41181	4/57	11/57	43887	9/50	4/64
40116	9/50	10/50	41195	9/52	11/57	43924	9/50	8/62
2P 4-4-0			**0F 0-4-0T**			43932	9/50	7/53
40423	1/51	8/52	41530	9/50	5/57		7/54	9/54
40486	8/52	5/53	41533	8/51	8/52	43978	9/50	3/53
40489	9/52	7/60	41534	8/55	11/55	44035	9/50	3/60
40501	7/60	7/60	41535	5/57	9/63	44045	9/50	4/64
40523	9/50	11/52	41537	9/50	9/63	44087	9/50	3/57
40530	9/50	1/51	**1F 0-6-0T**			44123	9/50	4/64
40540	8/52	2/62	41720	9/50	11/56	44135	11/52	10/53
40541	11/52	2/57	41727	9/50	3/52	44167	9/50	11/62
4P 4-4-0			41748	3/52	9/57	44175	9/50	11/56
40930	12/51	4/57	41769	6/57	8/57	44209	12/51	6/62

44272	9/50	7/61
	8/61	7/62
44293	11/52	3/57
44296	11/52	10/53
	6/57	6/63
44567	2/53	3/60
44587	2/53	3/57
44601	4/54	3/56
2MT 2-6-0		
46401	7/56	11/59
3F 0-6-0T		
47237	9/50	4/55
47417	12/55	1/63
47422	12/55	6/62
47506	6/54	2/63
47539	6/54	7/62
47607	9/50	11/55
47619	9/50	6/54
47620	9/50	6/54
47623	5/55	11/63
47635	9/50	5/53
	6/53	11/55

8F 2-8-0		
48172	11/62	4/64
48420	11/62	9/63
48463	11/62	3/64
1P 0-4-4T		
58034	9/50	9/50
58051	10/50	8/52
58063	9/50	5/51
58071	7/51	7/56
58073	3/53	5/53
58076	8/52	2/53
2F 0-6-0		
58165	7/57	12/58
58206	9/50	7/57
5MT 4-6-0		
73019	4/62	4/64
73021	9/62	4/64
73024	9/62	3/63
73028	1/64	4/64
73031	4/62	4/64
73050	7/62	11/62
73068	9/62	4/64

73091	9/61	4/64
73092	9/61	4/64
73093	9/61	4/64
73094	11/61	2/64
73096	6/62	4/64
4MT 4-6-0		
75002	1/60	9/61
75009	9/58	9/61
75023	9/58	9/61
2MT 2-6-0		
78001	1/64	4/64
78005	10/62	4/64
78006	9/62	4/64
78009	3/63	2/64
WD 2-8-0		
90148	12/61	2/62
90268	12/61	2/62
90315	4/60	6/60
90485	4/60	6/60
90565	11/59	7/60
90685	11/59	6/60

Gloucester GW
85B 8/50
Closed to Steam 12/65

14XX		
1401	9/52	10/58
1402	8/50	1/55
1404	8/50	1/56
1406	8/50	2/57
1409	8/50	5/53
	6/53	4/57
	6/59	4/63
1413	8/50	2/56
1420	9/64	11/64
1424	8/50	11/63
1426	9/58	5/60
	8/60	4/61
	10/61	4/62
1427	11/58	6/60
1428	4/56	5/59
1430	11/55	8/58
1431	1/60	4/61
1433	2/60	1/61
1440	5/61	6/61
	4/62	5/62
	3/63	12/63
1441	8/50	6/60
1444	12/63	11/64

1445	4/64	9/64
1451	11/63	7/64
1453	7/62	11/64
1454	7/59	12/60
1455	4/63	7/64
1456	8/50	6/52
1458	7/64	11/64
1461	9/57	5/58
1463	?/60 [N]	4/61
1464	8/50	7/58
1467	3/59	4/59
1472	3/59	11/64
1473	1/61	7/62
1474	4/64	9/64
16XX		
1605	10/57	2/62
1608	2/62	9/63
1612	8/50	4/52
	5/52	5/55
1616	8/50	9/59
1623	8/50	5/63
1625	8/50	11/56
1626	11/61	7/62

1627	9/50	8/59
	11/59	7/62
1630	2/51	9/55
	11/55	10/61
	11/61	3/62
1631	2/51	3/64
1632	2/51	5/62
1642	5/51	1/62
1647	2/60	4/60
1650	10/61	3/64
1666	9/63	3/64
1901		
1943	8/50	3/51
1989	8/50	9/50
1996	5/51	12/52
2009	8/50	1/51
2021		
2025	8/50	5/52
2034	8/50	5/51
2040	7/52	9/52
	3/54	4/54
2043	8/50	5/51
2044	8/50	7/51
2061	4/52	5/52

No.		
2080	8/50	3/52
2109	2/51	4/51
2121	8/50	6/52
2131	8/50	11/51
2144	8/50	4/52
2146	8/50	8/51
2153	8/50	12/50
2155	8/50	11/50
2251		
2201	5/58	5/58
2207	3/56	1/61
2228	10/52	2/53
2232	1/62	3/63
2242	11/64	5/65
2245	2/60	5/63
2248	8/50	8/60
2251	11/57	2/58
	3/58	5/58
2253	5/58	12/58
	2/59	12/63
2254	8/50	12/58
2273	6/61	9/62
2274	10/52	11/52
2278	11/55	6/57
2280	5/58	5/58
2281	1/58	5/58
2287	11/64	5/65
2288	6/61	12/61
2289	10/59	11/59
	12/60	5/63
2291	8/50	7/59
2292	6/53	7/54
2295	12/51	7/54
23XX		
2339	8/50	12/50
2350	8/50	1/52
28XX		
2809	4/56	6/57
2823	8/50	9/51
2829	5/58	1/59
2854	4/56	6/60
29XX		
2938	8/50	3/52
2951	8/50	6/52
ROD		
3022	2/53	4/56
3025	11/51	10/52
3048	2/53	4/56
31XX		
3101	10/52	11/52
3150		
3153	8/50	1/53
3163	8/50	6/57
3164	8/50	2/56
3171	8/50	6/57

No.		
3180	3/53	9/57
2251		
3203	10/52	12/63
3204	8/50	9/54
3205	8/50	6/55
	8/55	9/55
3213	8/50	10/54
57XX		
3609	8/50	7/60
3616	1/65	9/65
3633	8/63	10/63
3643	1/65	10/65
3675	1/65	12/65
3677	1/65	6/65
3693	7/63	7/64
3715	1/59	2/59
3721	12/60	12/63
3737	8/63	9/64
3740	11/56	12/58
3745	10/62	1/65
3759	3/65	12/65
3775	3/61	12/65
28XX		
3803	3/59	6/60
3848	8/50	11/50
	4/51	9/51
	3/58	6/60
40XX		
4059	8/50	8/52
4073		
4079	8/50	10/52
4082	8/64	9/64
4085	5/58	3/60
4093	6/64	9/64
51XX		
4100	6/57	10/65
4101	2/58	3/63
4104	3/63	7/64
4106	9/61	8/62
4109	9/61	4/64
4113	10/53	11/53
4116	8/58	8/62
4123	3/58	10/61
4131	4/54	6/54
4139	6/57	5/58
4140	10/50	9/54
4141	8/50	2/63
4142	7/60	9/63
4143	11/60	7/61
4148	11/54	7/55
4161	8/62	4/63
4163	1/61	9/62
4165	7/58	7/60
4174	8/50	6/56
4175	2/58	5/58

No.		
42XX		
4242	5/60	8/60
43XX		
4358	7/55	7/59
45XX		
4521	8/53	11/55
4534	8/50	10/52
4553	6/56	6/57
4564	8/50	7/58
	9/63	9/64
4567	8/50	6/51
4573	6/56	10/60
4586	5/51	3/56
57XX		
4611	3/63	12/63
4614	6/62	8/64
4624	8/63	9/64
4627	8/50	1/59
4628	8/50	12/60
4629	12/62	9/63
4659	8/50	7/58
4664	7/52	8/52
	11/57	5/58
4689	3/65	12/65
4698	8/63	4/64
	9/64	10/65
49XX		
4903	9/62	10/62
4929	8/50	3/65
4934	11/53	5/54
4935	2/62	6/62
4956	2/62	6/62
4958	6/64	9/64
4961	7/55	7/55
4974	9/61	4/62
4977	8/50	12/50
4985	6/64	7/64
4989	11/59	1/62
4992	6/63	11/63
4996	8/50	3/56
4073		
5007	3/61	8/62
5017	11/51	8/62
5018	3/51	7/51
	8/51	10/52
	12/52	4/58
5042	8/50	3/59
	7/64	6/65
5054	9/64	11/64
5055	7/64	9/64
5058	9/61	2/63
5064	9/61	8/62
5071	4/58	2/59
	4/59	6/59
	9/60	2/62

5086	3/58	4/58
5094	9/56	7/60
5099	9/62	1/63
	51XX	
5105	10/57	9/58
5112	8/50	12/52
5114	8/50	9/50
5154	8/62	4/63
5157	11/56	5/58
5162	10/56	5/58
5165	7/57	2/58
5173	11/59	6/61
	9/61	7/62
5177	7/58	3/60
5182	4/56	5/62
5184	8/62	11/64
5194	10/58	12/59
5198	7/58	11/58
	1/59	6/60
5199	2/63	3/63
	42XX	
5243	4/60	7/60
	43XX	
5312	8/50	1/54
5330	10/63	1/64
5336	8/50	6/53
5345	8/50	1/55
5347	8/50	2/56
5355	9/54	3/55
5368	10/52	5/53
5394	8/50	1/55
5398	8/50	1/59
	54XX	
5408	5/52	11/56
5413	1/57	9/57
5417	5/51	11/59
5418	1/55	6/60
5420	11/61	7/63
5421	10/57	5/60
	45XX	
5514	1/55	10/60
5518	8/50	5/51
	9/54	7/56
	9/63	7/64
5530	8/50	1/58
5538	8/50	1/60
5545	6/64	1/65
5574	8/50	9/53
	56XX	
5642	7/55	10/55
	57XX	
5763	1/59	5/60
	49XX	
5907	11/53	12/58
5913	11/60	1/61

5914	7/52	8/52
	1/58	3/61
	3/63	2/64
5936	3/63	2/65
5948	11/50	4/52
5951	8/50	11/51
	11/52	4/64
5968	10/61	8/62
5977	11/59	8/63
5979	3/63	9/64
5980	8/50	11/58
	3/62	8/62
5988	8/50	4/52
5990	8/50	3/56
5992	1/65	6/65
	61XX	
6113	9/64	11/64
	11/64	12/65
6126	12/60	5/62
6128	4/64	11/64
	1/65	4/65
6137	9/58	10/63
6160	7/65	12/65
	43XX	
6304	3/59	1/64
6308	12/52	4/53
6309	8/50	2/54
6319	6/63	8/63
6326	7/55	3/56
6330	8/52	8/62
6334	7/55	7/55
6341	8/50	6/56
	8/56	1/58
	7/60	10/61
6344	11/62	11/63
6346	3/64	9/64
6349	11/52	10/57
	9/63	8/64
6353	1/58	3/59
6354	12/58	1/59
6355	10/52	1/54
6363	11/59	8/60
6365	7/54	5/55
	6/55	10/63
6368	10/54	5/55
	12/59	6/60
	8/63	12/63
6373	8/52	9/61
6381	8/50	5/55
6385	8/50	6/54
6394	9/57	7/64
	64XX	
6412	8/64	11/64
6415	3/58	10/61
6419	7/60	8/60

6437	5/60	7/63
	56XX	
6631	8/50	4/57
6669	6/56	5/58
	5/58	8/62
6690	10/52	4/56
	6/56	12/60
6696	2/61	12/61
	68XX	
6865	10/55	12/55
	49XX	
6913	3/63	7/64
6917	8/50	6/61
6921	8/50	6/56
6924	10/52	3/53
6928	6/64	3/65
6936	6/51	6/53
6938	11/53	5/54
6940	8/50	2/51
	9/62	11/62
	9/63	5/64
6942	6/64	1/65
6943	2/62	12/63
6947	9/62	3/65
6948	9/62	11/63
6951	5/51	8/51
6956	9/61	6/65
6957	4/64	3/65
	6959	
6985	12/50	5/51
	11/52	9/64
6987	8/50	5/52
6989	9/62	
6992	8/50	6/51
6993	9/61	6/65
6995	4/64	9/64
	4073	
7000	5/59	2/63
7003	7/60	3/64
	6/64	8/64
7006	8/50	4/58
	7/60	8/60
7009	10/62	11/62
7022	9/64	6/65
7026	9/62	11/62
7029	9/64	12/65
7034	12/61	6/65
7035	9/53	10/56
	3/60	11/62
	72XX	
7227	11/58	12/58
7235	11/58	3/59
	43XX	
7303	8/50	5/53
7307	11/63	7/64

7312	8/50	6/57
	5/58	6/60
7318	6/64	11/64
7319	12/59	6/60
	12/63	9/64
7320	9/64	11/64
7322	(ex 9300 4/57)	
	8/61	10/61
7335	(ex 9313 7/58)	
	10/61	9/63
7338	(ex 9316 3/58)	
	12/59	8/60

74XX

7435	1/62	6/62

57XX

7723	8/50	11/59
7741	8/50	12/61
7750	5/58	12/58

78XX

7808	1/54	6/59
	9/60	1/61
	11/64	12/65
7809	12/58	4/59
7810	1/54	5/59
7813	11/64	3/65
7814	6/64	5/65
	6/65	9/65
7815	8/50	8/52
	12/58	12/59
	6/64	11/64
7816	6/65	12/65
7818	8/50	7/52
7824	2/51	8/52
7829	6/65	12/65

6959

7920	9/50	3/51
7926	11/50	9/62
	9/64	1/65

81XX

8107	9/60	7/61

94XX

8402	9/64	11/64
8403	9/64	1/65
8409	2/60	5/61
8421	5/59	12/59
8436	6/53	7/53
8471	7/63	1/65
8487	7/52	8/61
	1/62	8/62

8488	7/52	5/60
8489	10/61	2/62
8491	5/59	7/63

57XX

8701	8/50	8/52
	4/59	3/63
8717	8/50	1/62
8727	4/57	10/58
8729	5/60	1/63
8731	8/50	1/51
	3/51	4/51
	9/55	11/60
8743	2/59	1/64
8745	9/64	9/65
8749	7/64	9/64
8781	8/50	2/57

94XX

9430	11/64	1/65
9438	9/54	5/59
9441	4/51	1/61
9445	5/51	2/60
9453	3/60	4/64
	8/64	11/64
9464	3/52	10/61
9471	5/52	9/64
9475	7/52	7/60
9477	11/59	11/60
9480	10/52	12/52
9492	2/57	5/59

57XX

9606	7/64	9/64
	9/64	11/64
9620	10/63	7/64
9711	9/64	3/65
9727	8/50	4/61
9790	11/64	11/64
9798	12/62	12/63

4F 0-6-0

43887	4/64	7/64
	9/64	2/65
44045	4/64	11/64
44123	4/64	5/65
44264	5/65	10/65
44269	5/65	12/65
44422	2/65	5/65
44560	11/64	8/65

3F 0-6-0T

47539	7/62	10/62

5MT 4-6-0

73001	2/65	3/65
73019	4/64	11/64
73021	4/64	6/65
73028	4/64	11/64
73031	4/64	6/65
73068	1/65	4/65
73091	4/64	5/65
73092	4/64	7/64
73093	4/64	3/65
73096	4/64	11/64

4MT 4-6-0

75005	1/64	3/64
75025	1/64	3/64
75029	11/54	12/54

2MT 2-6-0

78001	4/64	12/65
78004	7/64	10/65
78005	4/64	9/64
78006	4/64	12/65

3MT 2-6-2T

82030	5/65	12/65
82039	5/65	6/65
82040	5/65	6/65
82042	5/65	6/65
82044	5/65	12/65

WD 2-8-0

90149	5/53	9/58
90179	8/50	4/51
90413	8/50	9/50
90485	4/57	6/57
90524	9/51	2/53
90573	5/53	9/58
90685	3/53	9/58
90691	8/50	10/50
	9/51	5/53
	5/53	9/58

9F 2-10-0

92000	3/65	6/65
92007	3/65	6/65
	10/65	12/65
92230	10/65	12/65
92238	3/65	7/65
92244	10/65	12/65
92246	10/65	12/65
92250	10/65	12/65

[N] After 1/60

14XX			**4981**	12/56	9/63	**6843**	9/56	11/56
1421	9/55	10/55	**4073**			**6869**	12/59	1/60
1423	8/50	9/57	**5039**	7/63	12/63	**49XX**		
1428	9/55	11/55	**5055**	7/63	10/63	**6900**	11/62	1/63
1431	8/50	4/58	**43XX**			**6909**	11/52	9/56
1452	8/50	8/57	**5395**	8/50	5/51	**6914**	6/63	9/63
1456	11/52	11/55	**57XX**			**6959**		
2251			**5713**	5/58	2/60	**6968**	2/62	7/63
2223	5/51	8/59	**5716**	8/50	3/58	**57XX**		
2271	9/59	6/62	**49XX**			**7747**	8/50	2/61
2278	6/57	8/59	**5905**	8/50	7/63	**6959**		
3206	8/60	6/62	**5908**	8/50	1/62	**7907**	11/61	2/62
3212	5/60	8/60	**5928**	8/50	5/62	**57XX**		
57XX			**5946**	6/62	6/62	**8739**	6/62	12/63
3637	8/50	9/62	**5947**	11/59	4/60	**94XX**		
3761	11/61	11/62	**5969**	12/59	7/61	**9436**	1/52	2/52
4621	7/63	8/63	**5972**	11/62	6/63	**57XX**		
4644	11/62	10/63	**5976**	6/63	9/63	**9602**	8/50	8/63
4677	10/54	9/62	**61XX**			**9603**	8/50	10/54
4699	9/55	10/55	**6116**	6/62	4/63	**9645**	1/60	9/63
49XX			**43XX**			**9666**	9/57	8/63
4927	1/62	6/62	**6338**	6/57	9/57	**9677**	8/57	12/63
4935	9/61	10/61	**6347**	10/57	5/60	**9714**	2/61	10/61
4947	11/61	1/62	**68XX**			**9760**	8/50	9/63
4962	5/62	9/63	**6823**	8/50	10/52			
				11/52	12/52			

10XX			**16XX**			**2043**	5/51	5/53
1022	7/59	10/59	**1613**	12/63	11/64	**2099**	8/50	2/52
AD 2-6-2T			**1617**	5/53	11/63	**2115**	8/50	9/50
1206	8/50	1/51	**1625**	11/56	6/60	**2138**	8/50	4/56
14XX			**1631**	3/64	11/64	**2144**	4/52	1/53
1420	2/62	9/64	**1657**	1/55	11/64	**2160**	8/50	2/55
1445	8/50	8/61	**1662**	11/56	12/63	**2251**		
1447	2/62	3/64	**1667**	5/55	11/64	**2205**	7/55	9/55
1455	8/50	9/61	**2021**			**2206**	9/55	6/57
1456	11/55	1/59	**2026**	8/50	4/51	**2225**	5/53	5/58
1458	11/63	7/64	**2034**	4/54	8/55	**2241**	5/58	7/63
1460	8/50	1/56	**2040**	8/50	7/52		8/63	2/64

2242	6/57	11/64
2243	8/50	5/52
2249	5/52	5/63
2256	6/61	8/62
2266	9/54	9/59
2274	11/52	3/58
2281	8/50	1/58
2286	8/50	7/53
	9/62	9/64
2287	2/64	11/64
2295	6/55	6/62

23XX

2349	8/50	3/52
2350	1/52	12/52
2474	7/53	10/54
2515	8/50	1/53
2538	1/53	7/53
2541	8/50	5/54
2556	2/53	5/53

28XX

2807	8/50	7/51
2879	2/53	5/53

29XX

2920	8/50	9/53
2937	8/50	5/53
2938	3/52	8/52
2944	8/50	11/51

2251

3204	12/62	2/63
3205	12/62	12/63
3209	8/50	6/55

33XX

3406	8/50	1/51

57XX

3683	6/64	9/64
3728	8/50	11/64
3729	9/60	11/62
	12/62	3/63
3789	8/50	11/56
3798	6/64	9/64

28XX

3848	11/50	4/51
3861	12/52	5/53

51XX

4107	9/63	11/64
4115	12/58	1/63
4135	4/62	5/64
4161	4/63	12/65

57XX

4600	8/50	11/56
4623	12/62	11/64
4641	5/51	3/53
4657	8/50	12/60
4659	7/58	7/64
4668	7/64	11/64

4678	8/50	5/62
	2/63	7/64

49XX

4905	10/53	6/56
4907	9/53	3/55
	4/62	8/63
4913	12/59	8/62
4916	6/62	11/63
4917	11/53	12/53
4943	2/58	5/58
4952	9/55	5/57
4975	10/53	5/58
4976	10/53	2/56
4990	10/59	4/62
4993	7/51	4/52

4073

5000	10/63	6/64
5025	10/63	11/63
5042	3/64	7/64
5054	11/63	3/64
5055	10/63	7/64
5056	3/64	6/64

51XX

5154	4/63	8/63
5156	10/57	5/58
	7/58	8/58

42XX

5226	10/55	11/59
5243	7/55	4/60
5245	10/58	3/60

43XX

5333	1/59	2/59
5337	5/58	5/58
5348	8/50	1/52
5350	2/58	12/59
5355	3/55	6/57
5377	8/50	5/58

57XX

5765	8/50	3/59

58XX

5807	8/50	6/57
5808	8/50	3/53
5814	8/50	6/57
5817	8/50	6/57
5818	2/53	11/56

49XX

5952	8/59	11/63
5970	6/62	10/63
5977	9/55	5/58
5998	9/55	5/58
	5/58	11/63

43XX

6308	4/53	9/55
6314	10/54	4/57

6326	8/50	7/55
	4/57	5/58
6338	12/53	6/54
6341	6/56	8/56
6348	12/60	2/62
6349	8/50	11/52
6352	8/50	7/54
6359	10/55	8/59
6362	12/52	6/54
6382	9/58	7/60
6395	8/50	9/56

64XX

6438	12/60	3/61

56XX

6606	3/55	7/55
6638	1/54	11/54
6681	8/50	12/53
6690	12/60	2/61

68XX

6806	7/55	12/55
6845	9/55	12/55
6849	7/55	12/55
6860	9/55	12/55

49XX

6905	8/50	2/53
6916	8/50	5/58
6936	8/50	6/51
6948	3/58	5/58
6951	8/50	5/51

6959

6984	8/50	5/58
6985	5/51	11/52
6989	8/50	3/56
	5/57	7/59
6992	6/51	9/59

4073

7022	11/63	3/64

72XX

7204	5/53	3/55
7222	5/53	11/55

43XX

7301	3/52	4/53
	1/54	6/57
7307	8/50	4/56
7308	8/50	6/57
7312	9/57	5/58
7314	8/50	4/56
7326	(ex 9304 5/58)	
	9/55	5/58
	7/58	2/61

74XX

7401	1/59	7/59
7413	8/61	7/63
7416	8/50	12/58
7418	7/59	2/62

7420	8/50	11/56
7426	8/58	2/61
7437	1/53	12/63
57XX		
7707	8/50	6/55
7719	5/59	8/60
78XX		
7805	10/53	5/58
6959		
7921	10/53	12/53
57XX		
8701	8/52	2/59
8702	3/63	7/64
8722	7/58	6/60
8731	4/51	5/53
8743	10/58	2/59
8781	2/57	5/62
8787	7/58	7/61
8791	3/61	6/61

43XX		
9304	9/55	
(renum 7326 5/58)		
57XX		
9619	8/50	8/58
9665	11/54	2/63
9717	11/54	1/63
3F 0-6-0		
43277	6/52	10/53
43491	6/52	10/53
43621	6/52	10/53
43822	6/52	10/53
8F 2-8-0		
48409	4/57	2/58
48452	4/57	2/58
48463	4/57	2/58
G1 & G2a 0-8-0		
48899	7/55	1/56
49028	11/54	3/55
49046	12/54	2/57

49051	11/54	3/55
49082	6/56	4/57
49146	11/54	4/57
49168	11/54	1/55
49226	12/54	4/57
G2 0-8-0		
49440	4/57	5/57
3F 0-6-0		
52449	11/51	6/52
2MT 2-6-0		
78004	6/57	1/64
3MT 2-6-2T		
82001	8/62	4/63
82002	9/62	4/63
WD 2-8-0		
90524	8/50	5/51

Kidderminster
85D 8/50   84G 1/61
2P 9/63
Closed to Steam 8/64

CMDP		
28	8/50	10/52
29	8/50	1/54
14XX		
1417	11/58	1/59
1457	11/58	1/59
16XX		
1661	3/55	10/57
2021		
2051	8/50	7/51
2101	9/51	5/53
2144	5/53	4/54
2251		
2207	5/53	3/56
57XX		
3601	8/50	8/64
3607	6/61	8/64
3619	5/62	8/64
51XX		
4100	8/50	6/57
4109	11/58	3/59
4114	9/54	3/55
	2/56	6/56
	7/56	11/63

4129	9/60	8/62
4139	4/57	6/57
4147	4/61	8/64
4153	8/50	8/64
4173	9/62	8/64
4175	8/50	2/58
	5/58	8/64
45XX		
4578	8/50	9/53
4584	8/50	6/51
4586	8/50	5/51
4594	8/50	3/52
4596	5/51	4/57
4599	8/50	6/51
57XX		
4614	12/53	10/55
	1/56	7/56
4625	8/50	4/52
	5/58	7/58
4629	5/59	12/62
4641	3/53	9/60
	10/60	5/62
51XX		
5110	8/50	10/59

5151	10/60	7/62
5153	8/62	8/64
43XX		
5333	2/59	5/60
5355	9/57	4/59
5394	1/55	12/58
5396	11/58	12/58
	3/59	5/59
45XX		
5518	5/51	9/54
	7/56	10/60
57XX		
5791	10/59	4/61
61XX		
6128	7/60	3/62
6144	7/60	5/62
43XX		
6314	4/57	7/63
6317	6/63	11/63
6326	3/56	4/57
6334	9/55	6/56
6340	5/57	6/57
6364	9/62	2/64
	8/64	8/64

6367	8/58	9/58		**68XX**			**57XX**	
6368	6/60	7/60	6832	10/58	11/59	8701	2/59	4/59
6382	8/50	9/53		**43XX**		8718	8/50	8/64
	9/55	9/58	7301	5/53	1/54	8727	8/50	4/57
6388	6/59	8/62		**57XX**		8731	5/53	9/55
6395	12/63	8/64	7700	8/50	5/61		**3MT 2-6-2T**	
	56XX		7777	5/58	10/58	82008	8/55	8/57
6669	5/58	5/58		**81XX**			12/57	1/58
6679	3/55	1/64	8101	8/50	3/61	82030	5/59	6/59
6690	4/56	6/56						

Laira
83D 8/50   84A 9/63
Closed to Steam 5/64

	4073			**14XX**		3862	12/53	6/62
111	8/50	6/53	1408	5/55	3/58	3864	8/50	3/51
	10XX		1420	7/59	?/?? [O]		**4073**	
1000	2/51	10/52	1421	5/58	7/60	4032	8/50	9/50
1002	3/53	5/53	1434	5/55	?/?? [P]		**40XX**	
	10/60	11/60		**16XX**		4054	8/50	2/52
1003	2/51	5/51	1624	5/53	9/53		**4073**	
	1/61	9/62	1650	11/54	7/60	4077	9/54	5/59
1006	8/50	6/54		**2021**		4086	2/53	4/57
	10/60	11/62	2038	2/52	3/53	4087	8/50	10/52
1008	7/58	1/59	2097	9/53	3/55		7/54	3/63
1010	2/51	2/53	2148	8/50	2/52	4088	8/50	11/53
	5/53	9/59		**2251**			9/54	4/58
1012	2/51	9/56	2258	8/50	9/50	4089	8/50	2/51
1015	2/51	9/59		**28XX**			2/52	6/54
	10/62	1/63	2809	9/58	2/60	4095	6/60	9/62
1016	10/52	11/52	2843	5/51	5/59	4097	8/50	2/51
1017	12/60	1/61	2846	5/60	7/60		**51XX**	
1018	9/54	10/54	2875	8/50	3/51	4133	5/51	8/51
	6/60	11/60		5/60	7/60	4167	10/54	11/54
1021	2/51	3/55	2899	2/59	11/62	4174	6/56	7/56
	7/55	11/59		**3150**			12/59	1/60
1022	8/50	2/51	3178	8/50	1/51		**44XX**	
1023	8/50	2/51	3186	8/50	6/57	4401	8/53	10/53
	10/55	11/55	3187	8/50	10/57	4403	5/51	12/52
1024	3/51	9/52		**57XX**		4406	11/54	1/55
1026	9/52	2/53	3629	8/50	9/58	4407	8/50	2/53
	1361		3639	8/50	10/58	4409	8/50	2/51
1361	8/50	12/53	3675	8/50	5/61	4410	4/53	8/55
	1/54	4/58	3686	8/50	1/62		**45XX**	
	5/58	1/60	3705	8/50	4/51	4517	8/50	11/50
1362	11/57	1/58	3787	8/50	12/61	4518	8/50	9/52
	2/58	7/58	3790	8/50	8/60	4524	8/50	10/55
1363	8/50	1/63		**28XX**		4528	8/50	12/50
1364	8/50	2/60	3832	8/50	3/51	4530	4/51	3/55
1365	8/50	4/55	3849	5/62	7/62	4534	10/52	1/55

Western

4542	8/50	8/55
4549	2/60	6/60
4553	7/58	11/58
4555	5/62	11/63
4561	7/61	5/62
4566	9/61	4/62
4567	4/62	8/62
4568	9/55	6/56
4570	6/62	1/63
4571	2/59	5/59
4574	7/62	2/63
4583	8/50	1/58
4588	11/61	6/62
4589	6/60	8/60
4590	5/51	9/58
4591	8/50	5/63
57XX		
4653	8/50	10/58
4656	8/50	2/59
4658	8/50	1/63
4679	8/50	4/62
4693	8/50	10/58
47XX		
4703	8/50	7/53
4705	1/57	6/61
4706	10/52	9/53
49XX		
4900	2/51	5/51
	6/56	9/56
4904	6/59	12/59
4913	6/59	9/59
4924	6/57	9/57
4928	7/57	9/57
	5/58	10/59
4936	10/54	12/58
4944	1/58	10/58
4950	5/53	9/57
	6/59	9/60
4954	2/51	3/51
4963	12/53	9/54
4965	12/54	9/55
4966	8/50	9/54
4967	11/59	3/61
4968	8/50	12/50
4972	8/50	11/53
4975	5/58	12/58
4976	6/56	10/58
	6/59	9/60
4977	6/56	9/56
4978	2/53	6/56
	9/62	6/64
4982	8/61	5/62
4992	8/50	10/57
4999	6/52	7/52

4073		
5003	12/56	2/57
	4/57	10/57
5012	8/50	10/52
5016	10/54	12/54
5020	1/57	4/57
	11/57	12/58
5021	8/50	10/52
	4/57	9/59
5023	8/50	10/52
	9/54	1/58
5026	8/50	12/50
5028	6/56	5/60
5029	11/59	11/62
5049	2/56	4/56
	1/57	5/58
5053	12/54	1/55
	11/59	9/61
5057	8/50	2/51
	2/52	6/54
5058	8/50	9/59
	11/59	9/61
5060	8/50	2/51
5069	7/54	2/62
5072	2/56	4/56
	2/57	4/58
5075	4/58	6/59
5090	8/50	10/52
5093	9/53	12/53
5095	8/50	2/51
5098	8/50	1/62
51XX		
5106	10/57	3/60
5148	8/50	12/59
5175	10/52	10/60
	12/60	4/61
5193	10/54	2/58
	10/60	11/60
43XX		
5318	8/50	8/51
5336	12/56	10/57
	1/58	9/58
5350	6/56	8/56
5356	8/52	6/53
	7/53	11/57
5376	8/50	4/52
	10/52	10/57
45XX		
5506	9/55	5/58
5511	10/58	12/61
5515	9/61	10/61
5519	6/59	6/60
5521	11/61	4/62

5531	11/50	10/54
	11/54	8/61
	9/63	11/63
5532	11/59	6/62
5540	8/50	5/51
5541	1/60	6/62
5544	7/61	8/62
5551	9/55	9/58
5552	3/55	7/55
5557	4/55	7/55
5558	7/55	8/55
	7/56	8/56
5560	9/60	9/61
5564	4/62	1/63
5567	8/50	2/60
5568	10/60	8/61
	9/61	1/63
5569	8/50	1/63
5572	2/58	9/60
	4/61	4/62
49XX		
5909	12/54	9/55
5913	6/53	9/54
5917	12/60	6/62
5926	2/52	10/52
5934	2/54	2/58
5943	6/56	10/56
5945	6/56	9/56
5952	7/55	9/55
5954	6/56	9/56
5961	12/53	9/54
5964	8/50	6/56
5968	2/51	10/51
5972	3/51	10/51
	11/58	7/59
5983	1/58	8/58
5993	2/51	10/51
5997	7/52	9/53
5998	8/50	5/53
	11/53	9/55
60XX		
6002	2/60	6/62
6004	3/54	9/59
6007	3/59	9/59
6008	7/52	1/59
6010	8/50	4/59
6012	8/50	7/54
6013	4/59	3/60
6014	10/52	3/54
6016	8/50	7/52
	1/59	6/62
6017	2/52	2/59
6021	9/56	9/59
6022	8/50	9/55
6023	8/50	6/56

Shed by Shed

6024	8/50	9/54	6849	6/57	6/59		**74XX**	
6025	8/50	6/59		6/60	9/60	7445	7/57	8/57
6026	8/50	2/60	6850	1/58	10/59		**57XX**	
6027	8/50	12/58	6854	2/60	9/60	7762	8/50	9/58
	1/59	11/59	6855	8/50	11/58		**78XX**	
6029	8/50	6/59	6856	6/57	9/57	7801	8/50	9/53
	61XX		6858	12/55	9/58	7804	8/50	6/54
6166	9/59	8/60	6860	6/53	9/53	7805	5/58	9/58
	43XX			6/61	5/62	7809	8/50	7/54
6301	6/56	3/62	6863	5/58	9/62		10/54	6/56
6319	8/50	12/59	6865	12/55	9/56		7/56	9/57
6328	6/56	2/58	6867	1/58	3/58	7812	12/56	9/59
6340	1/61	4/61	6868	6/62	9/62	7813	1/58	11/59
6373	5/52	8/52	6869	10/52	9/56	7814	8/50	6/54
6389	6/53	8/53	6871	5/58	12/58		9/54	7/55
	64XX			1/59	11/59	7815	8/52	7/54
6400	4/59	3/63	6873	8/50	12/58		12/54	9/55
6402	8/58	5/59		1/59	5/62		5/58	9/58
6406	8/50	6/60	6874	6/62	9/62	7820	12/54	11/59
6407	8/50	7/55	6879	5/58	12/58	7824	8/52	7/54
	9/55	7/58		**49XX**			12/54	9/55
6408	8/59	6/60	6907	8/50	9/55		12/56	1/57
6410	9/59	7/60	6912	2/51	9/55		**6959**	
6413	10/59	10/61	6913	8/50	9/60	7905	8/50	11/59
6414	8/50	5/59	6921	6/56	11/63	7909	8/50	9/58
6417	8/50	10/53	6925	5/55	9/55		9/62	11/62
6419	8/50	7/60	6933	6/53	10/54	7916	5/60	6/64
6420	8/50	12/59		4/59	11/59	7921	6/59	9/60
6421	8/50	7/60	6934	7/55	9/55		**94XX**	
	11/62	1/63	6938	11/59	10/62	8404	8/50	11/50
6430	5/62	1/63	6940	2/51	10/51	8422	4/51	5/61
6438	5/62	1/63		7/52	11/58	8425	3/51	10/58
	68XX		6941	6/56	5/60	8426	4/51	10/58
6802	2/53	9/57	6945	1/58	9/58		**57XX**	
6804	2/61	7/62	6949	8/50	9/53	8709	8/50	9/58
6805	5/58	10/58		**6959**		8719	8/50	5/58
	6/60	9/60	6965	2/51	3/58		**43XX**	
6812	6/62	9/62	6966	2/51	10/51	9313	5/58	
6815	6/61	7/62	6967	2/51	10/51		(renum 7335 7/58)	
6816	5/53	2/58	6978	12/53	1/57		**94XX**	
	5/60	9/60	6988	1/54	10/54	9433	1/51	1/61
6821	10/52	3/58		5/55	9/59	9467	4/52	5/62
6823	5/58	10/58		**4073**			**57XX**	
6824	7/62	9/62	7006	4/58	9/59	9671	8/50	4/55
6825	6/62	9/62	7022	1/57	11/63	9673	8/50	4/51
6826	6/62	9/62	7027	8/50	2/51	9711	8/50	7/61
6834	12/55	9/56	7029	12/56	4/57	9716	8/50	8/60
6836	5/60	10/61	7031	8/50	9/59	9765	8/50	4/53
6837	5/60	9/60		**43XX**		9770	8/50	2/59
6838	10/52	7/56	7321	6/56	8/56		**2MT 2-6-2T**	
6843	12/55	1/56	7326	2/61	3/61	41302	5/63	9/63
6845	6/60	9/60	7333	10/57	6/60	41315	5/63	9/63
6848	1/56	3/58	7335	(ex 9313 7/58)		41316	5/63	9/63
	5/58	9/58		5/58	10/61	41317	5/63	9/63

7MT 4-6-2			3MT 2-6-2T			92223	6/59	3/60
70016	7/53	12/56	82031	1/55	3/55		6/60	8/60
70019	9/51	12/56	WD 2-8-0			92224	6/59	7/60
70021	8/51	1/57	90148	8/50	7/52	92225	6/59	3/60
70022	9/51	4/52	9F 2-10-0			92249	6/60	9/60
70024	2/52	12/56	92208	5/59	3/60			
4MT 4-6-0			92209	6/59	8/59	[O] Before 2/62		
75025	5/54	6/56	92221	6/59	3/60	[P] Before 6/62		
75026	5/54	6/56		6/60	8/60			
75027	5/54	9/54	92222	6/59	3/60			
75028	6/54	6/56		6/60	10/60			
75029	6/54	9/54						

Landore
87E 8/50
Closed to Steam 6/61

14XX			4076	11/57	6/61	5006	7/60	6/61
1428	5/53	9/55	4078	8/50	1/58	5013	8/50	6/61
	11/55	4/56	4090	8/59	9/59	5015	6/60	1/61
2251				6/60	6/61	5016	8/50	10/54
2226	9/56	7/59	4093	10/52	6/61		12/54	6/61
2273	8/50	10/52	4094	6/57	6/61	5030	6/60	9/60
2284	8/53	5/59	4095	8/50	1/58	5039	6/52	7/52
2291	7/59	11/59	4097	6/57	5/60		3/53	5/53
28XX			4099	10/57	6/61		6/57	9/60
2821	1/59	5/59	51XX			5041	9/55	6/61
2844	1/59	5/59	4106	10/52	3/55	5043	2/53	5/53
57XX				4/55	6/56		3/55	4/55
3678	8/50	6/61		7/56	6/61	5051	8/50	6/61
3701	8/50	6/61	4107	10/52	6/56	5062	9/60	6/61
3713	8/50	1/60		7/56	6/60	5072	8/50	12/55
3768	8/50	7/54	4122	3/58	9/58	5074	7/55	7/56
	7/54	6/61	4134	8/50	1/52		7/60	6/61
3785	8/50	6/61	4147	7/60	8/60	5077	7/56	6/61
3797	8/50	6/61	42XX			5078	10/60	6/61
28XX			4207	8/50	10/52	5080	12/55	9/56
3849	1/59	5/59	4250	8/50	10/52		1/57	6/61
4073			49XX			5089	5/54	6/54
4000	10/56	5/57	4917	5/53	9/53		7/54	10/55
40XX			4918	7/55	9/55	5091	5/58	6/61
4003	8/50	7/51	4923	6/56	3/60	5093	8/50	7/52
4023	8/50	7/52	4924	7/55	9/55	51XX		
4073			4937	7/55	5/59	5162	8/50	9/53
4037	2/57	6/57	4965	7/54	10/54	42XX		
40XX			4978	9/51	2/53	5203	10/59	11/59
4039	8/50	11/50	4981	6/53	11/55	5211	8/50	3/51
4048	8/50	12/52	4073			5219	8/50	11/52
4050	8/50	2/52	5002	8/50	8/56	43XX		
4073				10/56	1/57	5341	8/50	11/50
4074	8/50	9/56	5004	4/58	6/61	5356	8/51	8/52
	7/57	5/60						

5361	10/59	12/59	6680	8/50	6/61	**57XX**		
54XX			6688	12/52	6/61	7787	8/50	4/56
5400	8/50	5/52	6695	8/50	6/61	**78XX**		
5408	8/50	5/51	**68XX**			7809	6/56	7/56
56XX			6816	2/53	5/53	**94XX**		
5604	8/50	5/58	6828	9/57	3/58	8439	10/59	9/60
5631	8/50	6/61	**49XX**			8463	9/53	2/60
5656	8/50	7/59	6903	8/50	2/59	**57XX**		
5673	10/52	6/61	6905	2/53	9/59	8788	4/56	6/60
57XX			6912	9/57	9/59	8789	8/50	6/61
5759	8/50	4/56		6/60	6/61	8794	7/56	6/61
49XX			6918	8/50	6/61	**94XX**		
5909	5/58	11/58	6933	11/59	2/60	9416	10/60	6/61
	6/60	6/61	**6959**			9436	7/56	7/60
5913	8/50	7/52	6963	10/59	11/59	9484	10/52	6/61
	11/55	11/60	**4073**			**57XX**		
5929	8/50	3/51	7002	8/50	10/56	9637	3/56	6/61
	5/51	10/58		5/58	12/59	9715	7/56	6/61
5955	10/50	6/56	7003	8/50	12/58	9738	8/50	1/60
	9/56	11/60	7009	8/50	9/60	9761	8/50	6/61
5958	5/53	12/53	7012	8/50	9/59	9775	8/50	1/60
	1/54	6/56	7016	9/56	9/59	9777	8/50	6/60
5959	4/57	6/57	7018	8/50	7/56		7/60	6/61
5988	5/53	3/60	7021	12/50	1/51	**4MT 2-6-4T Fairburn**		
5990	6/56	3/60		2/51	9/57	42182	11/60	6/61
61XX				6/59	6/61	42296	11/59	4/60
6114	6/59	6/61	7028	8/50	11/56	**4MT 2-6-4T Fowler**		
43XX				6/57	6/61	42305	8/59	6/61
6325	8/51	8/52	7035	2/59	3/60	42307	8/59	6/61
6368	6/54	10/54	**72XX**			42385	8/59	6/61
64XX			7200	10/52	6/60	42387	8/59	6/61
6412	8/50	7/56	7207	7/52	6/60	42388	8/59	6/61
6425	8/50	7/56	7209	10/52	7/60	42390	8/59	8/60
6431	8/50	7/56	7211	8/50	9/51	42394	8/59	6/61
56XX			7217	7/52	6/59	**4MT 2-6-4T Stanier**		
6602	6/60	6/61	7224	1/59	11/59	42566	12/60	2/61
6604	8/50	10/58	7225	8/50	10/51	42645	11/59	6/60
6641	9/59	12/59	7230	3/59	2/60	42651	11/59	4/60
6649	9/58	6/61	7236	10/52	6/60	**5MT 4-6-0**		
6650	6/60	6/61	7244	8/50	8/51	73022	12/53	1/54
6679	8/50	9/50	7248	9/54	6/57			

Leamington
84D 8/50   2L 9/63
Closed 6/65

2251			2267	11/60	10/61	3219	1/61	2/61
2201	9/61	2/62	**29XX**			**57XX**		
2210	9/61	11/64	2933	8/50	12/52	3619	9/51	5/62
2211	11/60	11/64	**2251**			3624	9/51	9/60
2257	11/60	6/62	3217	6/62	11/64	3631	8/50	12/61

51XX

4102	8/50	1/52
	4/52	5/52
4103	11/57	8/59
4112	8/50	3/62
4118	9/54	8/62
4120	9/62	11/64
4125	5/61	7/61
	1/62	3/65
4128	10/57	5/58
4133	10/62	10/64
4151	6/63	3/65
4162	10/58	7/60
4171	8/50	5/54
	9/54	10/64
4176	11/60	4/65
4178	8/62	10/64

49XX

4933	1/58	8/58
4987	7/51	10/52

51XX

5101	6/57	6/63
5104	8/50	2/58
5144	8/50	1/52
5153	8/64	11/64
5161	8/50	6/56
	7/56	4/57
5163	8/50	2/53
5177	3/60	5/61
5184	2/53	6/56
	7/56	5/58
	9/58	8/62
5185	8/50	5/58
5192	8/50	7/54
	10/61	6/63
5194	8/50	5/58
	12/59	4/61
5198	10/57	7/58

43XX

5315	3/51	5/51

56XX

5634	8/50	4/52
5640	9/62	7/63
5658	11/62	11/65

58XX

5813	4/57	10/57
5815	4/57	2/58

49XX

5923	2/51	5/51
5954	8/50	1/52
5966	2/51	10/52

61XX

6134	11/57	1/58

43XX

6364	2/64	8/64

56XX

6618	7/61	11/63
6624	8/52	10/57
6625	8/50	4/52
6632	8/50	1/52
6633	3/55	7/55
6639	6/63	10/63
6644	4/62	8/62
	10/63	6/65
6657	8/50	3/60
6663	5/62	6/63
6668	11/62	11/65
6671	2/62	6/65
6697	8/50	4/60
	9/64	6/65

68XX

6833	8/50	1/52
6835	5/51	6/51

49XX

6924	12/50	10/52
6942	12/50	8/55

72XX

7208	8/50	1/52
7218	8/50	1/52
7237	8/50	8/52

57XX

7702	8/50	8/60

78XX

7810	8/50	12/50

81XX

8100	8/50	9/62
8109	8/50	11/60

94XX

8454	8/50	8/51

57XX

9614	12/59	1/60
9733	12/59	1/60
9740	8/50	4/52

3MT 2-6-2T Stanier

40085	11/60	4/61

2P 4-4-0

40537	8/61	3/62

2MT 2-6-2T

41204	11/60	3/61
	3/64	6/64
41227	11/58	9/59
41228	11/58	2/60
41231	9/61	4/64
41232	2/64	11/64
41241	1/64	6/64
41272	7/63	11/64
41285	11/58	7/59
	1/60	3/60
	5/60	7/63

4MT 2-6-4T Stanier

42566	11/58	12/58
	2/59	12/60
	2/61	8/62

4F 0-6-0

44272	7/61	8/61

2MT 2-6-0

46428	10/64	6/65
46442	10/64	6/65
46457	10/64	6/65
46470	10/64	6/65
46505	10/64	6/65

8F 2-8-0

48412	11/62	1363/63

5MT 4-6-0

73026	10/64	6/65
73066	10/64	6/65
73069	10/64	6/65
73156	10/64	6/65

4MT 4-6-0

75000	8/62	9/63

4MT 2-6-4T

80072	9/63	6/65

3MT 2-6-2T

82007	5/58	5/58

WD 2-8-0

90010	11/51	9/53
	3/54	5/56
90261	6/56	8/59
90466	9/53	3/54
90483	11/51	9/53
	6/54	8/59
90563	9/53	4/54
90685	8/50	12/50
	2/51	6/51

Shed by Shed

Llanelly
87F 8/50
Closed 10/65

16XX		
1606	6/56	8/61
1607	8/50	9/65
1609	8/50	6/62
1611	10/59	10/65
1612	5/55	7/55
	8/55	9/55
	12/55	10/59
1613	8/53	10/59
1614	8/50	11/62
1615	1/57	6/61
1618	8/50	10/58
1622	5/52	6/62
1623	5/63	6/65
1628	5/53	6/59
1633	3/51	9/62
1638	4/51	7/62
1643	11/53	10/65
1644	4/52	9/59
1651	11/54	12/54
	4/55	10/65
1654	12/54	7/62
1655	1/55	3/65
1663	11/61	8/62
1665	4/55	8/64
1666	4/55	2/61
1669	8/64	10/65

1901		
1941	8/50	2/51
1957	8/50	4/51
1967	8/50	6/51
1991	8/50	12/52
2002	8/50	2/52
2012	8/50	5/55

2021		
2027	8/50	1/57
2042	8/50	12/51
2081	8/50	9/54
2083	8/50	11/51
2085	8/50	1/52
2098	8/50	5/51
2126	8/50	9/50
2150	8/50	1/52

BPGV 0-6-0T		
2162	8/50	3/55
2165	8/50	3/55

2167	8/50	1/53
2168	8/50	4/56
2176	8/50	3/55
2193	8/50	2/52
2196	8/50	12/55
2197	8/50	9/52
2198	8/50	3/59

28XX		
2803	8/50	9/51
2808	6/56	8/59
2824	8/50	5/54
	7/54	7/54
	12/58	7/59
2850	8/50	8/52
2855	8/50	10/52
2872	8/50	10/52
2888	8/58	2/59

57XX		
3610	6/64	7/64
3642	8/50	12/55
	7/57	4/61
3648	6/61	8/61
3661	8/50	9/59
3671	7/64	7/65
3678	8/62	12/63
3687	1/52	4/52
3690	12/51	5/62
3698	8/50	1/59
3701	6/61	7/64
3713	6/60	2/62
3719	8/50	1/63
3752	8/50	9/59
3761	8/50	11/61
	11/62	7/64
3771	8/50	1/63
3777	8/50	11/63
3781	5/62	8/63
3790	3/64	9/64
3796	1/63	7/64

28XX		
3803	8/58	3/59
3811	8/50	1/57
	2/57	9/63
3834	11/59	7/60
3851	8/50	6/64

4073		
4076	6/61	1/63
4078	6/61	6/62
4081	6/61	6/62
4093	1/63	2/63
4094	6/61	9/61
4099	6/62	8/62

51XX		
4169	11/54	12/54

42XX		
4213	8/50	10/59
4223	12/52	7/59
4225	9/62	1/63
4230	5/54	9/54
	7/61	8/62
4241	7/63	3/64
4242	8/60	12/61
4248	7/61	11/61
4254	8/50	8/52
4257	9/62	10/62
4260	12/53	5/59
4271	6/59	10/59
4272	10/59	6/62
	9/62	10/62
4273	1/62	5/62
4278	8/50	11/58
4279	6/60	11/62
4281	8/50	3/53
4283	8/50	9/54
4286	5/59	10/60
	12/62	8/64
4292	10/59	3/64
4294	6/63	9/64
4295	7/60	7/63
4296	10/63	12/63
4298	4/57	12/59
	7/60	6/63

57XX		
4604	9/64	7/65
4644	5/62	11/62
4668	5/65	7/65
4675	11/64	5/65
4676	8/59	10/65

49XX		
4907	5/53	8/53
4927	6/62	9/63

4928	6/62	1/63		**43XX**			6355	3/58	7/58
4938	8/61	1/63	5321	7/58	3/59		6357	6/62	9/63
4941	7/54	4/58	5323	5/58	5/58		6389	6/56	11/57
4952	7/54	9/55	5332	10/58	10/60		6395	9/62	12/63
4981	11/55	12/56	5335	8/50	9/58		6396	6/56	3/58
4988	11/62	9/63	5357	7/58	8/58		**56XX**		
4073				6/62	6/62		6602	12/63	11/64
5006	6/61	9/61	5361	5/59	10/59		6613	4/63	7/63
5016	6/61	8/62	5370	8/59	8/60			10/63	10/65
5020	6/62	11/62	5372	9/57	5/58		6623	3/63	6/63
5027	6/62	11/62	5378	8/50	3/53		6630	3/53	7/55
5037	6/62	10/62	5381	6/59	7/59		6641	2/60	4/60
	1/63	10/63	5385	6/62	6/62		6643	7/64	7/65
5039	1/63	4/63	5392	9/54	4/57		6652	11/62	12/63
5042	1/63	12/63		**56XX**			6653	9/59	12/63
5051	1/63	5/63	5602	7/60	7/63		6655	9/63	10/63
5054	1/63	11/63	5604	8/61	1/63		6688	8/50	6/51
5074	6/62	9/62	5612	10/53	4/63			7/51	12/52
5077	6/61	6/62	5634	9/61	11/61		6691	4/65	6/65
5080	6/61	4/63	5639	12/51	11/52		**68XX**		
5085	1/63	2/63	5656	12/59	11/62		6804	7/62	11/63
5087	12/61	8/63		12/63	2/64		6808	2/63	9/63
5091	6/61	9/61	5657	11/52	7/53		6810	8/50	9/61
5098	1/63	4/63		10/53	12/55			6/64	11/64
42XX			5675	8/50	1/53		6815	7/62	11/64
5200	3/65	3/65		2/53	8/53		6818	10/52	2/64
5201	11/61	6/63		6/63	1/65		6821	9/64	11/64
5203	8/50	10/59	5692	9/60	7/63		6824	8/50	2/52
	8/61	8/62		**57XX**			6828	6/57	9/57
5204	8/50	4/60	5702	8/50	5/60			3/58	11/58
	6/61	9/61	5705	8/50	7/59		6832	6/60	10/61
5209	8/50	4/63	5722	8/50	8/58		6837	9/60	11/64
5210	12/63	1/64	5782	8/50	10/58		6838	7/64	11/64
5213	8/50	9/60		**49XX**			6840	6/64	3/65
5215	8/50	4/59	5902	7/54	6/60		6843	1/56	9/56
	2/63	7/64	5903	6/59	5/60			11/56	3/64
5219	11/52	1/63		6/62	9/63		6844	7/52	11/61
5223	8/50	11/62	5909	11/58	6/60			7/62	3/64
5226	4/64	7/64	5913	9/54	11/55		6848	7/52	2/54
5230	8/50	10/59	5953	11/57	6/59		6851	7/60	9/60
	12/63	6/64	5955	8/50	10/50		6858	7/55	12/55
5240	8/50	8/52	5961	9/54	7/60		6860	9/60	11/60
	8/59	2/64	5976	6/62	6/63			9/64	11/64
5241	1/59	7/63	5980	6/59	7/59		6867	6/64	8/64
5242	10/62	7/64	5984	6/59	6/60		6871	7/60	9/60
5245	1/64	2/64		**43XX**			6878	3/64	4/64
5247	8/50	2/63	6310	10/58	5/60		**49XX**		
5248	8/50	11/62		1/61	6/62		6901	6/59	9/59
5249	12/52	4/59	6316	6/62	6/62		6909	9/56	6/60
5251	6/63	1/64	6323	3/58	5/58		6942	7/63	12/63
5252	3/65	3/65	6325	8/52	2/56		6958	6/59	9/59
5260	9/61	11/62	6328	3/58	12/58		**4073**		
5261	8/50	10/57	6345	6/59	7/60		7016	6/61	9/61
	11/57	12/58	6347	6/62	12/63		7021	6/61	12/61
5262	5/59	8/63	6349	6/62	9/63		7028	6/61	12/63

Shed by Shed

72XX

7200	10/60	7/63
7201	9/64	5/65
7203	3/55	11/59
7204	8/50	12/50
7211	9/51	8/59
	10/60	4/64
7215	8/53	10/57
	11/57	1/58
7217	7/63	6/64
7222	1/52	10/52
7223	11/63	11/64
7224	6/57	1/59
7225	10/51	1/58
	8/61	11/61
	1/63	4/64
7226	6/57	1/58
7228	8/50	2/60
7231	7/63	9/64
7232	1/59	6/63
	11/63	5/65
7235	11/57	4/58
	3/59	1/60
	10/60	4/64
7237	11/62	6/63
7239	11/62	10/63
7240	8/53	5/58
7242	7/63	7/64
7244	8/51	1/52
	11/62	3/64
	9/64	2/65
7248	12/63	6/65
7249	5/65	6/65
7251	10/57	4/58
7253	6/63	2/64

43XX

7307	4/56	11/63
7312	7/62	2/63
7314	4/56	6/60
7315	7/62	9/63
7318	8/51	9/54
7319	9/60	12/63
7320	8/51	5/59
7321	7/58	9/60
	7/62	8/62
7340	6/62	7/62

74XX

7437	12/63	3/65
7439	4/51	5/51
	3/64	5/65
7444	2/64	7/64
7446	12/63	7/64

57XX

7718	3/54	4/54
7745	8/50	3/61
7755	8/50	6/53
7765	8/50	6/62
7776	8/50	1/61
7785	8/50	5/62

78XX

7804	6/62	3/65
7811	12/62	2/63
	12/63	3/65
7814	9/63	6/64
7815	3/64	6/64
7826	11/63	3/65
7829	3/64	6/64

81XX

8103	6/62	9/63

94XX

8424	1/51	5/51
8467	3/51	2/62
	1/52	5/65
8475	3/52	5/52
8477	4/52	6/62
8488	7/64	5/65

57XX

8706	8/50	11/53
	8/59	6/61
8708	8/50	5/60
8726	7/60	4/61
8732	8/50	1/57
8736	2/59	3/62
8738	8/50	5/53
8749	8/50	7/64
8782	8/61	10/61
8783	1/63	5/63
8785	8/50	12/63

94XX

9408	6/61	4/63
9429	3/62	11/63
9443	5/51	10/56
9452	8/51	2/52
	11/63	5/65
9465	2/52	2/62
9468	4/52	11/56
9469	4/52	6/56
9472	5/52	2/57
	7/64	5/65
9474	6/52	2/57
9479	8/52	4/57
9485	9/59	7/64
9486	11/52	1/57
9492	12/54	9/56

57XX

9609	5/65	10/65
9621	1/61	9/64
9631	5/65	6/65
9632	3/64	7/64
9637	6/61	2/64
9648	6/64	7/64
9652	12/58	1/63
9677	7/64	11/64
9743	8/50	5/62
9744	5/61	5/62
9787	8/50	7/57
	8/63	9/63
9788	8/50	3/62

8F 2-8-0

48172	7/60	11/62
48307	12/61	6/64
48309	8/59	8/64
48328	9/59	9/64
48330	8/59	2/61
48400	8/59	9/64
48404	6/61	8/61
48409	8/59	8/64
48419	8/59	9/64
48420	9/63	3/64
48434	9/60	9/64
48438	8/59	6/64
48444	2/62	7/64
48452	8/59	6/63
48461	8/59	1/65
48463	8/59	11/62
48470	8/59	6/64
48524	8/59	3/64
48525	8/59	8/64
48706	8/59	5/65
48707	12/59	7/64
48730	8/59	7/64
48732	8/59	8/64
	11/64	10/65
48735	8/59	9/64
48760	8/59	8/64
	11/64	7/65
48761	8/59	1/65

5MT 4-6-0

73012	2/64	6/64
73021	5/60	6/62
73023	5/60	6/64
73024	9/63	6/64
73037	4/62	6/64
73050	3/64	4/64

2MT 2-6-0

78004	1/64	7/64

4MT 2-6-4T

80133	6/64	8/64
80134	3/64	8/64

WD 2-8-0

90167	6/60	8/60
90179	6/60	5/62
90207	6/60	5/62
90225	1/51	2/51
	6/60	8/60

90312	9/61	5/62	90676	9/61	5/62
90315	8/50	1/52	90693	8/52	11/52
90529	6/60	6/62			

Llantrisant
86D 8/50   88G 1/61
Closed 10/64

AD 2-6-2T			42XX			57XX		
1205	8/50	5/51	4208	8/50	12/59	5708	8/50	4/59
14XX			4222	4/64	9/64	5788	8/50	9/59
1421	8/50	11/52	4252	3/59	10/61	**64XX**		
1471	8/50	5/58	4261	8/50	3/59	6409	10/50	11/50
57XX			4267	12/59	9/62	6439	8/52	7/54
3612	8/50	9/64	4268	1/54	9/64	**56XX**		
3617	8/50	9/64	4273	9/57	6/60	6600	9/59	7/62
3644	8/50	9/64	4285	10/63	9/64	6639	3/61	6/63
3656	8/50	2/62	**57XX**			6670	8/62	7/63
3661	10/62	4/64	4620	8/50	9/64	**81XX**		
3663	4/59	12/61	4637	10/51	7/62	8103	9/63	10/63
3680	7/54	7/64	4662	6/56	9/64	**57XX**		
3691	8/50	2/51	4674	8/50	9/64	8739	8/50	9/55
3703	8/50	12/50	**42XX**			9746	8/50	11/62
3738	4/64	9/64	5228	6/63	4/64	9778	3/62	9/64
3776	2/51	3/58	5241	8/50	12/53	9780	8/50	7/61
51XX			5248	11/62	10/63			
4122	9/63	10/63						

Machynlleth
89C 8/50   6F 9/63
Closed to Steam 12/66

VoR			16XX			2219	8/50	11/53
7	8/50 [Q]		1603	8/50	1/54	2222	11/60	6/62
8	8/50 [Q]		1624	7/51	5/53	2223	8/50	5/51
9	8/50 [Q]		1636	1/54	7/59	2232	3/56	2/61
Cam R 0-6-0			**2251**			2233	7/52	9/52
849	12/52	9/54	2200	8/50	1/60		12/52	10/61
864	8/50	10/52		7/60	7/60	2236	9/61	6/65
873	7/53	9/53	2201	8/50	12/53	2237	7/56	5/59
892	8/50	3/53		1/54	3/54	2238	8/51	11/51
894	8/50	3/53		5/58	2/60	2239	9/61	5/62
895	7/53	9/53	2202	3/56	12/58	2244	3/56	8/62
14XX				1/59	9/60	2251	5/58	12/58
1434	3/55	5/55	2204	8/50	6/62		7/60	1/61
1449	9/58	6/60	2206	8/50	1/51	2255	7/55	5/62
1465	8/50	10/56	2214	8/60	12/60	2258	4/56	9/56
1474	8/50	9/51	2217	7/54	11/62			

2259	6/51	8/51
	9/51	11/51
2260	8/50	10/61
2264	4/56	6/60
2267	4/56	1/58
2268	6/64	6/65
2271	7/54	5/59
	6/62	8/62
2275	6/59	2/60
2276	6/61	8/62
2280	5/58	4/59
2281	5/58	12/59
2283	8/50	5/51
2285	6/56	12/59
2286	7/54	9/54
	7/55	9/62
2287	10/60	5/62
2289	7/56	1/58
	5/63	5/63
2292	8/50	1/51
	6/52	9/52
2294	10/59	8/62
2298	8/50	7/62
2301		
2323	8/50	4/53
2251		
3200	8/50	7/63
3201	8/50	7/55
3202	8/50	7/55
3205	4/61	6/61
3207	8/50	6/55
3208	6/63	6/65
3209	12/62	6/64
3213	7/60	11/62
57XX		
3630	5/60	8/62
43XX		
4377	10/55	12/58
45XX		
4501	8/50	2/53
4512	8/50	1/53
4530	8/50	1/51
4549	8/50	2/60
4555	8/50	9/57
4560	8/50	9/57
	1/58	7/59
4564	9/58	12/58
4571	8/50	2/53
4575	8/50	2/60
	6/60	7/60
4581	8/50	1/51
4584	6/51	11/51
4599	9/53	3/59
43XX		
5358	6/62	6/62

5395	5/51	9/55
45XX		
5507	8/50	7/58
5517	8/50	11/58
5521	6/51	11/51
5524	8/50	9/53
5538	6/61	7/61
5540	9/59	7/60
5541	8/50	1/60
5545	9/60	4/61
5553	12/58	11/60
5555	9/60	2/61
	6/61	7/61
5556	9/53	12/59
5560	8/50	9/53
5565	9/58	8/60
5570	8/50	3/60
57XX		
5700	9/51	2/56
58XX		
5801	11/55	8/58
5803	6/55	6/57
5809	8/56	7/59
43XX		
6333	6/60	9/60
6335	7/56	2/60
6336	6/61	4/62
6353	12/61	11/62
6368	6/62	9/63
6371	9/51	11/58
	1/59	8/60
6378	6/56	9/63
6383	12/52	4/56
6392	10/57	9/61
6395	6/60	8/60
	11/60	9/62
74XX		
7402	5/53	3/55
7406	8/50	3/62
7410	7/54	10/54
7417	8/50	11/60
	2/61	8/61
7428	9/60	9/62
7434	7/59	2/61
7442	9/61	2/62
	3/62	10/62
7446	4/62	7/62
78XX		
7802	8/50	11/62
	9/63	1/65
7803	8/50	6/59
	9/59	9/62
	3/63	1/65
7806	9/55	6/59
7807	12/63	11/64

7810	12/63	9/64
7814	2/59	12/62
7815	12/59	11/62
7818	1/60	1/65
7819	3/63	1/65
7820	8/52	10/52
7821	3/63	11/64
7822	12/63	1/65
7823	4/59	11/62
7827	12/63	1/65
7828	3/63	1/65
90XX		
9000	8/50	3/55
9002	8/50	4/54
9004	8/50	6/57
9005	8/50	7/56
9008	7/54	6/57
9009	8/50	6/57
9012	8/50	6/57
9013	8/50	11/58
9014	8/50	6/57
9015	7/56	6/60
9016	8/51	6/52
	7/54	6/57
9017	8/50	9/60
9018	6/53	7/56
	8/56	5/58
9020	7/54	6/57
9021	8/50	11/58
9022	9/54	7/57
9024	8/50	8/57
9025	8/50	7/57
9026	6/52	1/53
9027	8/50	9/54
9028	8/51	11/52
Stanier 3MT 2-6-2T		
40085	1/60	8/60
40086	2/60	10/60
40110	1/60	2/60
40205	1/60	3/60
2MT 2-6-0		
46446	5/63	12/66
46508	8/66	12/66
46519	3/63	2/65
46520	3/63	1/65
46521	3/63	10/66
46522	1/63	5/63
46523	1/63	8/63
4MT 4-6-0		
75002	9/62	12/66
75004	10/62	1/66
75006	9/62	3/63
75009	11/62	3/63
	7/66	12/66
75012	1/66	3/66

75013	6/65	12/66
75020	6/59	3/63
75021	5/62	3/63
75023	9/62	3/63
75024	11/62	3/63
	7/66	12/66
75025	7/60	11/60
75026	6/59	3/63
75027	11/62	3/63
75028	6/65	12/65
75029	11/62	3/63
75047	7/66	12/66
75052	7/66	12/66
75055	6/65	12/66

4MT 2-6-0

76038	6/66	8/66
76043	6/66	8/66
76086	6/66	9/66

2MT 2-6-0

| 78000 | 3/53 | 5/63 |

78001	3/53	5/54
78002	3/53	8/63
78003	3/53	3/58
	5/58	5/63
78004	5/53	1/54
78005	5/53	10/62
78006	9/53	9/62
78007	9/53	6/63

4MT 2-6-4T

80096	3/63	9/63
80097	6/64	8/65
80098	3/63	8/65
80099	7/63	5/65
80101	8/62	2/63
	3/63	7/65
80104	3/63	8/65
80105	7/62	8/62
	9/62	2/63
	3/63	8/65
80136	6/64	9/64

3MT 2-6-2T

82000	2/60	3/65
82003	6/62	3/65
82005	6/61	10/61
	11/61	4/65
82006	2/61	4/65
82008	6/61	9/61
82009	2/61	3/65
82020	3/60	4/65
82021	3/60	6/64
	6/64	4/65
82031	1/60	6/64
82032	7/61	11/61
82033	12/60	6/64
82034	4/61	3/65
82036	4/61	11/61

[Q] Locos still in service at end of normal steam operation on BR

Merthyr
88D 8/50
Closed 11/64

RR 0-6-2T

76	8/50	11/50
77	8/50	10/53
78	8/50	11/54
79	8/50	6/54
80	8/50	11/53
81	8/50	4/54
82	8/50	9/53
83	8/50	9/53

TV 0-6-2T

211	8/50	3/52
217	8/50	5/52
292	8/50	4/52
316	8/50	10/53
370	8/50	3/53
375	8/50	6/51
376	6/54	12/54
378	5/54	11/54
379	2/52	9/53
393	2/52	9/53
398	8/50	7/57

16XX

| 1629 | 11/50 | 12/50 |

2721

| 2760 | 8/50 | 10/50 |

57XX

3681	2/58	10/59
3690	11/63	11/64
3707	11/63	9/64

51XX

4101	9/53	9/55
4143	12/51	5/58
4152	12/51	5/58
4160	9/53	5/58
4161	9/53	4/58
4162	12/53	4/58
4163	9/53	5/58
4164	9/53	5/58

57XX

4616	5/52	5/58
4630	5/51	2/59
4632	8/50	11/58
	4/59	1/62
4635	8/50	5/64
4675	9/64	11/64
4684	6/52	7/52
4690	12/50	10/63

51XX

| 5195 | 9/53 | 12/53 |

56XX

| 5601 | 11/64 | 1/65 |

5602	11/63	7/64
5603	8/50	9/64
5605	8/50	6/64
	11/64	4/65
5609	12/63	11/64
5610	1/60	12/63
5615	11/54	9/58
	5/63	6/63
5617	8/50	1/52
	5/52	1/54
5618	7/60	3/65
5621	11/63	5/65
5622	8/50	1/57
	4/59	5/63
5623	9/50	10/50
5626	1/57	11/63
5630	5/58	1/61
5632	1/56	2/56
5635	8/50	1/61
5636	1/59	3/60
	1/61	5/62
5640	11/51	1/59
5650	10/55	6/63
5651	5/63	1/65
5652	8/50	8/62
5653	8/50	10/50

5654	8/50	10/50		**57XX**		6658	9/62	12/64
5655	8/50	5/65	5711	8/50	1/58	6685	6/63	3/64
5659	8/50	11/51	5721	8/50	9/53	6686	1/64	4/64
	6/64	4/65	5728	1/57	2/58	6691	1/64	4/65
5660	8/50	9/53	5769	8/50	6/57		**57XX**	
	1/54	9/64	5793	8/50	7/54	7717	8/50	10/58
5661	10/50	6/62		**64XX**		7766	8/50	10/58
5662	8/50	11/64	6408	8/50	1/58	7772	8/50	5/55
5666	8/50	7/63	6416	2/57	4/58		**94XX**	
5670	5/58	12/59		7/58	9/63	8465	6/51	2/52
	12/63	11/64	6423	3/56	7/58	8471	6/51	1/52
5671	8/50	7/53	6427	8/50	6/56		**57XX**	
	8/53	1/64		7/56	7/58	8723	6/62	1/63
5672	10/50	11/62	6433	9/53	1/63		2/63	4/63
5674	8/50	10/61	6434	8/50	5/57	8736	8/50	2/59
5677	8/50	2/54	6435	9/53	4/56		**94XX**	
	10/56	9/62	6436	9/53	11/55	9451	7/55	6/62
	11/62	4/65		12/55	6/62		**57XX**	
5681	11/54	5/65		**56XX**		9618	8/50	11/63
5683	8/50	10/50	6606	7/55	10/56	9622	8/50	7/55
5686	11/64	3/65	6608	7/63	7/64	9631	10/58	11/64
5687	11/62	11/63	6612	6/63	5/65	9638	8/50	11/63
5688	11/64	5/65	6613	2/63	4/63	9643	8/50	5/62
5692	8/50	10/50		7/63	10/63	9649	10/63	11/64
5694	8/50	6/56	6622	4/64	12/64	9675	8/50	4/64
5696	8/50	5/65	6627	10/50	9/53	9676	11/58	9/64
5698	8/50	9/53	6629	5/61	9/62	9679	10/58	11/64
			6649	11/64	2/65	9747	9/54	12/62
			6655	10/63	3/65	9776	11/58	5/64

Neath
87A 8/50
Closed 7/65

	RR 0-6-2T			**BPGV 0-6-0T**		3613	3/64	7/64
75	8/50	9/53	2192	8/50	4/51	3615	9/64	1/65
	16XX			**23XX**		3616	4/64	1/65
1612	7/55	8/55	2411	8/50	2/53	3621	8/50	7/63
	9/55	12/55		**2721**		3642	3/64	4/65
1643	10/53	11/53	2722	8/50	11/50	3647	3/64	6/65
1644	5/51	4/52		**28XX**		3650	10/61	10/63
1645	5/51	10/53	2818	4/63	10/63	3652	5/62	10/63
	11/53	9/62	2857	11/62	4/63	3654	3/64	6/65
1669	11/62	8/64	2874	11/62	5/63	3671	6/64	7/64
	1854		2890	3/64	11/64	3682	3/64	6/64
1855	8/50	12/50		**ROD**		3687	4/52	6/65
1858	8/50	10/50	3015	5/51	1/53	3690	11/64	6/65
	1901			**57XX**		3692	3/64	7/64
1964	1/51	5/51	3600	1/62	11/63	3693	6/62	7/63
1996	12/50	5/51	3603	6/64	7/64	3715	3/54	1/59
			3611	8/50	7/62	3731	5/62	7/64

Western

No.		
3741	8/50	8/62
3757	8/50	7/64
3766	8/50	7/63
3768	6/61	7/64
3774	8/50	5/62
3790	5/62	10/63
3797	6/64	11/64
3798	7/62	6/64
28XX		
3810	9/63	8/64
3814	4/64	11/64
3816	9/63	1/65
3822	11/62	10/63
3823	10/63	11/64
3832	4/63	4/64
3836	11/63	12/64
3847	6/63	3/64
3859	4/63	10/63
3860	4/64	8/64
3864	11/63	1/65
3866	4/64	11/64
4073		
4090	6/61	6/62
4093	6/61	1/63
4099	6/61	6/62
51XX		
4108	7/63	9/64
4110	5/63	11/64
4134	6/60	5/63
4142	9/63	12/63
4169	8/50	11/54
	12/54	7/64
42XX		
4221	8/50	7/55
	9/58	8/59
4232	8/50	4/56
4242	6/56	5/60
4243	5/53	2/59
	9/63	11/63
4252	8/50	3/59
	1/63	9/63
4255	9/59	3/64
4257	1/61	3/61
4258	10/63	9/64
4259	8/50	12/52
4264	9/55	7/60
4272	8/50	5/52
	9/59	10/59
4274	8/50	3/59
4275	6/56	1/64
4279	8/50	6/60
4281	3/53	12/60
4282	5/53	9/63
4284	8/50	9/64
4286	8/64	9/64

No.		
4288	8/50	9/60
4292	3/64	9/64
4293	8/50	1/57
4295	8/50	7/60
57XX		
4612	10/62	6/65
4621	8/50	7/63
4653	10/58	11/64
4657	3/64	7/64
4660	7/62	7/64
4669	4/64	6/65
4677	9/62	3/63
4682	5/62	10/63
4693	12/62	4/64
4695	3/64	7/64
4699	1/62	5/63
49XX		
4927	6/60	1/62
4932	9/64	11/64
4966	9/62	10/63
4967	6/62	8/62
4985	7/64	9/64
4988	6/60	11/62
4073		
5004	6/61	4/62
5013	6/61	6/62
5037	7/61	6/62
	10/62	1/63
5041	6/61	6/62
5044	6/61	7/61
	7/61	10/61
5048	7/61	7/61
	10/61	7/62
5051	6/61	1/63
5054	10/62	1/63
5062	6/61	7/62
5074	6/61	6/62
5075	7/61	1/62
5078	6/61	11/62
5085	10/62	1/63
51XX		
5102	10/52	6/56
	7/56	3/60
42XX		
5203	11/59	10/60
5204	9/61	1/63
5209	4/63	4/64
5210	1/64	2/64
5213	7/63	9/64
5216	4/63	10/63
5221	4/61	10/63
5222	6/56	4/64
5223	11/62	9/64
5225	8/50	4/59
5226	1/64	2/64

No.		
5238	4/63	1/64
5239	8/50	4/63
5241	9/63	6/64
5242	8/50	10/62
5245	3/64	9/64
5246	9/58	10/59
5254	8/50	2/52
	3/64	7/64
5257	10/63	9/64
5264	7/63	9/64
43XX		
5306	12/63	7/64
56XX		
5656	7/59	12/59
5673	6/61	9/63
5677	9/62	11/62
57XX		
5703	8/50	11/51
5720	8/50	1/62
5746	8/50	4/57
5761	8/59	5/62
5773	8/59	8/62
5778	8/50	1/52
	2/52	6/62
49XX		
5909	6/61	9/61
5953	11/60	1/61
5961	9/62	11/64
5972	6/60	11/62
5980	6/60	5/61
5981	6/62	8/62
5984	9/62	10/62
5989	7/61	6/62
61XX		
6149	12/63	7/64
43XX		
6357	9/63	6/64
56XX		
6613	7/58	9/59
6614	5/65	6/65
6628	11/64	5/65
6641	4/60	8/62
6649	6/61	7/63
6650	1/57	6/60
6695	6/61	10/63
57XX		
6700	2/57	4/57
6776	12/50	1/51
68XX		
6810	6/64	6/64
6832	10/61	1/64
6840	6/63	6/64
6867	6/63	6/64

Shed by Shed

49XX

6905	6/60	1/62
	7/62	7/64
6912	6/61	9/61
6918	6/61	9/61
6932	6/64	11/64

6959

6973	7/64	11/64
6975	9/62	11/63
6984	9/64	11/64

72XX

7203	6/62	1/63
7204	12/50	5/53
	6/61	3/63
7214	1/62	11/62
7220	10/52	3/54
7222	4/51	1/52
	10/52	5/53
7226	10/52	12/52
7229	3/64	6/64
7236	4/51	5/51
7240	4/51	5/51
7243	6/62	1/63
	3/64	8/64
7244	8/61	5/62
	3/64	9/64
7247	7/61	11/62
7248	4/51	12/52
	11/62	2/63
7252	3/64	9/64

43XX

7312	3/63	11/63
7315	9/63	12/63
7318	3/63	4/64
7320	3/63	4/64

57XX

7701	8/50	2/50
7737	8/50	3/60
7739	8/50	1/63
7742	8/50	6/59
7743	8/50	7/59
7757	8/50	8/60
7767	8/50	3/60
7769	8/50	7/59
7786	8/50	5/62
7799	8/50	5/62

78XX

7823	6/56	7/56
7828	4/51	10/52
7829	4/51	10/52

6959

7913	7/64	11/64

81XX

8102	12/60	3/63
8104	8/50	6/56
	7/56	9/62

94XX

8418	11/59	7/63
8420	8/50	5/51
8431	6/64	8/64
8439	9/60	9/62
8442	3/54	5/59
8465	11/50	12/50
8466	11/50	1/51
8475	6/64	7/64
8480	9/62	7/64
8488	6/64	7/64
8490	8/52	9/52

57XX

8715	8/50	4/62
8732	1/57	12/63
8737	5/62	1/63
8747	6/62	7/64
8760	4/60	1/62
8775	8/50	12/61
8782	8/50	8/61
8784	1/51	4/62
8788	6/60	5/62
8791	5/62	2/63

94XX

9412	6/61	2/63
9430	11/50	6/61
9436	2/51	1/52
	2/52	7/55
9442	4/51	10/62
	11/62	7/64
9446	5/51	7/63
	6/64	2/65
9448	6/51	9/56
	11/56	6/62
9451	8/51	7/55
9452	12/54	11/63
9455	9/51	11/51
9464	3/64	2/65
9472	6/64	7/64
9473	6/52	4/64
	6/64	7/64
9475	3/64	2/65
9478	8/52	6/62
9480	6/64	7/64

57XX

9600	11/64	5/65
9609	4/64	5/65
9615	3/64	1/65
9617	3/64	6/65
9625	5/62	6/65
9627	8/50	6/62
9631	11/64	5/65
9634	3/64	7/64
9637	2/64	9/64
9648	4/64	6/64
9656	3/64	5/65
9660	6/64	11/64
9666	8/50	10/52
9675	6/64	5/65
9677	6/64	7/64
9678	6/64	6/65
9716	8/62	6/65
9734	8/50	7/64
9742	3/64	7/64
9743	5/62	4/64
9748	5/62	3/63
9750	8/50	5/62
9756	8/50	11/59
9766	3/64	7/64
9777	6/61	7/64
9779	8/50	2/64
9780	6/64	1/65
9783	8/50	5/62
9786	8/50	7/64
9788	3/64	4/64
9792	8/50	5/59
	6/59	3/64

0F 0-4-0T

41535	6/64	9/64

8F 2-8-0

48732	8/64	11/64
48760	8/64	11/64

0F 0-4-0T

51218	6/64	9/64

4MT 2-6-4T

80133	3/63	6/64

WD 2-8-0

90315	1/52	9/54
90693	11/52	9/54
90701	2/53	5/53

9F 2-10-0

92216	10/63	9/64
92222	11/63	9/64
92225	10/63	6/64

Newport Pill
86B 8/50
Closed 6/63

AD 0-6-0T		
666	8/50	4/55
667	8/50	10/54
15XX		
1506	8/50	9/59
1507	8/50	4/60
1854		
1709	8/50	11/50
2021		
2033	8/50	3/51
2086	9/51	5/52
2136	8/50	7/52
2154	8/50	2/52
2159	6/51	8/51
28XX		
2805	5/51	9/54
2863	5/51	8/52
2883	5/51	8/53
ROD		
3025	4/51	11/51
57XX		
3652	2/56	6/56
	7/56	5/62
3663	8/50	4/59
3674	11/57	1/63
3700	11/54	11/57
3705	6/61	6/63
51XX		
4130	2/51	6/55
42XX		
4201	8/50	9/59
4211	8/50	12/54
	3/55	2/58
4214	4/54	6/63
4226	8/50	5/53
4229	8/50	6/53
4233	8/50	6/63
4235	8/50	11/60
4237	8/50	4/57
4238	1/58	6/63
4246	8/50	12/53
4253	8/50	4/63
4254	2/62	6/63
4258	8/50	10/57
	1/58	10/60
	4/63	6/63

4259	4/57	6/63
4263	9/50	3/55
4264	7/60	6/63
4269	8/50	4/54
4271	11/62	6/63
4276	1/58	1/63
4280	8/50	1/63
4285	5/53	1/58
4291	8/50	1/58
4294	7/60	6/63
4298	10/52	12/52
57XX		
4643	4/57	6/63
4652	2/61	3/61
4662	8/50	12/50
4682	1/58	5/62
42XX		
5200	8/50	6/63
5202	9/55	10/63
5205	8/55	10/55
	6/56	7/56
5231	8/50	10/63
5235	8/50	12/62
5244	8/50	6/63
5250	8/50	6/63
5251	12/62	6/63
5252	8/50	10/63
5256	10/59	6/63
5257	9/56	9/59
5260	8/50	5/52
56XX		
5638	8/50	5/51
57XX		
5706	2/51	3/59
5714	8/50	1/58
5733	5/53	7/58
5734	11/56	5/59
5736	2/56	1/58
5740	8/50	5/59
5741	11/56	6/57
5747	8/50	8/59
5750	8/50	10/51
5758	9/58	5/62
5768	6/57	3/61
5777	4/54	5/58

49XX		
5921	5/51	10/52
64XX		
6409	11/50	3/59
57XX		
6707	5/58	5/59
6710	8/50	7/57
6711	8/50	5/59
6724	9/57	10/62
6725	8/50	5/59
6726	8/50	5/58
6727	8/50	4/58
6728	8/50	6/60
6729	8/50	5/59
6730	8/50	8/57
6731	8/50	5/58
6732	8/50	5/58
6735	8/50	5/59
6739	1/55	6/62
6742	3/52	10/62
6743	8/50	4/59
6745	7/58	5/59
6750	4/58	8/59
6751	10/58	7/60
6752	7/60	1/61
6755	8/50	2/60
6756	8/50	7/60
6757	8/50	5/60
6758	9/60	6/62
6759	8/50	4/60
6760	8/50	10/62
6763	2/61	11/62
6764	8/50	5/61
6772	11/50	11/62
6775	7/60	7/60
49XX		
6932	5/51	8/51
57XX		
7703	1/58	3/60
7712	8/50	3/59
7721	9/51	3/59
	5/60	6/62
7748	5/51	4/53
7772	5/58	3/59
7774	8/50	4/54
7789	8/50	1/51

	94XX			57XX			WD 2-8-0	
8440	1/60	4/61	8791	6/61	5/62	90268	1/51	4/51
8499	12/59	4/61	8796	8/50	4/57			
			9664	1/63	6/63			

Newton Abbot
83A 8/50
Closed to Steam 6/62

	10XX	
1018	8/50	2/51
1019	8/50	2/51
	1361	
1362	8/50	9/52
	14XX	
1427	8/50	11/58
1439	8/50	7/55
	9/55	7/57
1452	8/57	7/59
1466	8/50	4/61
1470	8/50	5/61
1472	2/56	9/58
	16XX	
1608	8/50	1/56
	3/56	2/60
	2181	
2181	8/50	2/52
2182	8/50	7/55
2183	8/50	5/55
	28XX	
2805	9/58	5/60
2807	12/58	5/60
2809	8/50	5/51
	6/51	1/56
	5/58	9/58
2843	1/51	5/51
2846	7/54	5/60
2869	5/51	3/55
2873	9/50	5/51
2875	3/51	5/60
2881	8/50	2/60
2893	3/60	4/60
	57XX	
3600	8/50	10/58
3659	8/50	3/62
3796	8/53	1/63
	28XX	
3832	3/51	5/51
3834	9/50	11/59
3840	7/52	5/60

3841	7/52	5/60
3864	3/51	5/60
	4073	
4037	9/56	2/57
	6/57	6/62
4076	11/54	11/57
4077	8/50	9/54
	5/59	2/60
4080	5/53	7/54
	5/59	5/60
4083	4/58	9/60
4088	11/53	9/54
4098	8/50	6/62
4099	8/50	3/55
	51XX	
4105	8/56	4/58
	5/58	5/60
4108	5/58	9/59
4109	8/50	7/55
	9/55	11/58
4115	7/58	12/58
4117	9/58	3/59
4133	8/50	5/51
	8/51	10/53
4145	7/54	5/60
4148	2/62	9/62
4150	10/56	5/60
	7/61	6/62
4154	1/60	4/60
4165	7/60	2/61
4166	7/52	11/53
4174	9/57	12/59
	1/60	1/62
4176	9/55	5/60
4178	7/56	5/60
4179	8/50	4/61
	44XX	
4401	1/53	8/53
	10/53	9/54
4405	8/50	8/55

4406	1/55	8/55
	45XX	
4532	8/50	9/53
4547	8/50	3/55
4555	8/59	3/62
4561	11/58	7/61
4568	6/56	8/58
4574	9/61	7/62
4582	8/50	9/53
4587	8/50	9/53
4592	9/55	2/60
	49XX	
4900	5/51	10/51
4905	6/56	4/61
4920	12/58	?/6? [R]
4934	7/60	4/61
	6/61	6/62
4936	12/58	5/62
4950	8/50	11/50
4954	6/53	4/54
4955	9/57	11/59
4967	6/56	6/57
	10/57	11/59
4975	12/58	11/61
4978	10/61	9/62
4992	10/57	5/58
	4073	
5003	3/59	7/62
5005	1/57	4/58
5011	8/50	5/60
5024	8/50	5/62
5028	8/50	6/56
5029	5/59	5/59
	6/59	11/59
5032	4/58	3/60
5034	8/50	12/50
5041	8/50	9/55
5042	7/62	12/62
5047	8/50	11/54
5049	5/58	5/60
5053	1/55	11/59

5055	4/58	12/62					**74XX**	
5059	5/53	4/58		**57XX**		7427	8/50	3/59
5071	8/50	4/58	5796	8/53	1/55	7445	8/57	5/59
5078	8/50	5/58		3/55	7/56		**78XX**	
5079	8/50	5/60		9/56	9/58	7805	10/50	10/53
5089	10/55	5/58	5798	8/50	4/51	7806	12/51	7/55
5098	1/62	7/62		**49XX**			6/59	9/59
	51XX		5920	8/50	5/61	7808	6/59	9/60
5108	8/50	5/58	5967	1/55	3/60	7809	9/57	9/58
5113	8/50	9/55	5981	6/61	6/62	7812	8/50	6/56
5132	8/50	8/51		**61XX**			7/56	12/56
5140	8/50	6/53	6107	6/59	7/59	7813	8/50	6/56
5142	8/50	5/52	6119	6/59	11/59		7/56	1/58
5150	8/50	11/50	6166	6/59	9/59	7814	6/56	9/58
	12/50	7/60		8/60	1/62	7815	7/54	12/54
5153	8/50	2/59		**43XX**		7818	6/59	1/60
	3/59	8/62	6322	2/58	12/58	7821	6/59	9/61
5154	8/56	8/62	6330	4/52	8/52	7824	7/54	12/54
5157	8/50	6/53	6345	8/50	5/51		6/59	8/59
5158	8/50	4/61	6356	4/52	5/55		**6959**	
5164	8/56	10/61	6360	1/59	10/59	7909	10/60	9/62
5168	9/56	7/58	6363	4/59	5/59	7916	4/52	5/60
5178	8/56	3/60		**68XX**			**94XX**	
5183	8/56	4/61	6813	8/50	5/60	8403	8/50	12/56
5195	9/56	6/61	6814	8/50	2/58	8404	11/54	11/56
5196	12/52	12/59	6822	8/50	9/55	8422	10/50	1/51
5197	6/59	1/60	6829	8/50	5/60	8451	9/53	10/58
	43XX		6836	7/55	5/60	8466	11/56	11/58
5339	10/52	2/58	6848	4/54	3/55	8473	10/51	1/61
5350	8/50	5/51	6859	2/59	5/59	9434	6/56	7/56
5360	10/52	5/55	6860	7/55	9/55	9440	3/51	6/62
5362	8/52	1/55	6874	10/52	9/53	9462	3/52	10/60
5391	8/50	9/50		**49XX**		9463	3/52	4/52
	45XX		6904	8/59	2/60	9480	1/60	2/60
5505	8/50	12/53	6925	1/55	5/55	9487	11/56	7/60
5523	8/58	9/58	6933	10/54	4/59		**57XX**	
5525	7/61	8/62	6934	8/50	4/53	9623	8/50	8/60
5533	7/55	11/58	6938	1/56	11/59	9633	8/50	1/62
5536	9/56	6/57	6940	11/58	6/62	9668	8/50	7/55
5539	6/53	4/55	6951	7/55	9/55		8/55	7/58
5542	10/53	7/55		**6959**		9778	8/50	3/62
5543	10/53	7/55	6972	4/59	5/59	9792	5/59	6/59
5544	8/50	3/55	6988	10/54	5/55		**8F 2-8-0**	
5551	8/50	10/50		**4073**		48431	8/55	9/55
	11/50	9/55	7000	8/50	5/57		**7MT 4-6-2**	
5552	8/50	3/55		7/57	5/59	70019	7/51	9/51
5557	8/50	4/55	7029	8/50	12/56	70022	4/52	12/56
	7/55	9/55		4/57	7/62		**3MT 2-6-2T**	
5558	8/55	6/56		**72XX**		82001	7/55	9/56
	8/56	9/60	7200	8/50	10/52	82002	7/55	9/56
5564	9/60	4/62	7209	8/50	1/51	82004	4/55	7/56
5573	1/58	9/62	7220	8/50	10/52	82005	7/55	8/56
			7236	5/51	10/52	82006	7/55	7/56
			7240	5/51	10/52	82009	4/55	8/56
			7250	8/50	9/52	82031	3/55	5/55

Shed by Shed

82032 7/55 9/56
82033 1/55 9/56
82034 1/55 8/56
82038 5/55 9/55

WD 2-8-0

90148 7/52 4/54
90676 11/52 5/54

[R] Before 6/64

Neyland
87H 8/50
Closed 9/63

10XX		
1001	8/50	1/61
	9/62	5/63
1008	9/62	1/63
1009	8/50	1/55
1014	9/61	2/63
1020	8/50	9/56
	10/56	10/62
1027	12/50	11/59
	9/61	2/63
1029	12/53	7/61
16XX		
1601	11/50	7/60
1602	11/50	6/56
1606	11/50	6/56
1611	8/50	10/59
1613	10/59	12/63
1628	9/50	5/53
1637	3/51	6/60
1648	8/60	5/63
1666	2/61	11/62
	5/63	9/63
1669	7/60	2/62
1901		
1964	8/50	11/50
1996	8/50	11/50
2010	8/50	2/53
2011	8/50	11/50
2251		
2208	8/57	5/59
2209	9/57	10/57
2220	5/53	12/61
2226	5/53	9/56
2228	5/53	5/59
2229	10/53	11/59
2251	12/58	7/60
2259	12/58	4/59
2263	8/55	12/58
2271	5/59	9/59
2273	1/59	11/59
2283	5/51	8/63
2287	5/63	12/63

2288	8/50	11/59
2296	9/57	10/57
3214	1/62	10/63
57XX		
3624	9/60	5/62
3639	10/58	1/63
3654	8/50	12/63
3657	8/53	5/61
3678	6/61	8/62
3712	5/62	12/63
51XX		
4106	6/61	8/61
4107	6/60	9/63
4122	9/58	9/63
4131	6/54	9/55
4132	8/50	7/60
	6/62	9/63
4136	6/63	11/63
4159	11/60	6/62
4166	6/54	7/54
43XX		
4358	8/50	7/55
45XX		
4506	8/50	3/55
4515	8/50	3/53
4519	8/50	1/59
4541	10/52	9/55
4550	4/56	9/60
4553	8/50	7/55
4556	8/50	6/60
4557	9/53	8/62
4558	3/55	6/62
4569	7/61	4/63
4573	10/60	7/61
4576	8/50	8/58
4579	8/50	8/58
4594	12/55	10/60
57XX		
4654	8/50	12/63
4658	1/63	12/63
4699	3/54	9/55
	10/55	1/62

49XX		
4908	8/50	9/50
4957	8/50	11/53
4982	8/50	10/53
4983	2/63	9/63
4997	8/50	12/53
51XX		
5180	5/58	12/59
5193	11/60	6/62
43XX		
5310	8/50	10/53
5324	11/53	10/58
5353	8/50	10/53
5357	8/50	7/58
	8/58	6/62
	6/62	8/62
5368	8/50	10/52
5372	8/50	9/57
5392	8/50	9/54
5396	10/57	2/58
45XX		
5508	9/62	11/63
5509	7/60	11/60
5513	8/50	6/57
5520	9/55	8/62
5527	9/58	6/60
5545	9/62	11/63
5546	7/60	8/60
5549	8/50	1/62
5550	10/52	8/62
5554	9/62	8/63
5555	9/55	10/55
5560	9/57	7/60
5568	8/50	11/53
5571	3/62	11/63
5573	9/62	4/63
56XX		
5629	6/57	8/57
5634	9/62	8/64
5639	5/53	6/53
5646	1/52	9/55
5657	6/52	10/52

5661	8/50	10/50	6620	6/56	7/56		**81XX**	
5673	7/52	9/52	6623	6/60	7/60	8102	8/50	9/57
	57XX			10/60	11/60	8103	10/59	11/59
5748	5/54	9/54		1/61	3/63	8107	8/50	9/60
	12/54	8/60	6627	9/59	3/63		**57XX**	
5761	5/51	2/52	6644	7/55	8/55	8738	5/53	11/53
	49XX		6674	5/53	6/53		1/54	2/63
5903	7/54	6/59		**68XX**		8739	9/55	6/62
5921	10/52	11/53	6838	7/56	9/56		**43XX**	
5931	11/58	1/59		**49XX**		9305	6/54	9/54
	61XX		6909	6/60	7/60	9313	6/54	9/54
6105	4/55	5/55	6914	1/63	6/63	9315	6/54	9/54
6108	7/60	9/60		**6959**		9318	6/56	
6114	6/61	3/62	6984	2/63	9/63		(renum 7340 1/58)	
6118	1/63	9/63					**94XX**	
6125	6/61	4/62		**43XX**		9436	7/55	7/56
6148	10/60	7/61	7306	8/50	11/61	9452	2/52	12/54
	43XX		7318	9/54	2/63	9492	6/54	12/54
6306	8/58	6/60	7320	5/59	11/61		**57XX**	
6310	5/60	1/61		6/62	2/63	9652	8/50	12/58
6347	8/50	10/57	7321	5/58	7/58	9714	5/54	2/61
	6/61	9/61		9/60	2/61	9741	2/53	4/57
6348	6/57	9/57	7340	(ex 9318 1/58)		9748	3/63	12/63
6355	8/50	5/51		6/56	6/62		**4MT 2-6-4T Fowler**	
	7/58	3/59		7/62	9/62	42307	7/55	10/55
6371	8/50	9/51		**74XX**		42388	7/55	8/55
6388	5/58	10/58	7413	8/50	4/54		**3MT 2-6-2T**	
6389	8/50	6/53		**78XX**		82008	9/61	10/61
	11/57	8/60	7811	2/63	12/63	82042	9/61	10/61
	56XX		7814	2/63	9/63	82044	9/61	10/61
6602	8/50	5/51	7816	8/50	10/52			
	6/61	7/61	7825	10/61	12/63	[S] After 3/60		
6610	7/60	2/63		**6959**				
6616	?/6? [S]	8/62	7917	2/63	9/63			

Old Oak Common
81A 8/50
Closed to Steam 3/65

	10XX		1501	8/50	11/50	2276	8/50	5/60
1000	8/50	2/51	1502	8/50	12/50	2282	8/50	5/60
1003	8/50	2/51	1503	8/50	11/63		**28XX**	
1008	8/50	10/52	1504	8/50	4/63	2826	8/50	5/52
1010	8/50	2/51	1505	8/50	5/62	2835	8/50	5/52
1012	8/50	2/51	1506	5/62	11/63	2858	4/51	5/52
1015	8/50	2/51	1507	4/60	11/63	2868	8/50	5/52
1021	8/50	2/51		**2251**		2895	8/50	5/52
1024	9/52	10/52	2208	2/53	3/53		**ROD**	
1026	8/50	9/52	2222	12/52	5/60	3017	8/50	5/52
	15XX		2237	9/55	7/56		**57XX**	
1500	8/50	11/63	2243	5/52	11/58	3608	9/63	3/65

3618	8/63	7/64
3620	8/64	3/65
3622	8/64	9/64
3646	3/61	7/64
3648	8/50	1/61
3666	6/62	1/63
3685	8/50	4/54
3688	8/50	1/61
3710	8/50	9/50
3711	9/62	4/63
3715	3/51	3/54
	9/63	3/65
3750	9/61	8/62
3754	8/50	7/63
3763	4/63	3/65
28XX		
3813	8/50	5/52
3852	8/50	5/52
3853	8/50	5/52
4073		
4016	8/50	9/51
4037	8/50	6/56
4074	11/62	4/63
4075	8/50	12/50
	11/59	10/61
4078	4/60	6/61
4080	3/64	6/64
4082	9/63	8/64
4085	8/60	5/62
4089	2/51	2/52
	6/54	12/58
	7/60	12/63
4090	11/52	8/53
	12/55	8/59
4091	12/55	12/58
4096	4/58	6/62
	11/62	1/63
4097	2/51	6/57
4098	6/62	12/63
57XX		
4606	4/63	3/65
4609	8/63	3/65
4611	12/63	3/65
4615	8/50	9/64
4638	9/63	3/65
4644	8/50	12/59
	1/60	2/61
4666	8/50	9/50
4670	11/63	9/64
4698	8/50	4/54
4699	8/50	3/54
47XX		
4700	8/50	9/61
4701	8/50	10/62
	11/62	9/63

4702	8/50	9/61
4703	11/62	7/64
4704	10/51	10/62
	11/62	7/64
4705	8/50	1/57
	10/63	12/63
4706	9/63	3/64
4707	8/50	11/55
	10/63	7/64
4708	10/52	9/62
49XX		
4900	8/50	2/51
	9/56	4/59
4903	12/59	3/60
	10/62	6/63
4907	3/55	5/55
4908	5/52	9/52
	2/54	6/54
4915	10/58	1/59
4919	7/56	9/62
4921	12/59	4/60
4923	8/50	6/56
4925	11/56	4/58
4928	11/56	1/57
4930	6/62	9/62
4939	6/54	10/54
4941	5/52	8/53
4943	6/53	9/56
4945	6/53	9/53
	10/60	3/61
4958	8/50	4/51
4961	8/50	10/51
4962	6/53	8/53
	9/53	10/53
	9/63	11/63
	12/63	6/64
4965	7/56	9/56
4967	12/52	6/56
4970	6/62	9/62
4977	9/56	12/58
4978	4/51	9/51
4982	2/61	8/61
4983	10/60	9/62
4986	3/53	3/55
4073		
5001	1/57	9/58
	7/60	2/63
5004	8/50	6/56
5005	4/58	9/58
5006	6/54	4/58
5007	4/57	2/59
5008	11/56	8/62
5010	4/58	1/59
5011	10/60	8/62
5012	2/56	3/56

5014	8/50	6/64
5015	1/61	9/62
5022	2/56	3/56
	4/58	7/61
5029	8/50	4/58
5032	3/60	8/62
5034	12/53	8/62
5035	8/50	9/60
5036	10/60	8/62
5037	6/60	7/61
5038	8/50	4/58
5039	8/50	6/52
	2/56	3/56
	4/63	7/63
5040	8/50	10/61
5041	6/62	12/63
5042	4/60	7/62
5043	8/50	6/52
	2/56	4/62
5044	8/50	7/60
5045	8/50	12/50
5050	9/60	8/61
5052	1/57	8/60
5054	11/59	11/60
5055	8/50	4/58
5056	8/50	7/63
5057	2/51	2/52
	4/60	3/64
5060	2/51	3/63
5065	8/50	1/63
5066	8/50	8/62
5069	8/50	10/52
5070	11/62	3/64
5074	1/57	7/60
5076	5/51	7/51
	4/63	6/64
5081	8/50	12/54
5082	11/52	6/62
5084	7/55	6/62
5085	8/50	9/52
5087	8/50	12/61
5090	10/60	5/62
5092	3/55	2/58
5093	7/52	9/53
	12/53	9/63
5095	2/51	2/57
5098	4/63	3/64
5099	1/57	5/58
57XX		
5717	10/50	5/60
5764	8/50	5/60
49XX		
5900	10/62	11/62
5906	5/52	4/54
5907	12/59	3/60

No.		
5918	8/50	12/50
5919	10/62	8/63
5923	3/58	10/61
5929	10/58	2/62
5931	8/50	11/58
	1/59	11/59
5932	8/50	6/52
	7/52	4/63
5936	8/50	5/59
5937	8/50	8/53
5938	8/50	8/53
5939	8/50	9/62
5940	8/50	6/59
5941	8/50	6/59
5945	9/56	9/58
5947	8/50	3/53
5952	8/50	10/50
5954	9/56	10/59
5958	10/58	2/62
5962	8/50	8/53
5967	10/60	7/63
5971	3/63	6/64
5976	1/59	?/60 [T]
5977	10/58	12/58
5984	10/62	4/63
5985	3/63	7/63
5986	8/50	10/54
5987	8/50	11/59
5988	10/62	6/63
5994	12/50	1/51
5996	8/50	4/57

60XX

No.		
6000	9/52	1/63
6001	8/50	9/54
6002	8/50	2/60
6003	8/50	6/62
6004	9/59	6/62
6005	9/62	1/63
6007	8/50	3/59
6009	8/50	8/62
6010	4/59	9/61
6011	9/62	1/63
6012	7/54	4/62
6013	8/50	4/59
	3/60	5/61
6014	8/50	10/52
6015	8/50	6/62
6016	12/54	12/58
6017	8/50	2/52
6018	8/50	1/63
6019	8/50	9/60
6021	8/50	9/56
	9/59	8/62
6022	9/55	6/59
6023	6/56	6/62

No.		
6024	9/54	9/61
6025	6/59	1/63
6026	2/60	8/62
6027	11/59	1/60
6028	8/50	1/63
6029	6/59	6/62

61XX

No.		
6108	11/59	7/60
6109	10/53	6/56
6110	6/53	12/59
	7/60	10/60
	7/64	8/64
6113	9/57	7/60
6117	8/50	5/52
6120	8/50	10/60
6121	8/50	9/53
	10/53	7/60
6124	4/63	4/64
6125	10/59	11/59
	4/62	8/64
6132	12/55	10/60
6135	8/50	9/64
6137	8/50	7/55
6141	8/50	3/60
	10/60	8/64
6142	8/50	8/64
6144	8/50	1/60
6145	5/58	6/65
6149	8/50	11/59
6155	8/50	2/56
6156	7/64	8/64
6157	11/59	6/61
6158	8/50	7/61
6159	8/50	11/59
6163	1/60	8/64
6164	10/60	6/62
6165	7/64	8/64
6168	8/50	5/61
	9/61	3/62
6169	10/60	4/64

68XX

No.		
6821	5/52	10/52
6834	5/52	10/52
6874	5/52	10/52

49XX

No.		
6900	8/50	10/51
6910	8/50	9/50
6920	3/58	9/62
6926	8/50	5/51
6927	5/52	8/53
6932	8/50	5/51
	8/51	9/51
	5/52	8/53
6942	10/58	7/63
6944	8/50	10/54

No.		
6953	8/50	10/50
6954	7/51	8/51

6959

No.		
6959	8/50	6/64
6960	8/50	9/53
6961	5/52	10/63
	9/64	1/65
6962	8/50	1/63
6963	12/60	4/64
6966	9/58	1/64
6973	8/50	5/59
	8/59	9/59
	12/59	4/63
6974	8/50	12/61
	12/63	2/64
6978	1/57	10/63
	9/64	2/65
6983	8/50	9/53
6985	8/50	12/50
6990	8/50	12/50
	1/52	10/63
6996	5/52	7/54
6998	1/61	6/64

4073

No.		
7001	8/50	8/61
7004	8/50	7/60
7006	3/62	12/63
7008	9/56	9/64
7009	6/61	2/62
	11/62	3/63
7010	11/52	1/64
7012	11/60	6/61
7013	8/50	5/60
	3/64	6/64
7014	2/56	3/56
	8/61	6/62
7015	9/62	4/63
7017	7/54	1/63
7018	10/61	9/63
7019	?/60 [U]	5/61
7020	1/57	6/64
7021	12/61	9/63
7024	8/50	8/61
7025	8/50	7/60
7027	2/51	5/60
7029	7/62	9/64
7030	8/50	1/63
7032	8/50	9/64
7033	8/50	1/63
7035	2/63	6/64
7036	9/50	6/62
	9/62	9/63

57XX

No.		
7722	2/58	3/60
7734	8/50	4/59

7791	8/50	12/59
6959		
7902	8/50	7/64
7903	8/50	10/63
7904	8/50	1/64
	3/64	4/64
7910	11/63	4/64
7911	8/50	1/52
7921	9/60	12/63
7923	9/64	2/65
7927	9/58	9/60
94XX		
8420	6/62	1/64
	8/64	5/65
8432	3/53	12/55
8433	3/53	11/55
	2/63	5/65
8434	3/53	5/59
8435	10/60	2/62
8436	5/62	11/64
8458	10/60	8/63
8459	1/59	5/65
8464	7/63	8/63
8472	10/62	2/63
8481	2/63	5/65
8486	8/64	3/65
8487	8/62	11/63
8498	7/63	3/65
57XX		
8707	8/50	12/55
8743	1/64	6/64
8750	8/50	12/52
8751	8/50	4/60
8753	8/50	2/62
8754	8/50	10/60
8755	12/55	11/57
8756	8/50	9/62
8757	8/50	8/62
8759	8/50	1/63
8760	8/50	4/60
8761	8/50	5/59
	8/60	5/62
8762	8/50	7/61
8763	8/50	7/62
8764	8/50	3/60
8765	8/50	8/62
8767	8/50	7/63
8768	8/50	9/64
8769	8/50	5/59
8770	8/50	7/60
8771	8/50	6/62
8772	8/50	8/60
8773	8/50	9/62
43XX		
9302	8/50	8/51

9304	8/50	8/51
9305	8/50	11/50
9306	8/50	8/51
9308	8/50	8/51
9309	8/50	3/51
9315	8/50	5/51
94XX		
9400	11/55	12/59
9401	8/50	5/51
9402	8/50	5/51
9403	8/50	10/51
9404	8/50	5/51
	8/64	5/65
9405	8/50	5/51
	6/56	7/56
	5/59	7/64
	8/64	3/65
9406	8/50	5/51
	11/63	9/64
9407	8/60	6/62
9410	5/51	6/62
9411	5/51	5/65
9412	5/51	6/61
9414	5/51	7/60
9415	11/63	5/65
9416	11/55	10/60
9418	8/50	3/65
9419	8/50	2/63
9420	5/51	3/64
9422	8/50	11/58
	11/63	12/63
9423	9/51	2/63
9435	7/63	9/64
9440	6/62	7/63
9455	10/62	4/63
9463	7/63	3/65
9469	5/59	3/62
9470	7/63	9/64
9477	11/60	3/65
9479	11/58	7/63
9495	7/62	3/65
9498	7/63	9/64
57XX		
9640	11/60	7/63
9642	8/64	11/64
9658	8/50	7/63
9659	8/50	3/65
9661	8/50	7/63
9700	8/50	10/63
9701	8/50	1/61
9702	8/50	5/62
9703	8/50	12/61
9704	8/50	11/63
9705	8/50	9/61
9706	8/50	11/64

9707	8/50	11/63
9708	8/50	12/58
9709	8/50	5/62
9710	8/50	9/64
9725	8/50	1/63
9751	8/50	6/61
9754	8/50	4/61
9755	4/62	4/63
9758	8/50	5/62
9763	8/63	9/63
9784	8/50	4/63
9789	8/63	3/65
8F 2-8-0		
48410	1/60	10/62
48412	1/60	11/62
48431	1/60	11/62
7MT 4-6-2		
70015	8/53	12/56
70017	7/51	12/56
70018	9/51	12/56
70020	8/51	12/56
70023	9/51	2/57
4MT 2-6-4T		
80070	7/62	11/62
80098	7/62	8/62
80102	7/62	11/62
80104	7/62	11/62
80131	7/62	8/62
80132	7/62	11/62
WD 2-8-0		
90101	8/50	12/50
90105	8/50	12/50
90585	9/51	10/51
9F 2-10-0		
92000	3/62	6/62
92203	10/60	3/63
92204	10/60	3/63
92211	9/59	6/61
92220	9/62	10/62
92226	10/61	10/62
92229	10/58	1/60
92230	10/58	1/60
	9/62	10/62
92238	12/58	8/60
92239	12/58	8/60
92240	11/58	8/60
92241	11/58	10/60
92243	11/62	9/63
92244	11/58	10/60
92245	11/58	10/60
92246	11/58	10/60
92247	12/58	2/62

[T] Before 12/60
[U] After 1/60

Oswestry
89A 8/50   89D 1/61
6E 9/63
Closed 1/65

	W&L 0-6-0T			2251			3209	5/58	8/62
822	8/50	7/61	2202	12/58	1/59	3214	9/60	1/62
823	8/50	6/62	2210	8/50	10/58		57XX	
	Cam R 0-6-0		2219	11/53	10/59	3600	2/59	1/62
844	8/50	1/53	2236	11/58	10/59	3770	9/59	4/63
	4/53	7/54	2239	4/56	9/61	3789	11/56	11/62
849	8/50	12/52	2244	8/50	9/53		28XX	
855	8/50	9/54	2251	1/61	11/62	3821	7/64	9/64
873	8/50	1/53	2255	8/50	7/55	3825	7/64	9/64
	3/53	7/53	2261	4/56	7/56	3850	10/64	1/65
	9/53	2/54	2275	4/56	6/59	3855	10/64	1/65
887	8/50	10/52	2285	4/56	6/56		45XX	
893	8/50	1/53	2286	9/54	7/55	4546	10/52	1/58
895	8/50	7/53	2287	12/59	10/60	4560	9/57	1/58
	9/53	9/54	2289	4/56	7/56	4564	7/58	9/58
896	8/50	12/52		11/59	1/60		12/58	2/59
	14XX		2294	11/58	6/59	4578	3/58	7/58
1412	8/50	10/56		23XX		4580	3/58	5/58
1423	9/57	12/58	2323	4/53	5/53	4588	1/59	3/59
1428	8/50	5/53	2327	8/50	3/53	4595	8/58	11/58
1432	8/50	7/63	2354	8/50	10/52		43XX	
1438	1/60	1/63	2386	8/50	12/50	5386	2/58	9/58
1440	6/61	11/61	2407	2/51	1/52		54XX	
1447	5/59	8/59	2408	8/50	12/52	5400	2/57	4/59
1458	12/58	7/63	2409	8/50	12/52	5401	12/52	1/57
1459	8/50	5/57	2452	8/50	9/52	5405	12/52	9/57
	16XX		2482	8/50	10/50	5421	5/60	8/62
1602	6/56	8/60	2483	8/50	10/50	5422	10/57	6/60
1603	1/54	5/59	2484	8/50	4/54		57XX	
1604	8/50	7/60	2516	8/50	2/53	5726	7/53	9/59
1628	6/59	10/62		5/54	4/56		58XX	
1635	3/51	8/53	2538	8/50	11/52	5803	8/50	3/53
1636	3/51	1/54		7/53	5/57	5806	8/50	6/57
	7/59	6/62	2543	8/50	1/53	5812	8/50	6/57
1638	7/62	1/65	2556	8/50	2/53		43XX	
1663	11/62	4/63	2572	8/50	11/52	6335	6/56	7/56
1666	11/62	5/63		2251		6342	10/58	11/60
1668	7/60	1/65	3200	7/63	8/63	6383	10/52	12/52
	2021		3201	7/55	11/58		64XX	
2032	8/50	6/51	3202	7/55	6/60	6404	3/59	5/59
2054	8/50	3/51	3203	8/52	9/52		74XX	
2068	8/50	12/52	3204	5/58	10/58	7405	8/50	11/62
2075	8/50	3/51	3207	6/55	11/58	7410	8/50	7/54
2090	7/51	9/51	3208	8/50	6/63		10/54	1/61

7417	11/60	2/61
7434	8/50	7/59
	2/61	9/62
7446	7/62	12/63
	57XX	
7794	7/59	8/59
	78XX	
7800	8/58	1/63
7801	8/58	1/63
7803	6/59	9/59
7807	8/50	12/53
	8/58	12/63
7808	8/50	12/53
7809	4/59	1/63
7810	5/59	12/63
7812	9/60	11/61
7819	8/50	1/63
7820	12/50	8/52
	10/52	12/53
7821	12/50	11/53
7822	12/50	4/54
	8/58	12/63
7827	8/58	12/63
	81XX	
8103	8/50	10/52
	90XX	
9001	8/50	3/54
9003	8/50	9/55
9005	7/56	6/59
9008	6/52	1/53
9010	6/52	1/53
	6/54	6/57
9016	8/50	8/51
	6/52	1/53
9018	7/56	8/56
	6/59	6/60
9020	8/50	1/53
9022	8/50	9/54
9026	8/50	6/52
	7/54	7/57
9027	9/54	7/57
9028	8/50	8/51

	3252	
9084	8/50	4/51
9089	1/51	7/51
	57XX	
9629	5/60	11/62
9681	4/56	12/60
	2MT 2-6-2T	
41204	11/59	1/60
41285	7/63	7/64
	2MT 2-6-0	
46401	11/59	3/63
46503	11/52	3/63
46504	11/52	3/63
46505	11/52	3/63
46506	11/52	12/56
	10/59	7/60
46507	11/52	12/54
	6/56	1/63
46508	12/52	12/54
	11/59	1/63
46509	12/52	1/63
46510	12/52	1/65
46511	12/52	1/65
46512	12/52	1/65
46513	12/52	1/65
46514	12/52	1/65
46515	1/53	1/65
46516	1/53	7/53
	10/59	1/65
46517	1/53	7/53
46518	2/53	5/53
	10/59	6/63
	6/63	1/65
46519	2/53	3/63
46520	2/53	3/63
46521	2/53	3/53
	10/59	3/63
46522	3/53	4/53
	10/59	1/63
46523	3/53	4/53
	1/55	1/63

46524	3/53	4/53
	3/59	2/63
46525	9/62	2/63
46526	12/56	3/62
	9/62	12/62
46527	1/58	3/62
	9/62	12/62
	8F 2-8-0	
48122	11/64	1/65
48345	11/64	1/65
	4MT 4-6-0	
75002	9/56	1/57
75005	2/54	8/58
75006	12/53	8/58
75020	11/53	8/58
75023	12/53	8/56
75024	12/53	2/58
75026	1/57	8/58
75028	6/56	8/58
	2MT 2-6-0	
78000	12/52	3/53
78001	12/52	3/53
78002	12/52	3/53
78003	1/53	3/53
78004	3/53	5/53
78005	3/53	5/53
78006	3/53	9/53
78007	3/53	9/53
78008	5/53	6/53
78009	5/53	6/53
78029	5/63	5/63
	4MT 2-6-4T	
80097	7/63	6/64
80131	1/63	1/65
80132	1/63	1/65
80135	1/63	9/64
80136	1/63	6/64
	2MT 2-6-2T	
84000	4/63	1/65
84004	4/63	1/65

Oxford
81F 8/50
Closed to Steam 12/65

	14XX	
1420	8/53	9/58
1425	8/53	1/56
1435	5/58	1/62
1442	3/51	9/53
	12/53	10/62
1444	9/59	3/60
	6/60	12/63
1447	3/59	5/59
1448	8/50	11/50
1450	8/50	4/51
	8/59	6/62

1462	10/52	11/52	3857	6/56	10/60		**51XX**	
1468	1/62	3/62	3866	8/50	4/52	5190	1/56	1/61
	16XX			**40XX**		5198	11/58	1/59
1617	8/50	5/53	4021	8/50	9/52		**43XX**	
1627	7/62	7/64		**4073**		5322	3/53	5/53
1630	10/62	7/64	4092	10/60	12/61		10/54	8/56
	1901			**51XX**		5323	8/50	7/54
1935	8/50	10/51	4103	8/59	12/61		**54XX**	
	1/52	3/53	4105	5/53	6/53	5413	8/50	1/57
	2021		4125	11/57	5/58		**56XX**	
2076	8/50	10/51		7/58	5/61	5697	8/59	3/60
	2251		4147	5/53	7/60		**58XX**	
2202	5/52	6/53		8/60	4/61	5803	3/53	6/55
2206	6/57	8/57	4148	11/57	2/62	5808	3/53	1/57
2221	12/60	1/61		**45XX**		5811	2/57	5/57
	1/62	6/62	4511	8/50	9/53	5816	6/57	6/57
2236	9/53	10/58	4513	8/50	10/50	5818	6/57	8/59
2249	8/50	5/52	4558	8/50	11/53		**49XX**	
2262	11/54	12/54		**57XX**		5904	8/50	1/52
2289	9/54	4/56	4645	8/50	10/50	5907	11/59	12/59
	1/58	10/58	4649	12/60	4/64	5918	9/61	8/62
2292	11/52	6/53	4676	8/50	2/58	5922	10/61	1/64
2294	6/55	10/58	4680	8/50	7/53	5923	10/61	11/63
	23XX			**49XX**		5932	12/63	3/64
2579	5/51	12/53	4902	8/50	12/59	5933	11/60	7/65
	28XX		4903	8/50	12/59	5942	9/59	12/59
2803	9/51	6/53	4907	5/55	3/58	5945	5/55	6/56
2815	10/52	6/53	4908	10/61	7/62		9/62	3/63
2827	8/50	8/52	4919	9/62	1/63	5955	11/60	6/64
2836	12/58	8/59	4921	8/50	12/59	5956	9/62	3/63
2845	8/50	11/50	4922	6/63	7/63	5957	11/59	7/64
2858	12/50	4/51	4928	8/50	9/54	5960	8/50	5/51
2860	8/50	8/53	4933	8/52	9/55		1/52	8/62
2880	3/58	5/59	4938	8/50	12/59	5965	8/50	3/59
	ROD		4945	5/53	6/53	5966	5/55	8/62
3012	7/54	10/54	4951	9/62	1/63	5969	4/56	6/56
3023	7/54	10/54		1/64	7/64		9/56	5/58
	2251		4954	8/56	12/59	5971	12/64	1/65
3217	4/54	6/55	4962	6/65	10/65	5985	7/63	9/63
	57XX		4965	10/54	12/54	5987	6/63	1/64
3608	8/50	8/58	4966	10/63	11/63	5989	11/60	7/61
3653	12/60	10/63	4969	8/52	2/56	5994	4/53	5/53
3677	9/65	12/65	4975	6/63	9/63		**61XX**	
3722	8/50	7/60	4976	3/63	7/64	6104	5/52	7/52
3751	1/65	9/65	4979	5/58	12/63	6106	8/53	2/63
3794	10/63	1/65	4981	9/63	10/63		9/65	12/65
	28XX		4987	5/58	7/58	6108	9/64	9/65
3814	3/58	4/64	4988	9/63	2/64	6109	8/50	1/51
3823	8/58	10/63	4995	5/58	2/60	6110	3/65	6/65
3835	8/50	9/54		**4073**		6111	8/50	12/65
3843	1/60	2/60	5012	12/52	2/56	6112	3/51	9/59
3846	9/52	3/53		3/56	4/62	6113	1/53	9/57
3847	8/50	6/53	5026	12/50	4/58	6122	8/50	9/56
3854	1/51	7/52	5033	5/58	8/62	6123	6/60	4/62
	6/56	1/57				6124	1/62	4/63

6126	4/64	12/65
6129	11/60	8/62
6132	9/65	10/65
6133	11/59	1/60
6134	9/65	12/65
6135	9/65	12/65
6136	6/65	12/65
6138	8/50	6/62
6139	11/59	3/60
6143	10/65	12/65
6144	5/62	11/63
6145	6/65	12/65
6149	6/61	12/63
6150	1/61	3/65
6154	7/60	6/65
6156	6/61	7/64
	10/65	12/65
6161	9/65	10/65
6163	1/58	1/60
6168	5/61	9/61
43XX		
6300	8/50	5/52
6304	5/58	9/58
6313	8/50	5/53
6336	10/54	1/58
6379	4/54	3/55
56XX		
6664	8/58	4/60
68XX		
6812	4/64	3/65
6821	3/58	11/59
6822	3/58	1/60
6824	10/63	3/64
6834	7/55	12/55
6841	7/64	5/65
6848	9/58	11/59
6849	10/63	12/65
6854	3/55	2/60
6858	9/58	2/60
6859	5/59	7/59
6862	3/55	5/65
6864	3/55	7/59
6868	10/63	10/65
6874	10/63	9/65
49XX		
6910	9/62	1/65
	6/65	10/65
6920	4/53	3/58
6921	6/65	10/65
6922	9/54	12/59
6923	3/63	12/65
6924	5/55	3/59
	11/64	10/65
6925	8/50	1/52
6927	5/58	10/65

6931	9/65	10/65
6932	5/65	12/65
6933	8/50	9/52
6936	11/63	2/64
6937	8/50	2/60
	6/65	12/65
6947	3/65	11/65
6952	4/60	5/60
6953	10/50	1/65
	6/65	12/65
6956	2/61	6/61
	6/65	12/65
6957	3/65	10/65
6959		
6959	9/65	12/65
6960	8/63	9/63
6961	6/65	9/65
6963	6/65	7/65
6966	1/64	9/64
6967	11/63	12/65
6970	8/50	7/64
6973	9/59	12/59
6974	2/64	8/64
	11/64	5/65
6983	6/65	9/65
6990	12/50	1/52
6991	6/65	12/65
6993	6/65	12/65
6998	9/65	12/65
6999	5/65	12/65
4073		
7008	8/50	9/56
7010	8/50	11/52
7035	11/62	2/63
72XX		
7209	?/6? [V]	10/62
7212	6/53	6/56
7218	1/60	11/60
7238	6/53	11/60
7239	6/53	9/62
7246	6/53	6/56
7249	4/54	5/54
7252	4/54	5/54
43XX		
7324	(ex 9302 2/57)	
	6/53	9/58
74XX		
7404	8/50	12/63
7411	8/50	5/59
7412	8/50	7/63
7436	8/50	5/58
7445	5/59	7/62
57XX		
7760	8/50	12/61

6959		
7900	2/52	1/65
7906	6/63	8/64
	9/64	3/65
7909	6/65	12/65
7910	11/64	2/65
7911	1/52	12/63
7917	6/65	9/65
7919	6/65	12/65
7922	7/65	12/65
7925	10/65	12/65
7927	10/65	12/65
94XX		
8424	2/58	1/61
8432	12/55	6/59
8486	11/63	8/64
8494	9/59	12/60
57XX		
8761	2/60	8/60
90XX		
9015	9/53	7/56
9018	11/52	6/53
9028	11/52	6/53
43XX		
9302	6/53	
(renum 7324 2/57)		
9311	5/53	11/56
9316	8/50	6/54
9317	8/50	5/53
94XX		
9403	10/51	5/59
9416	8/50	11/55
9450	7/58	12/60
	3/62	4/62
9455	2/61	10/62
57XX		
9611	8/50	8/60
9640	10/50	11/60
9653	5/53	7/65
9654	8/50	11/64
9773	11/64	12/65
9789	3/65	12/65
5MT 4-6-0		
73003	6/65	12/65
73021	6/65	9/65
73023	9/64	6/65
73024	9/64	11/64
73030	6/65	9/65
73031	6/65	9/65
73037	9/64	4/65
73044	1/65	3/65
73049	9/64	3/65
73162	1/65	5/65
73164	9/64	1/65
73166	6/65	12/65

4MT 4-6-0		
75000	2/61	6/62
75001	9/54	3/63
75004	9/54	7/55
75007	9/58	3/63
75008	10/58	7/64
75021	10/60	5/62
75022	9/61	4/64
75024	12/58	3/59
75027	12/54	2/59

75029	12/54	10/58
	1/59	2/59
	11/60	1/61
WD 2-8-0		
90251	6/56	7/59
90284	6/56	7/59
90312	11/52	8/56
90529	8/50	6/56
90573	3/53	5/53

9F 2-10-0		
92001	9/62	11/62
92220	10/62	8/63
92224	10/62	8/63
92244	10/62	11/62
92245	9/62	10/62

[V] After 7/60

Oxley
84B 8/50   2B 9/63
Closed to Steam 3/67

28XX		
2809	6/57	1/58
2819	9/54	11/58
2825	8/50	9/50
2830	8/50	12/58
2832	8/50	11/52
2833	8/50	9/57
2841	12/53	1/57
2850	6/56	2/60
2854	8/50	3/56
2856	4/61	6/61
	9/61	3/63
2857	2/59	4/59
2858	7/52	11/52
2859	2/59	12/59
2865	7/52	12/52
2868	7/52	11/52
2882	7/52	1/55
2888	2/59	4/59
	4/61	11/61
ROD		
3016	12/52	9/56
3024	6/56	11/56
3028	6/51	10/51
	9/53	7/56
3029	8/53	4/56
3031	8/50	10/52
	2/53	4/56
3033	8/50	9/51
3043	6/56	8/56
3047	12/52	5/53
57XX		
3605	10/62	9/66
3631	12/61	8/65
3694	1/54	3/54
3698	1/59	4/64

3744	8/50	3/54
	8/64	8/66
3745	8/50	4/54
3776	8/64	4/66
3778	?/6? [W]	3/64
3782	1/65	10/66
3788	12/64	10/65
3792	8/50	5/53
	9/63	10/65
3793	8/50	5/53
28XX		
3802	5/52	10/62
3813	7/52	3/63
3820	3/59	12/60
3821	9/61	12/61
3825	10/51	1/55
3829	10/57	7/60
3831	9/61	3/63
3837	5/55	4/59
3842	9/59	12/60
3845	5/55	1/57
3848	6/57	3/58
3854	9/59	7/60
3860	7/51	1/57
3861	9/54	7/60
3863	5/52	6/59
3865	11/53	10/62
51XX		
4146	9/59	1/60
4148	6/63	9/65
4154	6/65	9/65
4165	6/63	9/65
4176	4/65	9/65
4178	6/65	9/65
4179	6/63	4/64

57XX		
4602	4/64	11/64
4625	7/61	5/62
4687	4/64	11/64
47XX		
4708	8/50	10/52
49XX		
4901	1/57	6/57
	7/60	8/60
4903	12/61	9/62
4906	11/60	8/62
4912	4/59	7/62
4913	1/57	10/57
	11/57	6/59
4918	5/53	7/55
4919	12/50	7/56
4923	9/61	6/64
4924	11/52	7/55
4926	12/52	7/54
4934	3/53	5/53
4943	2/51	4/53
4950	11/50	4/53
4951	2/57	4/57
4954	7/64	11/64
4955	8/50	7/55
4957	1/58	2/60
4959	10/52	5/55
4963	9/54	6/56
	9/56	5/61
4965	9/55	7/56
4966	9/54	9/62
4977	12/50	3/52
4984	9/56	6/61
4986	3/55	6/56
4991	8/50	8/52
4997	9/55	9/61

	4073	
5000	6/64	11/64
5026	9/63	11/64
5031	9/63	10/63
5056	6/64	11/64
5063	9/63	2/65
5089	9/63	11/64
	43XX	
5300	11/50	6/52
	9/52	12/52
5307	10/50	6/52
5309	8/50	5/52
	6/52	12/52
5312	5/54	9/58
5313	8/50	2/52
	5/55	5/58
5325	7/55	7/56
5336	6/53	12/56
5341	11/50	9/57
5375	2/53	8/58
5378	3/53	12/56
5379	8/50	1/52
	6/56	8/56
5381	3/53	10/57
5386	8/50	10/52
5390	8/50	5/52
	8/52	1/58
5391	11/52	6/54
	10/55	1/56
	56XX	
5606	8/50	11/50
	10/60	3/64
5624	8/50	10/52
5657	8/50	6/52
	10/52	11/52
5684	8/50	1/58
	9/63	3/64
	57XX	
5748	8/50	2/54
	3/54	5/54
	49XX	
5900	11/55	10/62
5910	11/60	8/62
5916	2/57	6/62
5919	3/59	10/62
5921	8/50	5/51
5942	11/50	7/52
5944	12/50	8/52
	1/53	10/60
5945	8/50	7/54
	9/54	5/55
5958	9/56	1/58
5959	6/57	6/57
5965	3/59	6/62
5966	10/52	5/55
5972	10/52	7/54
5985	4/58	11/62
5991	8/50	4/61
5993	5/52	7/52
5995	11/50	4/63
5996	7/61	10/61
	12/61	7/62
5997	5/52	7/52
	43XX	
6301	3/62	6/62
6302	4/53	5/53
6311	10/58	11/58
6324	2/54	1/58
6335	8/50	5/51
6338	6/51	5/52
	4/53	5/53
6353	3/59	1/60
	3/60	11/60
	2/61	12/61
6355	1/54	8/56
6361	8/50	4/53
6362	8/50	1/52
	6/54	9/54
6363	2/51	5/53
6365	5/55	6/55
6367	6/54	7/54
6375	3/62	6/62
6383	8/52	10/52
6396	2/53	5/53
	56XX	
6600	8/50	5/51
6609	8/50	1/51
6610	8/50	2/59
6631	8/62	9/63
6638	8/50	10/52
6640	8/50	8/62
6644	8/62	10/63
6645	8/50	7/62
	57XX	
6755	2/60	7/60
6757	5/60	7/60
	68XX	
6803	9/62	9/65
6806	11/56	6/61
6808	9/63	8/64
6811	4/64	8/64
6812	6/51	7/52
6817	5/58	6/61
6823	9/61	7/65
6827	4/64	9/65
6828	9/61	7/63
6830	4/62	9/65
6831	4/62	10/65
6833	5/62	10/65
6835	4/62	5/62
6839	4/54	12/60
	9/61	4/64
6844	10/51	7/52
6845	9/60	11/62
6848	2/52	7/52
6851	9/60	6/65
6854	9/52	3/55
	9/61	6/65
6855	9/62	5/65
6856	8/50	5/52
	9/52	12/56
6857	9/57	5/65
6858	9/62	6/65
6860	10/51	10/52
6861	4/53	11/55
6862	8/50	3/55
6863	4/58	5/58
6864	5/62	5/65
6870	9/61	8/65
6871	9/60	10/65
6879	8/50	5/52
	9/52	5/58
	49XX	
6907	9/55	1/64
6917	6/61	1/65
6920	8/50	4/53
6924	3/53	5/55
6925	9/55	4/64
	6/64	11/64
6926	3/53	5/58
6933	9/61	4/64
	6/64	11/64
6934	9/55	7/60
6940	2/52	7/52
6951	4/53	7/53
6956	8/50	12/50
6963	5/52	7/52
6964	10/53	11/53
6967	8/50	2/51
	10/51	11/51
6975	8/50	7/54
	9/55	12/58
	5/59	9/62
6980	4/59	10/64
6994	6/64	11/64
	4073	
7001	9/63	9/63
7011	6/64	2/65
7012	9/63	11/64
7014	9/63	6/64
7019	9/63	2/65
7023	6/64	2/65
7024	9/63	2/65
7026	9/63	6/64

72XX

7207	8/50	7/52
7208	1/52	10/52
7213	11/60	9/64
7217	9/59	12/59
7218	1/52	8/52
	11/60	11/62
7226	8/50	10/52
7227	8/50	11/52
7238	8/50	2/53
	11/60	10/61
7243	8/50	11/52
7247	3/55	1/60

43XX

7305	3/55	5/58
7311	8/50	10/52
7329	(ex 9307 11/56)	
	5/53	5/58
7336	(ex 9314 5/58)	
	8/50	1/59
7339	(ex 9317 9/56)	
	5/53	9/61
7341	(ex 9319 6/57)	
	7/56	5/58
	8/58	11/59
	7/60	9/61

57XX

7759	8/50	3/60
7796	8/50	4/54
7797	8/50	2/54
	9/54	9/59

78XX

7806	8/62	11/64
7811	7/52	1/53
7818	7/52	3/53
7820	10/64	9/65
7821	11/64	9/65
7824	7/62	11/64

6959

7915	5/51	10/62

94XX

8417	8/50	3/59
8428	3/51	9/62
8449	7/54	1/58
8462	9/58	10/58
	1/59	7/59
8464	11/59	7/63

57XX

8713	1/56	2/56
8739	5/64	11/64
8767	7/63	4/66
8798	8/50	5/53

43XX

9307	5/53	
	(renum 7329 11/56)	

9312	8/50	5/52
	6/52	7/54
	1/56	9/56
9314	8/50	
	(renum 7336 5/58)	
9316	6/54	1/55
9317	5/53	
	(renum 7339 9/56)	
9318	5/53	9/54
9319	7/56	
	(renum 7341 6/57)	

94XX

9408	8/50	6/61
9474	7/60	10/61

57XX

9640	7/63	7/66
9658	7/63	10/66
9661	7/63	11/64
9714	8/50	5/54
9715	8/50	7/56
9730	8/50	4/54
9739	8/50	6/61
9742	8/50	4/51
9747	8/50	2/54
9752	8/50	4/62
9768	8/50	1/65
9769	8/50	2/54
9776	5/64	4/66

4MT 2-6-4T Fairburn

42069	5/65	7/65
42071	5/65	7/65

5MT 2-6-0 Stanier

42946	4/65	11/65
42957	4/65	12/65
42983	4/65	12/65

5MT 4-6-0

44663	11/66	12/66
44691	3/65	8/66
44777	4/66	9/66
44805	3/65	3/67
44808	3/65	12/66
44812	3/65	3/67
44841	3/65	10/66
44843	6/65	3/67
44856	3/65	2/67
44865	11/66	3/67
44876	10/65	3/67
44914	10/66	12/66
44919	3/65	12/66
44944	9/65	3/67
44945	9/65	10/66
44965	9/65	8/66
45006	3/65	3/67
45040	3/65	3/67
45186	3/65	3/67

45263	3/65	12/66
45264	6/65	11/65
	4/66	3/67
45272	3/65	9/65
45283	3/65	1/67

8F 2-8-0

48016	1/65	6/65
48035	12/65	2/66
	11/66	3/67
48061	12/65	2/66
	11/66	3/67
48105	2/67	3/67
48120	1/65	6/65
48177	2/67	3/67
48180	2/67	3/67
48220	11/64	2/65
48402	12/65	3/67
48415	6/65	7/66
48450	7/66	3/67
48460	7/66	3/67
48474	6/65	3/67
48475	11/64	10/66
48477	2/66	2/66
48531	7/66	3/67
48628	9/65	9/66
48674	3/66	2/67
48680	3/66	9/66
48705	3/66	2/67
48724	3/66	3/67
48738	1/65	8/65
48752	3/66	2/67
48755	1/65	6/65

G1 & G2a 0-8-0

49082	5/57	6/57

7MT 4-6-2

70045	6/65	9/65
70047	6/65	9/65
70053	6/65	9/65

5MT 4-6-0

73000	1/65	3/65
73010	1/65	3/65
73011	1/65	3/65
73013	1/65	6/65
73014	1/65	6/65
73019	11/64	4/66
73025	1/65	3/65
73028	11/64	4/66
73033	10/56	5/58
	1/65	3/65
73034	10/56	5/58
73035	10/56	5/58
73038	1/65	3/65
73067	1/65	3/65
73071	1/65	3/65
73090	1/65	3/65

Shed by Shed

Loco	Date	Date
73096	11/64	3/65
73157	1/65	3/65
73160	1/65	3/65
73163	11/64	3/65
73165	11/64	3/65
4MT 2-6-0		
76022	11/64	8/66
76037	9/65	2/67
76039	9/65	3/67
76041	9/65	3/67
76042	5/66	7/66
76052	5/65	7/65
76087	5/66	1/67
76088	3/66	2/67
2MT 2-6-0		
78008	11/62	10/66
WD 2-8-0		
90010	10/51	11/51
90069	10/51	2/53
90125	9/51	10/51
90141	8/50	11/50
90152	9/51	11/51
90188	10/60	12/60
90251	11/51	5/52
90284	5/52	9/53
90323	10/60	11/60
90466	7/53	8/53
90485	9/51	1/52
90691	10/60	5/62

[W] After 1/60

Penzance
83G 8/50
Closed to Steam 9/62

Loco	Date	Date
10XX		
1001	1/61	9/62
1002	5/53	6/60
	11/60	2/61
1004	8/50	11/51
	12/60	8/62
1006	10/54	7/55
	9/55	6/60
1008	5/58	7/58
	1/59	2/61
1013	9/51	12/51
1018	2/51	12/51
	10/54	6/60
	11/60	8/62
1019	2/51	12/51
1021	3/55	7/55
1022	2/51	5/58
1023	2/51	9/51
2021		
2097	11/50	11/51
57XX		
3635	3/61	5/62
4073		
4037	6/56	9/56
4087	10/52	7/54
4090	8/50	11/52
4095	1/58	5/60
4099	3/55	10/57
51XX		
4114	6/56	7/56
4136	8/58	?/62 [X]
4148	6/56	7/56
45XX		
4500	8/50	7/53
4505	10/56	9/57
4508	5/58	5/58
4509	8/50	6/51
4525	8/50	6/53
4537	8/50	1/55
4545	8/50	8/58
4547	3/55	9/58
4548	8/50	9/57
4549	6/60	8/60
	6/61	12/61
4553	5/58	5/58
4554	5/58	8/58
4563	11/54	9/61
4564	4/59	12/59
4566	8/50	9/61
4568	8/58	1/59
4570	7/54	6/62
4571	5/59	3/61
4574	8/50	1/57
4577	1/58	9/59
4587	9/53	7/54
4588	3/59	9/61
49XX		
4908	12/54	3/60
4931	12/54	10/59
4940	4/52	7/52
	8/52	10/52
4946	8/50	6/53
4947	8/50	12/50
	2/52	6/52
4950	9/57	6/59
4965	8/50	4/54
4967	9/57	10/57
4968	2/52	3/52
4976	10/58	6/59
4990	12/56	5/57
4999	2/52	6/52
4073		
5020	12/58	5/60
5023	10/52	9/54
51XX		
5107	6/56	7/56
5161	6/56	7/56
5184	6/56	7/56
45XX		
5508	11/61	9/62
5515	2/61	9/61
5524	2/59	4/59
5537	1/62	7/62
5545	4/61	9/62
5562	3/62	8/62
49XX		
5915	8/50	9/56
5934	2/58	11/59
5952	12/54	7/55
5959	10/54	9/56
5969	8/50	3/56
5972	9/55	11/58
5985	7/56	4/58
5990	4/56	6/56
5998	5/53	11/53
43XX		
6318	8/50	6/53
6354	8/50	9/50
68XX		
6800	8/50	10/53
	12/53	6/62
6801	8/50	9/60
6805	5/60	6/60
6806	8/50	9/54
	12/55	11/56

6808	8/50	9/62	6854	11/60	4/61		**78XX**	
6809	8/50	1/58	6855	6/59	11/59	7806	9/50	3/51
6812	9/61	6/62	6858	2/60	4/60	7824	1/57	6/57
6814	2/61	6/62	6860	12/53	7/55		**6959**	
6816	2/58	5/60		12/55	9/60	7925	11/50	10/59
6817	8/50	9/54	6864	2/62	4/62		**94XX**	
6824	2/52	7/62	6868	2/61	6/62	8409	8/50	9/59
6825	8/50	9/60	6869	8/50	10/52	8473	9/51	10/51
	10/61	6/62		1/60	4/62	9433	1/61	6/62
6826	8/50	6/62	6870	2/57	9/61	9434	6/59	6/60
6830	1/62	4/62	6871	12/58	1/59	9462	1/52	3/52
6831	1/62	4/62	6873	12/58	1/59	9463	2/52	3/52
6833	2/62	5/62	6874	1/62	6/62		4/52	11/58
6835	1/62	4/62	6875	1/58	6/60	9475	7/60	9/62
6836	5/53	10/53		10/61	9/62		**57XX**	
	12/53	7/55		**49XX**		9665	2/54	11/54
6837	11/52	5/60	6911	8/50	1/56	9717	8/50	11/54
6838	8/50	10/52		5/59	11/59	9748	8/53	5/62
6842	1/62	4/62	6919	2/54	4/54			
6845	12/55	6/60	6933	2/60	3/60	[X] Before 12/62		
6849	6/59	6/60	6934	12/54	7/55			
			6945	12/59	3/60			

Plymouth Friary
72D 8/50   83H 2/58
Closed 5/63

	T1		30183	8/50	7/53		**BB/WC**	
30007	8/50	6/51		10/53	6/56	34011	8/50	4/51
	M7			7/57	9/61	34012	8/50	11/50
30034	3/51	7/62	30192	3/53	8/61	34013	8/50	5/51
30035	8/50	1/60	30193	5/57	4/62	34021	8/50	11/50
30036	3/51	7/62	30199	5/57	7/57	34032	3/51	5/51
30037	8/50	5/58	30200	4/62	7/62	34033	9/51	11/51
30039	3/51	6/55	30207	8/50	3/53	34034	11/50	3/52
30040	9/52	6/55	30216	8/50	12/57	34035	11/50	12/57
	B4		30225	4/54	3/62	34036	11/50	12/57
30083	9/51	10/53	30236	8/50	12/55	34037	5/51	12/57
30084	8/50	11/51		**M7**		34038	5/51	12/57
30088	8/50	6/52	30356	8/50	3/51		**2MT 2-6-2T**	
	9/53	9/58	30374	1/51	3/51	41203	7/61	10/61
30089	3/52	9/58	30375	8/50	3/51	41214	12/61	1/63
30094	8/50	3/57		**757**		41295	7/61	1/63
30102	8/50	9/58	30757	8/50	6/56	41302	1/57	5/63
	M7		30758	8/50	6/56	41310	2/60	8/61
30107	8/50	9/51		**N**		41314	11/56	1/57
	G6		31870	10/50	11/50	41315	1/53	5/63
30162	8/56	3/58	31871	8/50	11/50	41316	11/56	5/63
	O2			**E1/R**		41317	5/57	5/63
30182	8/50	3/53	32094	8/50	4/55			
			32095	9/53	11/56			
			32096	6/55	11/56			

Pontypool Road
86G 8/50
Closed 5/65

TV 0-6-2T

349	8/50	5/51
385	8/50	6/52

14XX

1422	8/50	10/55

16XX

1635	12/58	1/59

2021

2021	8/50	6/51
2035	8/50	9/52
2094	8/50	5/52
2117	8/50	6/51

2251

2296	2/59	9/59

23XX

2385	8/50	10/51
2414	12/51	5/52

28XX

2800	8/50	12/50
2801	8/50	11/58
2802	8/50	5/58
2803	2/59	4/59
2807	5/58	5/58
2811	8/50	3/52
2813	8/50	1/51
2817	5/58	3/59
2821	3/53	9/56
2825	5/58	3/59
2833	5/58	12/58
2834	5/58	12/58
2839	12/59	7/64
2841	3/53	4/53
2845	6/59	6/62
2848	5/58	5/59
2855	5/58	1/59
2857	5/58	2/59
	4/59	8/60
2859	12/59	8/64
2862	8/50	8/52
2864	8/50	11/53
2866	1/59	7/62
2867	6/59	11/62
2872	8/62	11/62
2883	10/59	6/60
2884	8/50	11/59
	5/63	4/64

2888	8/50	1/53
2893	8/50	10/52
2896	1/63	7/64
2897	6/62	2/63

ROD

3012	8/50	7/54
3018	8/50	10/52
3023	8/50	7/54
3024	9/54	6/56
3026	9/54	11/54
3036	5/52	6/56
3038	8/50	7/56
3040	8/50	6/56
3042	8/50	7/56
3043	9/54	6/56
3044	8/50	6/56

57XX

3627	1/60	2/60
3628	8/50	1/63
3640	3/52	5/62
3651	8/50	3/63
3661	4/64	4/65
3682	1/62	8/62
3683	11/50	6/64
3685	4/54	3/64
3690	8/50	12/51
3692	8/50	9/53
3703	12/50	5/62
3708	9/50	5/65
3717	8/50	5/65
3730	8/50	7/55
3779	8/50	11/63

28XX

3804	6/59	2/61
3815	2/59	9/59
3818	2/59	2/61
	4/64	7/64
3822	8/50	6/60
3824	6/56	11/59
3826	8/50	8/64
3828	8/50	3/59
3829	7/60	6/62
3841	8/62	3/64
3842	5/59	9/59
3844	5/59	9/65

3854	6/57	9/59
	7/60	6/62
3855	3/53	3/58
3859	2/58	11/62
3861	7/60	8/64
3862	8/50	12/53

51XX

4121	8/50	2/53
4130	8/50	12/50
4131	8/50	4/54
4135	8/50	4/62
4138	8/50	4/57
	5/57	1/58
	4/58	5/58
4142	2/53	9/54
	3/55	9/55
4157	4/63	11/64
4158	8/50	12/52
4174	4/63	6/64

42XX

4229	6/53	10/58
4230	9/54	6/59
4243	4/64	7/64
4271	8/50	11/50
	5/53	1/59
4285	11/64	4/65
4290	10/50	5/53
4295	4/64	1/65

43XX

4303	8/50	11/51

45XX

4522	6/52	6/54
4533	8/50	9/51
	1/52	3/55
4541	8/50	10/52
4553	8/57	1/58
4593	8/50	1/52
	10/56	6/59
4597	9/51	12/53

57XX

4600	11/56	4/64
4603	9/61	4/64
4611	8/50	9/51
4616	2/64	11/64
4639	8/50	5/65
4642	8/50	1/64

4668	8/50	7/64	**5573**	12/53	1/58		**64XX**	
	11/64	5/65		**56XX**		**6400**	8/50	4/59
4678	5/62	2/63	**5602**	10/51	5/52	**6403**	8/50	1/58
	49XX		**5620**	9/50	1/54	**6424**	8/50	11/59
4901	6/54	10/55		6/62	3/63	**6426**	4/57	9/57
4912	8/50	12/50	**5625**	3/54	11/62	**6429**	8/50	12/58
4916	12/59	6/62	**5629**	8/57	10/57	**6430**	8/50	9/54
	11/63	6/64	**5638**	5/52	3/64	**6432**	8/50	3/59
4926	5/58	8/61	**5645**	1/58	4/63	**6434**	9/57	10/57
4932	8/50	12/50	**5659**	7/55	4/64		**56XX**	
4933	8/50	12/50	**5665**	3/65	6/65	**6622**	12/64	1/65
4937	11/59	4/62	**5679**	11/59	4/62	**6634**	5/51	4/64
4943	5/58	12/63		**57XX**		**6636**	8/50	6/63
4955	1/63	10/63	**5728**	8/50	1/57	**6651**	1/63	5/63
4958	11/59	6/64	**5750**	6/56	5/60	**6652**	7/62	11/62
4964	9/62	10/63	**5756**	6/52	8/61	**6653**	5/51	3/58
4968	1/58	3/58	**5759**	4/56	11/57	**6658**	12/64	5/65
4974	5/58	11/58		3/58	8/60	**6663**	8/50	11/51
4983	6/59	10/60	**5768**	8/50	6/57	**6675**	11/51	6/63
4985	1/63	6/64	**5775**	3/56	1/63	**6676**	6/59	4/65
4989	6/63	7/63	**5789**	1/57	5/62	**6685**	6/52	6/63
4990	10/52	12/56	**5792**	8/50	9/56	**6687**	8/50	5/53
4991	11/53	2/56		**58XX**		**6688**	1/63	2/64
	51XX		**5818**	8/50	2/53	**6690**	2/61	5/62
5103	7/58	12/60		**49XX**		**6693**	3/52	1/63
5164	10/61	3/63	**5916**	8/52	12/56		**57XX**	
	42XX		**5929**	6/63	10/63	**6742**	8/50	3/52
5206	11/64	5/65	**5948**	5/52	8/63		**68XX**	
	43XX		**5962**	10/63	6/64	**6802**	10/57	7/61
5306	9/59	10/61	**5970**	6/59	6/62	**6809**	1/58	2/58
	11/63	12/63	**5975**	8/50	12/50	**6810**	9/61	6/63
5315	5/58	8/58	**5976**	9/63	7/64	**6812**	3/56	1/61
5318	8/52	10/54	**5998**	11/63	3/64	**6819**	10/53	6/61
	6/57	6/59		**61XX**			8/61	6/64
	9/59	8/61	**6107**	10/53	11/53	**6820**	4/61	6/61
5321	3/59	8/59	**6114**	11/63	6/64	**6821**	11/59	6/61
5322	9/59	4/64	**6115**	2/61	6/64		8/61	6/63
5330	2/58	6/59	**6151**	4/63	11/63	**6822**	11/62	6/64
5334	12/53	3/54		**43XX**		**6829**	3/63	6/64
5345	11/58	5/59	**6300**	3/60	6/60	**6836**	10/61	6/64
5355	8/50	9/54	**6317**	12/53	3/54	**6837**	10/52	11/52
5362	9/56	10/56	**6318**	6/57	12/58	**6838**	10/61	6/64
5369	9/62	11/63	**6325**	2/56	10/57	**6840**	12/50	6/63
5381	9/58	6/59	**6328**	2/58	3/58	**6848**	11/59	1/64
5382	6/57	10/57	**6333**	8/50	8/51	**6849**	12/50	9/54
5388	9/55	3/59	**6335**	9/61	7/63	**6850**	3/63	6/64
	54XX		**6338**	7/63	7/64	**6860**	9/53	12/53
5421	10/52	11/52	**6361**	4/53	3/56	**6861**	11/50	4/53
	45XX		**6368**	5/55	6/59	**6867**	5/58	6/63
5516	8/50	4/57	**6370**	8/50	5/52	**6871**	9/51	12/56
5532	8/50	8/52		8/60	1/63	**6872**	4/51	6/64
5534	5/58	3/59	**6381**	5/55	11/63	**6876**	10/61	6/64
5539	4/55	10/56	**6386**	10/52	11/53		**49XX**	
5545	11/51	9/53	**6393**	12/53	7/55	**6901**	9/59	7/64
5564	4/57	8/59		9/59	2/50	**6903**	2/59	1/64

6928	10/57	6/64	8493	7/59	3/63	48424	6/56	5/58
6941	1/64	4/64	8495	6/59	7/64	48430	3/58	5/58
6942	12/63	6/64	**57XX**			48444	6/56	10/57
6946	1/58	7/64	8707	12/55	7/64		1/58	5/58
6958	9/59	6/64	8709	5/60	8/62	48460	6/56	11/58
72XX			8716	8/50	4/64	48470	6/56	11/58
7201	3/55	7/64	8755	8/50	12/55	48524	1/58	11/58
7204	3/55	12/59	8777	9/53	3/56	48760	1/58	11/58
7205	3/65	5/65	8781	5/62	8/62	**G1 & G2a 0-8-0**		
7206	8/50	6/59	8786	10/50	12/52	49113	9/55	12/58
	12/62	4/64		11/57	4/58	49157	8/57	12/58
7210	2/58	5/65	8788	8/50	4/56	49168	9/55	9/57
7220	9/54	9/64	**94XX**			49174	9/55	9/57
7227	5/59	6/63	9488	11/63	7/64	**G2 0-8-0**		
7233	8/50	6/57	**57XX**			49403	11/54	3/58
	10/63	9/64	9602	3/65	3/65	49409	2/58	3/58
7234	8/50	6/57	9611	8/60	8/62	49422	11/54	3/58
7235	8/50	11/57	9629	4/64	9/64	49440	10/57	3/58
7240	6/63	9/64	9644	11/63	5/65	**WD 2-8-0**		
7246	2/58	9/63	9650	8/50	1/65	90069	10/54	12/54
7251	4/58	9/63	9655	5/62	7/64	90167	1/51	3/58
43XX			9723	3/54	4/54	90179	3/53	12/54
7302	12/61	7/62	9730	4/54	7/64	90192	9/54	2/61
7318	4/64	6/64	9796	11/52	2/65	90268	8/50	1/51
7320	4/64	6/64	9797	8/50	8/62	90315	9/54	4/60
7325	(ex 9303 5/58)		**3MT 2-6-2T Stanier**			90563	8/50	2/53
	7/63	4/64	40091	1/54	8/59	90630	4/51	6/51
74XX			40098	10/54	3/55	90691	5/53	5/53
7426	8/50	6/55	40145	12/53	8/59	90701	1/58	7/59
57XX			**2MT 2-6-2T**			**9F 2-10-0**		
7712	3/59	7/60	41203	9/55	4/56	92231	7/58	1/59
7724	8/50	8/62	**8F 2-8-0**			92232	7/58	1/59
7740	8/50	12/60	48308	1/58	5/58	92233	8/58	1/59
7771	9/60	10/61	48344	10/57	5/58	92234	8/58	1/59
7796	4/54	2/62	48408	3/58	5/58	92235	8/58	1/59
94XX			48415	6/56	5/58	92236	8/58	9/58
8440	12/59	1/60	48417	6/56	5/58			
8461	9/60	11/63	48418	6/56	5/58			

Reading GW
81D 8/50
Closed 1/65

PM 0-4-0T			1442	9/53	12/53	2206	12/59	12/61
1153	5/53	1/54	1444	8/50	9/59	2208	8/50	2/53
MSWJ 2-4-0			1447	8/50	3/59	2210	11/59	6/61
1335	8/50	8/52	1474	4/60	5/60	2212	5/58	1/63
1336	8/50	2/54	**1901**			2221	11/52	10/54
14XX			1925	12/50	4/51	2245	8/50	2/60
1407	8/50	2/60	**2251**			2248	11/63	9/64
1421	7/60	10/62	2201	1/64	7/64	2249	5/63	9/64

No.		
2253	9/55	5/58
2257	11/62	9/64
2261	5/55	4/56
	9/61	9/64
2262	9/55	12/59
2264	8/50	4/56
2299	8/50	8/59
23XX		
2474	10/54	4/55
2516	2/53	5/54
2573	8/50	1/53
28XX		
2815	9/51	10/52
2820	5/54	9/56
2821	9/51	9/52
2824	5/54	7/54
	7/54	12/58
2825	9/50	12/52
2835	12/56	6/57
2841	9/59	3/63
2842	2/60	11/61
2845	11/50	7/52
2853	9/59	5/62
2867	12/56	10/57
2879	4/63	12/63
2887	9/63	12/63
2889	5/62	4/63
2898	5/63	1/64
ROD		
3025	8/50	4/51
3047	8/50	12/52
2251		
3213	9/63	12/63
3219	11/53	1/61
	2/61	11/63
33XX		
3453	8/51	11/51
3454	8/50	11/51
57XX		
3697	8/50	11/50
3715	8/50	11/50
	5/62	9/63
3723	8/50	4/62
3736	8/50	9/50
3738	10/50	9/60
3740	3/56	11/56
28XX		
3835	12/56	4/57
3836	3/55	7/55
	7/55	9/55
3840	8/50	7/52
	6/61	9/61
3841	8/50	7/52
3843	2/60	6/60
3845	8/50	9/52

No.		
3846	8/50	9/52
3858	9/59	9/63
4073		
4074	5/60	11/60
4078	5/58	11/58
4084	11/59	1/60
4085	8/50	4/58
4086	9/59	12/59
	5/61	4/62
4089	12/63	9/64
4092	4/58	10/60
4095	9/62	1/63
4096	6/62	11/62
45XX		
4539	4/51	9/55
57XX		
4606	11/50	2/59
4609	8/50	8/63
4661	8/50	3/63
4665	8/50	7/60
4670	8/50	11/63
4697	2/56	6/56
49XX		
4903	3/60	12/61
4908	3/60	10/61
4913	9/59	11/59
4915	1/62	2/63
4920	8/50	6/53
4921	4/60	8/62
4931	8/50	2/51
4939	8/50	3/51
	10/54	12/56
4941	4/58	9/61
4943	8/50	2/51
	4/53	6/53
	9/56	2/57
4948	10/50	1/53
4949	9/62	10/62
4950	4/53	5/53
4951	4/57	9/62
4960	10/52	2/59
4961	7/55	5/60
4962	8/50	6/53
	10/53	6/60
4965	9/56	1/58
4969	2/56	2/59
4975	11/61	6/63
4977	12/58	5/61
4979	9/57	5/58
4986	12/60	3/61
4987	11/55	5/58
	7/58	9/61
4989	8/50	11/59
4993	7/52	12/59
4994	8/50	4/53

No.		
4995	8/50	5/58
4998	8/50	5/52
	10/52	11/62
4073		
5002	3/64	6/64
5010	1/59	9/59
5011	5/60	10/60
5018	4/58	3/64
5034	12/50	12/53
5036	8/50	10/60
5038	10/62	9/63
5039	1/64	7/64
5061	5/58	12/59
5067	5/61	6/62
5076	4/60	4/63
5085	7/62	10/62
5092	2/58	4/58
5098	3/64	7/64
43XX		
5322	12/58	6/59
5324	10/58	4/59
5326	5/54	10/57
5330	6/53	7/55
5367	5/58	8/58
5368	9/53	8/58
5375	8/50	2/53
5390	5/52	8/52
5391	1/56	1/57
56XX		
5675	5/58	1/59
57XX		
5737	2/51	2/53
5762	8/50	2/56
5763	8/50	1/59
5766	8/50	2/56
5772	8/50	1/56
49XX		
5901	8/50	9/61
	4/62	7/64
5906	4/54	5/62
5907	12/58	11/59
	3/60	10/61
5914	6/62	3/63
5915	9/56	5/58
	8/58	2/60
5932	4/63	12/63
5933	8/50	2/58
5936	5/59	3/63
5942	7/52	9/59
5948	8/50	11/50
5956	8/50	9/62
5957	8/50	11/59
5959	8/50	10/54
	9/56	12/56
5971	9/64	12/64

Shed by Shed

Loco			Loco			Loco		
5973	8/50	8/62	6363	8/50	2/51	7814	7/55	6/56
5976	?/61 [Y]	6/62	6366	8/50	2/58	7816	9/62	8/64
5977	12/58	11/59	6379	8/50	4/54	7817	9/62	7/64
5979	8/50	3/63		3/55	9/57	7825	12/63	5/64
5982	12/58	8/62		6/61	6/63	7829	6/64	8/64
5986	9/61	9/62	6383	8/50	8/52	**6959**		
5987	4/63	6/63	6385	11/59	10/63	7904	1/64	3/64
5993	7/52	5/63	6391	5/61	8/62		4/64	1/65
61XX			6393	8/50	3/53	7906	9/50	6/63
6100	8/50	8/58	6394	3/55	6/57		8/64	9/64
6101	8/50	12/60	**56XX**			7910	4/64	11/64
6103	8/50	3/55	6627	9/53	9/59	7914	4/55	3/64
	4/55	1/65	6654	5/58	6/60	7919	8/50	1/65
6104	7/52	6/60	6655	5/58	9/59	7926	4/64	7/64
6105	8/50	9/53	**68XX**			7927	11/50	9/58
6106	2/63	1/64	6802	8/50	2/53	**94XX**		
6107	8/59	1/65	6812	9/62	4/64	8401	6/56	12/56
6109	2/53	10/53	6825	9/62	4/64	8420	1/64	8/64
6112	9/59	11/60	6826	9/62	4/64	8430	1/53	4/63
6114	9/58	6/59	6834	10/52	7/55	8464	8/63	12/63
6115	7/55	9/56		3/63	4/63	8486	8/63	11/63
6117	5/52	7/58	6863	9/62	4/64	8496	1/61	7/63
6118	9/63	11/63	6864	8/50	3/55	**43XX**		
6119	11/59	2/63	6865	8/50	7/55	9303	8/50	11/53
6122	5/59	8/64	**49XX**			9305	11/50	6/54
6123	7/55	7/58	6913	9/60	3/63	9306	8/51	7/56
6125	11/59	7/60	6921	4/64	8/64	9307	8/50	5/53
6126	12/52	4/57	6923	11/50	3/63	9308	8/51	7/56
6129	7/51	11/60	6924	3/59	11/64	9309	5/55	
6130	8/50	5/61	6927	9/53	5/58	**(renum 7331 5/59)**		
6131	7/58	9/64	6933	9/52	6/53	9313	8/50	6/54
6134	3/58	1/65	6938	10/62	1/65	9315	5/51	6/54
6135	9/64	1/65	**6959**			9318	8/50	5/53
6138	6/62	8/63	6960	9/53	8/63	9319	8/50	11/53
6140	7/58	6/59	6963	4/64	1/65	**94XX**		
6145	8/50	5/58	6968	8/50	5/60	9401	5/51	1/57
6153	8/50	1/51	6974	8/64	11/64	9402	5/51	8/59
	3/55	1/62	6991	4/63	1/65	9404	5/51	8/64
6157	1/58	9/58	6996	8/50	5/52	9405	5/51	6/56
6161	5/52	1/65	**4073**				7/56	1/57
6162	8/50	2/61	7004	9/63	1/64		7/64	8/64
6163	8/50	4/55	7010	1/64	3/64	9410	8/50	5/51
6164	6/62	11/63	7027	8/63	12/63	9411	8/50	5/51
6165	12/63	7/64	**43XX**			9412	8/50	5/51
43XX			7318	8/50	8/51	9420	8/50	5/51
6302	8/50	4/53	7320	8/50	8/51	9423	8/50	9/51
	5/53	12/59	7331	(ex 9309 5/59)		9447	4/59	1/61
6312	8/50	1/55		5/55	8/62	9450	4/62	6/64
6313	5/58	10/59	**57XX**			9488	10/63	11/63
6324	1/58	4/62	7708	8/50	6/60	**57XX**		
6333	11/59	2/60	7777	8/50	1/56	9722	8/50	11/50
6334	8/50	7/55	7788	8/50	3/62	9749	8/50	9/60
6337	5/62	11/63	**78XX**			9763	8/50	8/63
6338	5/52	4/53	7808	9/62	8/64	9789	1/62	8/63
	5/53	12/53	7813	10/62	8/64	9791	8/50	11/59

4MT 4-6-0				WD 2-8-0		[Y] After 1/61
75027	9/54	12/54	90485	11/59	1/60	
75029	9/54	11/54				

Severn Tunnel Junction
86E 8/50
Closed to Steam 11/65

15XX			2865	6/60	1/63	2251		
1508	8/50	6/56	2866	6/53	1/59	3212	6/62	10/63
2251			2867	2/59	6/59	**57XX**		
2231	6/54	2/65	2869	3/55	5/59	3652	6/56	7/56
2283	10/63	12/63	2872	9/54	8/62	3686	3/65	7/65
2287	12/63	2/64		11/62	8/63	3699	2/65	2/65
2292	9/54	6/62	2873	5/51	2/54	3700	3/63	2/65
23XX				7/56	9/59	3786	5/60	6/60
2414	8/50	12/51	2879	7/55	10/55		7/60	3/63
	5/52	2/53	2882	3/52	7/52	3796	2/65	4/65
2460	8/50	3/54	2883	8/53	10/59	**28XX**		
28XX				6/60	10/60	3800	9/59	10/60
2803	6/53	2/59	2884	11/62	5/63	3801	6/59	8/64
2804	8/50	11/52	2885	5/63	2/64	3802	3/63	4/64
2806	5/54	3/60	2887	8/50	1/62	3803	6/60	7/63
2807	5/60	3/63	2888	1/53	8/58	3806	8/50	5/54
2808	5/54	6/56	2889	7/55	3/58		7/54	6/62
2809	5/51	6/51	2890	2/64	3/64	3808	8/50	5/54
2811	3/52	6/56	2892	8/50	12/50		7/54	9/56
2813	9/54	6/56		2/59	5/63	3812	3/55	7/63
2815	6/53	12/59	2893	10/52	10/57	3813	5/52	7/52
2816	1/58	3/58		2/59	10/59	3815	8/50	2/59
2821	12/58	1/59	2895	5/52	7/57	3816	1/65	7/65
2826	3/55	5/58		1/60	3/63	3818	8/50	2/59
	9/58	8/59	2896	3/55	1/63	3822	6/60	9/62
2829	8/50	1/56	**29XX**			3823	7/55	5/58
2832	3/55	12/59	2952	8/50	9/51		11/64	6/65
2836	10/63	7/64	**3150**			3826	8/64	1/65
2837	1/59	5/60	3150	8/50	8/57	3832	5/51	2/57
2838	8/50	7/59	3154	8/50	10/50	3834	7/60	11/62
2839	5/51	2/57	3157	8/50	9/52	3835	6/60	11/64
2844	5/51	1/59	3161	8/50	11/52	3838	8/50	6/64
2847	1/58	3/58	3167	8/50	8/52	3841	5/60	8/62
	12/58	3/60	3168	8/50	9/50	3842	12/63	7/65
2854	6/60	10/63	3170	8/50	11/54	3843	8/50	7/56
2857	8/61	2/62	3172	8/50	9/57		12/60	9/62
2858	5/60	1/63	3174	8/50	3/58		9/63	10/63
2859	5/51	2/57	3176	8/50	10/57	3844	8/50	5/59
	4/57	7/57	3177	8/50	9/57	3845	10/61	9/62
2860	8/53	4/62	3183	8/50	9/57	3847	6/53	9/62
2861	12/58	2/63	3185	8/50	1/56	3848	6/60	4/64
2862	10/52	4/64	3188	8/50	10/52	3849	5/51	1/59
2864	4/54	10/57	3190	8/50	3/58	3850	8/50	2/59

3852	5/52	10/62
3853	5/52	3/59
	9/63	12/63
3856	12/59	11/64
3857	10/60	10/62
3859	11/62	4/63
	10/63	6/64
3863	9/59	6/64
3864	5/60	11/63
3866	4/52	4/59
51XX		
4106	3/55	4/55
4107	11/64	5/65
4110	5/65	5/65
4114	3/55	2/56
4115	1/63	6/65
4119	8/50	6/56
	1/58	9/63
4121	2/53	7/58
	4/64	6/65
4125	10/57	11/57
4127	10/57	1/63
4128	9/62	6/64
4130	6/55	7/55
	2/58	7/64
4131	4/61	7/61
4132	9/63	7/64
4136	?/62 [Z]	6/63
4137	11/53	6/62
	8/62	9/64
4142	7/51	2/53
	9/54	3/55
4144	8/50	8/57
	11/62	5/65
4145	11/53	7/54
	10/60	1/63
4146	6/62	7/62
4150	7/62	6/65
4151	5/51	6/62
	8/62	6/63
4152	3/60	8/62
4156	11/53	6/65
4157	11/64	6/65
4159	6/62	6/64
4160	9/64	5/65
4164	9/58	2/60
42XX		
4200	8/50	2/56
4215	3/56	9/59
4217	2/57	6/59
4229	10/59	7/60
4241	8/59	7/63
4243	8/50	5/53
4248	2/62	5/63
4254	6/63	12/64

4258	3/65	4/65
4271	6/62	11/62
4275	4/51	6/56
4277	8/50	7/53
	6/63	3/64
4282	8/50	5/53
4286	8/50	2/54
4289	7/53	8/61
4297	8/59	1/60
4298	2/53	4/57
57XX		
4621	3/65	7/65
4671	9/64	12/65
49XX		
4908	9/50	5/52
4927	7/59	6/60
4932	11/64	11/64
4941	8/53	7/54
4952	5/52	7/54
4970	4/51	5/51
4978	8/64	9/64
4983	9/63	11/63
4988	7/59	6/60
4989	9/64	11/64
4990	3/52	10/52
4992	1/65	4/65
4993	1/65	2/65
51XX		
5155	4/53	2/60
5166	10/57	5/61
5169	12/50	8/60
5181	10/57	7/62
5191	11/57	7/64
42XX		
5201	1/51	12/53
5205	8/50	8/55
	10/55	6/56
	7/56	7/56
5208	4/64	5/65
5212	11/53	5/62
5213	4/63	7/63
5214	8/50	3/63
	11/63	1/64
5224	2/54	3/62
5226	3/65	3/65
5228	8/50	12/53
5235	11/63	11/64
5236	7/55	6/61
5243	7/60	11/62
	4/64	1/65
5253	8/50	4/63
5256	9/63	1/64
5260	7/56	5/58
5262	8/50	6/56
5264	6/63	7/63

43XX		
5306	1/63	11/63
5318	6/52	8/52
5336	2/59	10/63
5339	5/59	1/60
5362	8/50	8/52
5381	7/59	8/59
5382	10/57	4/59
56XX		
5620	8/50	9/50
	9/55	6/62
5624	10/63	12/63
5625	8/50	3/54
5626	8/50	11/53
5645	8/50	7/53
5679	2/59	11/59
57XX		
5706	8/50	2/51
5727	11/57	1/58
5729	8/50	9/55
5750	9/55	6/56
49XX		
5902	7/52	7/54
5923	5/51	7/54
5932	8/64	4/65
5948	4/52	5/52
5961	11/64	3/65
5972	7/59	6/60
5974	8/64	1/65
5980	7/59	6/60
5989	8/57	10/57
61XX		
6102	10/53	11/53
	1/58	7/59
6114	10/53	11/53
	1/58	6/58
	3/62	6/62
	1/63	11/63
	6/64	10/64
6115	6/64	11/64
6118	7/58	6/62
6119	3/56	7/56
	11/56	6/59
6125	5/61	6/61
6132	11/55	12/55
6134	1/58	3/58
6140	11/59	1/64
6155	2/56	6/60
6158	7/61	10/63
6166	10/57	6/59
43XX		
6320	9/61	11/63
6325	10/57	12/59
6338	10/57	8/58
	9/58	7/63

6346	6/63	3/64
6357	6/64	7/64
6362	10/57	6/61
	8/61	8/62
6363	10/59	11/59
6369	11/53	1/63
6373	9/61	12/63
6375	10/53	6/56
6380	11/63	12/63
6384	6/56	6/63
6386	8/50	9/51
	11/53	6/61
	8/61	8/62
64XX		
6424	11/59	4/62
6430	3/59	8/61
56XX		
6633	10/62	11/63
6639	8/50	7/55
6642	11/55	1/63
6654	10/52	10/53
6666	8/50	7/63
6672	8/53	6/56
	7/56	12/63
6673	8/50	6/56
6676	8/50	9/54
6689	8/50	8/55
68XX		
6812	7/52	10/52
6815	7/65	12/65
6850	6/64	1/65
6859	7/65	12/65
6871	8/50	9/51
6872	12/50	4/51
	6/64	11/64
6876	6/64	1/65
49XX		
6905	9/59	6/60
6909	4/51	10/52
6912	9/59	6/60
6926	5/51	3/53
6928	8/57	10/57
6932	11/64	5/65
6944	9/65	12/65
6955	8/64	2/65
6959		
6973	11/64	4/65
6978	2/65	3/65
6984	9/63	11/63
	11/64	4/65

6999	1/65	5/65
72XX		
7203	9/63	12/63
7205	5/65	6/65
7206	6/59	12/62
7208	2/53	11/60
7210	8/50	9/50
7211	4/64	7/64
7212	8/50	6/53
	9/60	1/63
7216	8/50	5/51
7217	2/61	12/62
7223	8/50	10/61
7224	8/50	10/53
7225	4/64	7/64
7226	12/63	11/64
7228	9/61	9/62
7229	8/50	3/54
7230	8/50	1/56
	2/59	3/59
7232	8/50	9/50
7233	6/63	10/63
7237	8/52	6/59
7239	8/50	6/53
7246	8/50	6/53
7250	2/62	7/62
7251	8/50	4/56
7252	1/65	6/65
7253	4/65	5/65
43XX		
7306	12/63	9/64
7308	1/60	1/63
7310	11/63	7/64
7312	11/63	12/63
7320	6/64	8/64
7322	10/57	6/61
7325	8/62	7/63
7328	(ex 9306	5/58)
	10/57	4/62
7339	12/63	7/64
74XX		
7403	8/60	1/64
7426	6/55	8/58
7427	6/61	1/64
57XX		
7764	8/50	5/62
7789	1/51	12/59
7793	1/60	4/60
78XX		
7804	7/65	9/65

6959		
7913	11/64	3/65
7917	9/63	11/63
94XX		
8401	11/50	6/56
8450	9/50	6/56
57XX		
8799	8/50	7/56
43XX		
9306	10/57	
(renum 7328 5/58)		
57XX		
9616	9/64	9/65
9619	8/58	7/65
9656	7/65	12/65
9675	7/65	10/65
9745	8/50	3/59
WD 2-8-0		
90179	5/52	3/53
90201	8/50	3/55
90323	5/53	10/55
90355	8/50	10/55
90573	5/52	11/52
90716	8/50	3/53
9F 2-10-0		
92007	7/65	10/65
92209	7/65	10/65
92214	7/64	9/65
92216	9/65	10/65
92226	7/64	10/64
	6/65	9/65
92231	1/59	2/59
92232	1/59	2/59
92233	1/59	2/59
92234	1/59	2/59
92235	1/59	2/59
92236	11/64	4/65
92237	11/64	3/65
92238	7/65	10/65
92242	10/64	5/65
92243	11/64	2/65
92246	9/65	10/65
92250	7/64	10/65

[Z] After 1/62

Shrewsbury
84G 8/50   89A 1/61
6D   9/63
Closed 3/67

10XX

No.		
1002	10/62	9/63
1003	5/51	1/61
1004	12/51	2/53
1008	1/63	9/63
1013	12/51	9/63
1014	2/63	9/63
1016	11/52	9/63
1017	12/51	12/60
	1/61	1/63
1018	12/51	1/53
1019	12/51	1/53
	9/62	2/63
1022	5/58	7/59
	10/59	9/62
1023	9/62	2/63
1024	11/50	3/51
1025	11/50	2/63
1026	9/55	8/62
1027	2/63	9/63

SHT 0-4-0T

No.		
1142	6/57	12/59
1143	12/59	10/60

16XX

No.		
1632	5/62	6/62
1663	4/63	5/63

2251

No.		
2203	1/52	2/52
2206	3/51	7/55
2210	10/58	11/59
2214	5/60	8/60
	12/60	8/63
2222	5/60	6/60
2228	8/50	10/52
2229	8/50	8/53
2231	8/50	6/54
2232	5/53	3/56
2233	8/50	7/52
	9/52	12/52
2234	8/50	9/58
2235	8/50	7/54
2244	9/53	3/56
2274	3/58	3/59
2276	5/60	6/61

No.		
2289	10/58	10/59

2721

No.		
2744	8/50	11/50

28XX

No.		
2822	8/52	3/53
	4/54	9/54
2823	9/51	9/52
2826	9/54	3/55
2832	11/52	3/55
2841	8/50	3/53
	4/53	12/53
2854	3/56	4/56

ROD

No.		
3033	3/53	4/53
3041	8/53	10/55

2251

No.		
3203	3/52	8/52
	9/52	10/52
3204	7/61	12/62
3205	7/60	4/61
	6/61	12/62
3207	6/59	6/60
3217	8/50	5/53

94XX

No.		
3400	10/58	5/62

57XX

No.		
3602	8/50	2/62
3702	8/50	10/55
3709	11/62	11/65
3754	7/63	11/65
3769	1/59	9/62
3782	8/50	1/52
	2/52	7/64
3788	8/50	11/64

28XX

No.		
3820	10/52	1/54
3836	9/59	11/63
3861	5/53	12/53
3865	4/53	11/53

40XX

No.		
4040	8/50	6/51
4044	8/50	1/53
4046	8/50	11/51
4052	8/50	5/53

No.		
4061	8/50	11/50

4073

No.		
4080	5/60	7/60
4081	6/59	7/59
4083	9/50	1/51
4090	6/62	9/62

51XX

No.		
4105	6/53	11/55
4118	8/50	9/54

42XX

No.		
4212	3/59	5/59

45XX

No.		
4564	12/59	9/63

57XX

No.		
4602	8/50	8/52
4617	3/62	10/63
4623	8/50	12/62
4644	12/59	1/60
4672	8/50	2/57
4693	1/59	1/62

49XX

No.		
4904	8/50	9/54
	6/57	6/59
4912	11/58	4/59
4913	10/57	11/57
4915	10/54	5/55
	7/55	10/58
4918	3/59	5/59
4919	8/50	12/50
4924	6/62	10/62
4933	9/63	8/64
4937	10/54	7/55
4944	6/62	7/62
4946	4/60	6/63
4957	3/60	5/60
4968	3/58	10/59

4073

No.		
5001	9/58	7/60
5004	6/56	9/57
5029	5/59	6/59
5032	8/50	12/51
5038	4/58	10/62
5050	8/50	9/60
5059	5/59	6/62

5061	8/50	2/51
5064	8/50	12/50
5073	8/50	4/58
5086	8/50	12/50
5091	5/53	9/55
5095	5/58	5/58
	9/60	7/62
5097	8/50	6/59
51XX		
5110	10/59	11/59
5112	12/52	2/53
5154	8/50	11/55
5167	9/59	1/60
5168	8/50	11/55
43XX		
5300	6/52	9/52
5312	1/54	4/54
5319	3/55	7/55
	7/58	12/59
5324	4/59	8/60
5328	11/53	1/58
5331	10/54	10/60
5347	2/56	4/58
5355	6/57	9/57
5362	10/56	5/58
5379	2/56	6/56
45XX		
5538	7/61	9/61
5555	7/61	9/61
5564	8/59	1/60
56XX		
5634	4/52	2/54
	6/55	5/60
5642	8/50	10/52
5651	10/58	12/58
5673	8/50	7/52
5690	10/54	5/60
57XX		
5791	6/57	10/59
49XX		
5942	12/59	6/63
	9/63	12/63
5958	1/58	10/58
5962	8/53	1/54
	10/62	11/62
5967	8/52	11/52
5968	4/56	10/61
5971	7/59	11/62
5977	5/58	10/58
5981	8/50	12/56
5986	10/54	7/55
	9/55	8/57
5991	4/61	8/64
5994	8/50	12/50
	11/62	3/63

5998	5/58	5/58
43XX		
6303	10/58	4/59
6307	8/50	10/52
6317	3/54	4/58
6338	8/50	6/51
	6/54	9/54
6339	11/53	9/54
6342	11/60	8/62
6348	8/50	10/52
6357	6/57	1/58
	2/58	5/58
6374	10/60	7/62
6375	10/62	2/63
6378	2/56	6/56
6380	6/61	2/63
6395	6/57	6/60
56XX		
6606	8/50	3/55
6620	1/56	6/56
6624	5/51	8/52
6633	8/50	3/55
6681	4/57	10/58
6683	8/50	5/51
	12/52	5/53
6698	12/52	5/53
	2/59	6/60
68XX		
6800	6/62	6/64
6858	9/54	7/55
	5/60	7/60
49XX		
6903	1/64	7/64
6904	2/60	9/60
6907	1/64	6/64
6915	2/61	7/64
6916	5/58	6/64
6922	12/59	11/64
6926	11/58	5/59
6928	4/57	6/57
6929	8/52	11/52
6934	4/61	10/64
6942	8/55	12/56
6944	10/54	9/60
6949	3/60	5/61
6956	1/53	3/54
	11/58	2/61
6959		
6963	8/50	12/51
6964	6/57	11/64
6976	8/50	12/51
6980	8/50	5/55
	7/55	4/59
6994	3/63	6/64
6998	3/58	1/61

4073		
7011	7/59	10/59
7015	11/59	9/62
7025	7/60	9/62
7035	8/50	9/53
43XX		
7300	9/61	8/62
7309	3/54	8/62
7314	9/61	8/62
	10/62	2/63
7319	8/50	10/52
7329	5/58	1/63
7330	(ex 9308 6/57)	
	10/56	8/62
7336	1/59	8/62
7341	5/58	8/58
74XX		
7431	10/60	2/61
57XX		
7797	2/54	9/54
78XX		
7800	1/63	8/64
7801	1/63	7/65
7802	1/65	10/65
7803	1/65	4/65
7809	1/63	4/63
7810	12/50	1/54
7811	1/53	9/61
7812	1/63	10/65
7817	9/58	10/58
7819	1/63	3/63
	1/65	10/65
7820	4/63	10/64
	9/65	10/65
7821	11/53	12/53
	9/65	10/65
7822	1/65	10/65
7824	9/55	12/56
7827	1/65	9/65
7828	10/52	5/61
	1/65	9/65
7829	10/52	3/53
6959		
7908	7/55	9/55
7912	5/55	7/55
7913	5/55	7/55
7921	8/58	6/59
7922	8/58	8/62
94XX		
8449	1/58	8/62
57XX		
8718	7/66	7/66
43XX		
9308	10/56	
(renum 7330 6/57)		

9318	2/56	6/56

94XX

9401	8/57	10/57
9463	7/59	7/63
9470	4/56	7/60
9472	2/57	11/62
9498	11/57	7/63

57XX

9641	7/63	11/64
9656	8/50	11/62
9657	8/50	4/66
9672	8/50	6/56
9719	8/50	8/52
9740	4/52	2/56
	3/56	6/56
9741	10/60	11/60

3MT 2-6-2T Fowler

40005	8/50	9/58
40008	8/50	11/58
40048	8/50	11/52
40058	8/50	8/58

3MT 2-6-2T Stanier

40085	8/60	11/60
40086	10/60	4/61
40110	2/60	4/61
40126	3/60	7/60
40205	3/60	4/61

2MT 2-6-2T

41202	4/62	1/64
	6/64	6/64
41203	4/62	8/63
41207	7/63	8/65
41209	11/62	7/65
41240	3/60	4/60
	9/62	8/63
41304	7/63	8/65

1F 0-6-0T

41725	9/50	8/55

4MT 2-6-4T Fowler

42320	2/59	8/59
42362	2/59	9/59
42372	2/59	9/59
42395	2/59	9/59
42418	2/59	9/59
42420	2/59	9/59

3F 0-6-0

43277	6/52	6/52
	10/53	2/59
43357	8/50	7/53
43394	8/50	7/58
43491	6/52	6/52
	10/53	2/58
43570	8/50	2/59
43581	8/50	6/55
43600	8/50	5/55

43621	6/52	6/52
	10/53	2/59
43679	8/50	2/59
43757	8/50	5/58
43760	8/50	9/58
43822	6/52	6/52
	10/53	2/59

5MT 4-6-0

44661	11/66	3/67
44711	9/66	3/67
44775	12/65	12/66
44777	9/66	3/67
44780	9/66	3/67
44800	4/66	3/67
44814	9/65	3/67
44821	9/65	3/67
44835	8/50	10/64
44897	4/66	3/67
44908	8/50	4/52
44942	9/66	3/67
44966	9/65	9/66
44971	9/66	3/67
44981	9/65	1/67
45045	9/65	11/65
45051	11/66	11/66
45052	11/66	3/67
45058	10/65	9/66
45112	8/50	11/51
45132	9/65	3/67
45134	9/66	12/66
45143	8/50	10/64
	9/65	12/65
45145	8/50	6/64
	9/65	3/67
45149	9/66	3/67
45180	8/50	8/51
45183	8/50	9/51
45185	9/65	7/66
45190	8/50	10/64
45245	8/50	8/51
45272	4/64	6/64
45279	9/66	3/67
45281	8/50	11/51
	2/59	9/59
45283	8/50	9/64
45285	8/65	3/67
45287	9/66	3/67
45298	8/50	6/64
45310	9/66	3/67
45311	9/65	10/66
45318	8/50	8/51
45330	8/50	8/51
45348	9/65	7/66
45384	8/50	9/51
45400	8/50	11/51

45406	8/50	10/64
45422	8/50	9/64
45430	10/65	9/66
45436	8/50	8/51
45447	9/66	3/67
45493	9/66	3/67

6P 4-6-0 Jubilee

45572	9/61	1/64
45577	9/61	8/64
45651	9/61	9/62
45660	9/61	7/64
	9/64	9/64
45662	9/61	9/62
45699	9/61	11/64

2MT 2-6-0

46446	12/66	12/66
46508	12/66	12/66
46510	1/65	9/65
46511	1/65	9/65
46512	1/65	2/65
	6/65	9/65
46519	2/65	9/65
46524	2/63	2/65
46525	2/63	12/64

Sentinel 0-4-0T

47180	7/51	7/53
47181	8/55	11/56
47183	8/50	9/51
	6/53	9/55

8F 2-8-0

48020	10/63	9/64
48110	12/50	11/62
48122	1/65	8/65
48172	11/50	7/60
48207	8/50	9/50
48269	10/63	6/64
48307	8/50	12/61
48308	8/50	1/58
48309	11/50	8/55
48328	8/50	9/59
48344	11/50	10/57
48345	1/65	8/65
48347	8/50	4/59
	6/59	12/61
48354	11/50	9/64
48369	8/50	9/64
48373	8/50	9/50
48402	8/55	5/58
48404	2/62	8/66
48418	12/60	8/66
48436	12/61	2/67
48438	11/50	4/59
48444	10/57	1/58
48460	11/58	9/59
48468	12/50	1/62

48471	12/61	5/66
48474	8/50	6/62
48478	8/50	8/62
48660	11/50	3/55
	8/55	2/62
48688	8/50	9/50
48707	1/51	2/51
	12/51	8/59
48724	8/55	8/62
48730	11/50	12/50
48732	11/50	12/50
48737	10/59	12/61
48738	12/52	9/64
48739	12/51	9/64
48757	1/63	3/63
48760	12/50	1/58
48768	10/59	6/64

G1 & G2a 0-8-0

48893	12/51	3/53
	6/53	7/54
48901	8/50	6/52
48921	3/58	4/58
48945	8/50	3/59
49028	3/55	1/56
49051	3/55	2/57
49082	6/57	2/59
49117	2/52	12/52
49138	8/50	2/52
49157	5/52	8/57
49243	11/54	5/59
49260	12/51	4/58
49276	8/50	10/58
49345	11/54	2/58

G2 0-8-0

49424	4/56	3/58
49440	8/50	4/57

3F 0-6-0

52414	8/50	12/51
52428	8/50	9/51
52525	8/50	6/52
52551	8/50	6/52

0F 0-4-0T

56027	8/50	10/50

2F 0-6-0

58162	1/54	8/55
58194	6/53	2/56
58203	5/52	7/55
58207	5/52	7/55
58211	8/50	5/53
58213	8/50	2/59
58241	5/52	6/55
58258	5/52	1/54
58322	8/50	1/52
58327	8/50	6/52
58330	8/50	6/52
58333	8/50	1/52
58346	2/52	3/52
58354	2/52	6/52
58360	4/52	4/52

2F 0-6-2T

58881	8/50	9/50
58900	6/54	7/54
58904	8/50	7/55
58926	9/50	5/54
	9/55	10/58

Y3

68164	10/56	8/57

5MT 4-6-0

73000	3/65	4/66
73001	3/56	11/56
73003	3/63	9/63
73012	9/53	11/56
73013	9/53	7/55
73014	9/53	7/55
73015	9/53	3/56
73017	9/53	6/56
	6/56	11/56
73018	9/53	11/56
73020	9/54	11/56
73021	4/60	5/60
73024	9/54	6/56
	4/60	6/62
	3/63	9/63
73025	9/53	7/54
	4/59	1/65
	3/65	4/66
73026	9/53	7/54
	4/59	10/64
73033	9/53	10/56
73034	9/53	10/56
	5/58	4/66
73035	9/53	10/56
	5/58	7/65
73036	9/53	10/56
	1/58	9/65
73037	9/53	10/56
	1/58	4/62
73038	7/65	9/65
73045	6/64	9/64
73047	7/64	1/65
73049	4/60	6/62
73050	4/64	4/66
73053	7/64	7/65
73067	3/65	4/66
73070	6/64	4/66
73071	3/65	7/65
73090	9/58	1/65
	3/65	9/65
73091	9/58	9/61
73092	9/58	9/61
73093	9/58	9/61
73094	9/58	9/61
	5/64	7/65
73095	9/58	8/65
73096	9/58	6/62
73097	9/58	7/65
73125	6/56	8/58
73126	6/56	8/58
73127	7/56	8/58
73128	8/56	8/58
73129	8/56	8/58
73130	9/56	8/58
73131	9/56	8/58
73132	9/56	8/58
73133	10/56	8/58
73134	10/56	8/58
73167	8/64	8/65

4MT 4-6-0

75000	9/51	12/53
75001	9/51	9/53
75002	9/51	9/53
75003	9/51	12/53
75004	10/51	9/53
	1/66	3/67
75005	9/51	9/53
75006	4/52	9/53
	11/65	3/67
75007	10/51	9/53
75008	10/51	10/53
75009	11/51	9/53
	12/66	3/67
75012	3/66	1/67
75013	12/66	3/67
75014	9/64	12/66
75016	6/65	3/67
75020	12/65	3/67
75021	3/66	7/66
75024	2/58	12/58
75029	8/66	3/67
75033	1/67	3/67
75038	10/64	12/65
75047	1/67	3/67
75053	9/64	8/66
75055	9/64	10/64
	12/66	3/67
75063	9/64	7/66

2MT 2-6-0

78003	1/66	12/66
78017	10/66	12/66
78018	4/66	11/66
78035	9/65	12/65
78036	11/66	11/66
78038	9/65	8/66
78039	4/66	9/66
78058	9/65	12/66

78060	9/65	9/66		**3MT 2-6-2T**		90148	6/57	3/58
78063	4/66	12/66	82000	11/55	1/59	90176	10/55	1/58
	4MT 2-6-4T		82004	5/59	10/59	90261	10/53	6/56
80048	9/64	7/65	82005	4/61	6/61	90323	3/53	5/53
80070	11/62	2/63		10/61	11/61	90327	9/50	12/50
	3/63	4/65	82007	11/55	5/58	90356	10/53	1/58
80072	6/65	8/65	82009	5/59	1/60	90366	8/50	12/50
80078	7/62	2/63	82020	1/60	3/60	90413	9/50	12/50
80096	7/62	11/62	82021	1/60	3/60	90466	8/53	9/53
80098	8/62	11/62	82030	5/55	12/55		3/54	7/55
80100	7/62	8/65	82031	5/55	1/59	90483	9/53	6/54
80101	7/62	8/62	82032	4/61	7/61	90527	7/53	9/53
80102	11/62	6/64		11/61	6/64	90535	8/50	11/50
	9/64	4/65	82036	11/61	6/62	90548	8/50	12/50
80105	8/62	9/62	82038	9/55	11/55	90561	8/50	12/50
80131	8/62	1/63		**WD 2-8-0**		90563	2/53	9/53
80132	11/62	1/63	90010	9/53	3/54		4/54	10/54
80135	7/62	1/63		6/56	1/58	90589	9/50	12/50
	9/64	8/65	90069	2/53	10/54	90701	5/53	1/58
80136	7/62	1/63	90110	8/50	2/51	90715	9/50	12/50
	9/64	8/65	90113	8/50	11/50	90716	3/53	4/55
			90123	8/50	12/50			

Slough
81B 8/50
Closed 5/64

	14XX		3715	11/50	3/51	6107	8/50	12/50
1411	7/54	9/56	3738	8/50	10/50	6108	8/50	11/59
1437	8/50	1/59	3740	5/52	3/56	6109	2/57	7/60
1442	8/50	3/51	4606	8/50	11/50	6113	8/50	1/53
1444	3/60	6/60		2/59	4/62	6114	8/50	7/51
1445	9/61	12/63	4638	5/52	9/63	6115	8/50	7/55
1447	8/59	5/61	4650	8/50	5/60		9/56	2/61
1448	11/50	6/60	4680	7/53	7/57	6116	8/50	9/51
1450	4/51	8/59	4691	8/50	2/61	6117	7/58	2/64
1453	4/60	11/61		**51XX**		6119	8/50	3/56
1465	10/56	11/56	5153	2/59	3/59	6122	9/56	5/59
1474	1/61	6/61		**54XX**		6123	8/50	7/55
	6/62	8/63	5409	8/50	7/54		7/58	6/60
	16XX		5410	11/59	12/59	6124	8/50	11/59
1622	6/62	7/64		**57XX**		6126	4/57	12/60
1654	1/63	7/64	5715	8/50	7/58	6127	8/50	3/62
	1901		5717	8/50	10/50	6128	3/62	4/64
1935	10/51	1/52	5737	8/50	2/51	6131	8/50	7/58
	2021		5755	2/56	7/60	6132	7/51	11/55
2112	8/50	11/52	5766	2/56	5/62	6133	8/50	11/59
	57XX		5783	8/50	11/52	6136	8/50	8/60
3608	8/58	9/63		**61XX**		6140	8/50	7/58
3665	6/62	1/63	6104	8/50	5/52	6143	8/50	6/64
3697	11/50	3/62	6106	8/50	8/53	6146	8/50	7/60

6150	8/50	1/61
6151	8/50	6/62
6152	8/50	1/62
6153	7/51	3/55
6154	8/50	7/60
6157	8/50	1/58
6160	8/50	6/57
	8/57	6/64
6161	8/50	5/52
6164	8/50	11/59
64XX		
6410	7/60	1/63

56XX		
6655	9/59	3/60
6664	4/54	8/58
74XX		
7441	8/50	5/52
7442	8/50	5/52
94XX		
8486	3/62	8/63
57XX		
8770	7/60	3/61
94XX		
9406	5/51	9/63

9414	8/50	5/51
9415	8/50	7/62
9421	8/50	2/62
9422	11/61	9/63
9424	8/50	8/60
9463	11/58	7/59
9495	5/62	7/62
57XX		
9640	8/50	10/50
9653	8/50	5/53
9722	11/50	6/62
9781	8/50	2/61
9789	8/50	3/56

Southall
81C 8/50
Closed to Steam 1/66

14XX		
1402	1/55	5/55
1406	2/57	3/58
1407	2/60	6/60
1410	3/54	7/55
1415	5/55	1/57
1420	9/58	7/59
1426	12/51	9/58
1431	4/58	1/60
1436	10/55	9/58
1438	11/57	9/58
1443	8/50	6/57
1446	7/55	8/58
1458	1/58	9/58
1462	8/50	10/52
	11/52	10/55
1474	9/51	9/58
	5/60	1/61
	6/61	6/62
15XX		
1501	11/50	1/61
16XX		
1605	8/50	9/53
1654	7/62	1/63
1669	1/60	7/60
1901		
1925	8/50	12/50
2251		
2285	8/50	4/56
28XX		
2821	9/52	3/53
2835	6/57	3/58
2841	3/63	12/63

2843	8/50	1/51
2845	7/52	2/53
2851	3/63	5/63
2853	7/56	9/58
2856	3/63	4/64
2858	8/50	12/50
	11/52	4/54
2859	9/64	1/65
2873	11/62	1/65
2875	3/63	11/63
2879	12/63	8/64
2880	9/51	3/58
2890	9/55	10/58
2899	5/52	2/59
	11/62	3/65
57XX		
3608	3/65	6/65
3618	8/50	8/63
3620	8/50	8/64
	3/65	6/65
3622	11/60	8/64
3665	1/63	1/64
3704	8/50	1/61
3715	2/59	2/60
3727	8/50	4/57
3750	8/50	9/61
3763	3/65	6/65
3799	8/50	1/61
28XX		
3803	8/50	5/52
3810	8/64	11/64
3812	3/65	6/65
3814	10/55	3/58

3818	3/65	5/65
3820	1/65	6/65
3823	5/58	8/58
3834	11/62	6/63
3836	9/55	5/59
3838	9/64	1/65
3845	9/52	5/53
3848	4/64	6/65
3851	1/65	6/65
3854	8/50	1/51
	11/62	6/65
3855	8/50	3/53
3856	8/50	10/58
3857	8/50	6/56
3859	9/64	5/65
3866	11/64	6/65
4073		
4080	6/64	8/64
43XX		
4381	8/52	4/53
57XX		
4608	8/50	9/64
4609	3/65	5/65
4610	8/50	1/57
4611	3/65	6/65
4622	1/64	7/64
4638	3/65	6/65
4673	8/50	7/60
4695	8/50	6/57
4697	6/64	8/64
47XX		
4700	9/61	9/62
4701	10/62	11/62

No.				No.				No.		
4702	9/61	6/62		**57XX**				6149	11/59	6/61
4703	9/62	11/62		5727	8/50	6/57		6156	8/50	7/60
4704	10/62	11/62			7/57	10/57			8/64	9/64
4705	9/62	10/63		5751	8/50	9/53			5/65	10/65
4706	9/62	9/63		5753	8/50	8/59		6157	9/58	11/59
4707	11/55	10/63		5755	8/50	2/56		6159	11/59	7/60
49XX				5799	8/50	6/59		6160	6/64	7/65
4903	9/63	9/64		**49XX**				6161	1/65	9/65
4907	3/58	11/59		5901	9/61	4/62		6162	2/61	3/62
4908	9/52	2/54		5914	3/61	6/62		6163	8/64	10/65
	6/54	12/54		5917	6/62	8/62		6165	8/50	12/63
4917	8/50	5/51		5918	12/50	10/59			8/64	10/65
4919	1/64	9/64		5925	10/58	9/62		6167	6/64	10/65
4925	4/58	7/62		5929	11/62	6/63		6169	8/50	10/60
4931	2/51	12/54		5933	2/58	5/60		**43XX**		
4934	2/58	7/60		5945	3/61	9/62		6300	5/52	2/53
4939	3/51	6/54		5952	10/50	12/54		6313	10/56	5/58
4944	8/50	1/58		5953	3/53	11/57		6325	8/50	8/51
	7/62	8/62		5971	11/62	3/63		6388	8/50	2/53
4945	3/61	10/61			6/64	9/64		**56XX**		
4956	12/50	6/56		5983	8/50	1/58		6654	1/54	5/58
	6/62	9/62		5985	11/62	3/63		6655	9/53	5/58
4969	11/61	8/62		5989	8/50	6/57		6664	9/53	4/54
4976	4/62	3/63		5990	3/56	4/56		6809	9/62	6/63
4978	8/50	4/51		5996	4/57	11/59		6834	9/62	3/63
4979	3/53	9/55		**61XX**				6841	9/62	7/64
4986	3/61	5/62		6102	8/50	12/50		6869	9/62	7/64
4987	9/61	4/62		6106	1/65	9/65		6875	6/63	2/64
4989	1/62	6/63		6109	6/56	2/57		**49XX**		
4995	2/60	6/62		6110	8/50	6/53		6934	4/53	12/54
4996	10/58	11/59			12/59	7/60		**6959**		
4073					10/60	7/64		6959	6/64	9/65
5002	6/64	9/64			8/64	3/65		6961	8/50	5/52
5076	6/64	9/64		6112	11/60	2/62			10/63	9/64
43XX					12/64	9/65		6967	9/58	11/63
5356	8/50	8/51		6117	2/64	9/65		6974	12/61	12/63
5360	8/50	12/51		6119	7/56	11/56		6977	6/62	9/62
54XX				6125	8/50	10/59		6978	10/63	9/64
5401	8/50	12/52			8/64	1/65		6986	11/62	3/65
5405	8/50	12/52		6126	8/50	12/52		6991	9/54	4/63
5410	8/50	11/59		6128	8/50	7/60		6994	2/62	3/63
5414	8/50	9/54			11/64	1/65		6998	6/64	9/65
5415	8/50	6/57		6132	10/60	9/65		**4073**		
5416	8/50	3/54		6133	1/60	11/63		7020	6/64	9/64
5418	8/50	1/55		6134	1/65	9/65		**43XX**		
5420	8/50	1/58		6135	1/65	9/65		7309	12/50	2/51
45XX				6139	8/50	9/53		**57XX**		
5508	11/63	1/65			1/64	1/65		7730	8/50	3/59
5531	11/63	1/65		6141	3/60	10/60		7731	8/50	4/59
5545	11/63	6/64			8/64	10/65		7732	8/50	3/55
5564	11/63	1/65		6142	8/64	9/64		**6959**		
5569	11/63	1/65		6143	6/64	10/65		7910	8/50	11/63
5570	11/63	12/63		6144	1/60	7/60		7922	11/62	7/65
5571	11/63	11/64		6147	8/50	11/60		7923	9/58	9/64
5573	12/63	1/64		6148	8/50	10/60				

	94XX	
8413	1/57	1/61
8422	5/61	6/62
8426	12/62	11/63
8451	5/59	10/61
8456	11/58	11/63
8465	7/62	11/63
8498	3/65	5/65
	57XX	
8731	11/60	6/62
8750	12/52	5/60
8752	8/50	1/63
8758	8/50	12/58
8761	5/59	2/60
8769	5/59	4/61
8770	3/61	1/63
8774	8/50	5/60
	93XX	
9300	8/50	10/52
	2/53	7/54
9301	8/50	10/52
	2/53	9/55
9302	8/51	10/52
9304	8/51	6/54
9305	9/54	7/58
9309	3/51	5/55
9310	8/50	6/54
9311	8/50	5/53
9313	9/54	9/55
9315	9/54	9/55
	94XX	
9405	1/57	5/59
9406	9/63	11/63
9407	8/50	11/55

9409	8/50	11/55
	1/56	5/62
9413	11/55	11/63
9415	7/62	11/63
9417	11/55	5/59
9418	3/65	5/65
9422	11/58	11/61
	9/63	11/63
9463	3/65	5/65
9469	6/56	5/59
9477	3/65	5/65
9479	4/57	11/58
9490	12/59	3/60
9495	11/61	5/62
	3/65	5/65
	57XX	
9641	8/50	7/63
9642	4/59	8/64
9659	3/65	6/65
9707	11/63	8/64
9726	8/50	6/64
	1/65	6/65
9789	3/56	1/62
9791	11/59	2/62
	WD 2-8-0	
90069	9/62	11/62
90149	9/62	11/62
90152	11/51	7/59
90174	6/52	1/63
90207	7/51	3/58
90268	4/51	6/59
90284	8/51	9/51
	11/54	3/55
90312	3/60	3/61
90313	4/54	4/58

90355	6/56	1/63
90356	1/58	1/63
90466	2/59	8/62
90485	11/52	4/57
	1/60	2/60
90529	6/56	3/58
90544	10/62	3/64
90565	11/60	3/61
	9/61	1/63
90572	9/62	11/62
90573	9/62	11/62
90579	9/62	11/62
90630	6/56	1/63
90685	10/60	11/62
90693	9/61	1/63
	9F 2-10-0	
92004	2/60	10/60
92204	10/60	10/60
92207	2/60	11/64
92208	3/60	11/61
92209	5/65	6/65
92210	12/63	6/64
92216	9/64	9/65
92222	9/64	4/65
92224	7/60	10/62
92226	7/60	10/60
92229	11/63	6/64
92238	8/60	12/61
92239	8/60	6/61
92240	8/60	9/65
92241	11/63	6/65
92245	10/62	1/65
92246	11/63	9/65
92250	11/63	6/64

St Blazey
83E 8/50
Closed to Steam 4/62

	10XX	
1002	6/60	10/60
1006	6/60	10/60
	14XX	
1419	8/50	4/61
1468	12/60	7/61
	16XX	
1624	9/53	2/62
1626	8/50	8/61
	9/61	11/61
1627	8/59	11/59
1664	4/55	12/61

	2021	
2050	8/50	10/51
2097	11/51	9/53
	57XX	
3635	8/50	3/61
3705	4/51	6/61
3731	9/61	5/62
3790	8/60	5/62
	51XX	
4167	5/53	10/54
	11/54	9/60

	42XX	
4206	12/52	12/59
4215	8/50	2/51
4242	11/55	3/56
4247	12/52	1/58
4273	6/60	1/62
4294	9/57	7/60
4297	11/52	12/52
4298	8/50	10/52
	45XX	
4503	8/50	1/51

4505	8/50	10/56	5519	8/50	6/59	**57XX**			
4508	4/51	9/56	5521	11/51	8/58	7709	8/50	7/60	
4516	8/50	11/52	5523	9/58	6/60	7711	12/54	9/56	
4517	11/50	12/52	5531	8/50	11/50	7715	8/50	1/62	
4523	8/52	7/55		10/54	11/54	**78XX**			
4526	8/50	1/58		8/61	?/62 [a]	7805	9/50	10/50	
4529	8/50	3/52	5534	1/60	8/60	7806	3/51	12/51	
4547	9/58	2/60	5539	2/58	4/62		9/59	9/60	
4552	8/50	8/61	5551	9/58	2/60	7816	10/52	9/60	
4555	3/62	5/62	5553	11/60	10/61	7820	6/60	9/60	
4559	8/50	9/60	5557	9/55	9/60	7823	12/55	1/56	
4564	2/59	4/59	5564	1/60	9/60	**6959**			
4565	8/50	9/61	5570	3/60	8/61	7916	9/50	4/52	
4568	8/50	9/55	5572	9/60	4/61	7929	1/60	9/60	
4569	8/50	7/61	**49XX**			**94XX**			
4570	8/50	6/53	5926	8/50	2/52	8404	10/54	11/54	
4577	9/59	12/59		10/52	5/57	8409	9/59	2/60	
4584	11/51	1/59	5985	1/56	7/56	8422	1/51	4/51	
4585	5/52	9/59	**43XX**			8426	2/51	4/51	
4598	8/50	5/53	6300	2/53	9/56	8485	1/59	5/59	
57XX			6305	10/52	7/58	**57XX**			
4665	7/60	8/62	6309	2/54	10/54	8702	2/56	1/62	
49XX			6330	8/50	4/52	8713	9/59	11/59	
4906	6/57	11/60	6356	8/50	4/52	8719	1/59	5/62	
4940	8/50	4/52	6388	2/53	10/53	8733	1/52	2/62	
	7/52	8/52	6397	10/52	8/59	8737	9/59	5/62	
	10/52	9/53	**68XX**			8783	8/50	1/52	
51XX			6812	6/61	9/61	**57XX**			
5160	7/58	10/58	6814	2/58	10/60	9655	8/50	5/62	
5193	7/53	10/54	6825	9/60	10/61	9673	4/51	5/60	
	2/58	10/60	6832	1/58	10/58	9680	7/60	2/62	
5198	6/60	12/60	6875	6/60	10/61	9716	8/60	8/62	
42XX			6879	6/59	11/59	9755	8/50	2/62	
5201	10/61	11/61	**49XX**			**2MT 2-6-2T**			
5215	3/60	5/60	6911	1/56	5/59	41304	5/59	7/60	
5240	3/55	4/55	6931	5/58	7/60	**WD 2-8-0**			
43XX			6942	12/56	4/57	90701	3/51	6/51	
5378	12/56	8/57	**72XX**						
45XX			7209	1/51	10/52	[a] Before 12/62			
5502	8/50	5/58	**74XX**						
5518	11/60	?/62 [a]	7446	8/50	4/62				

Stourbridge
84F 8/50   2C 9/63
Closed 7/66

14XX			1458	12/50	1/58	1621	8/50	8/60
1401	1/52	6/52	1459	5/57	11/57	1624	6/51	7/51
1410	10/50	1/51	1465	1/57	4/57	1663	1/60	4/61
1414	8/50	4/57	**16XX**			**2021**		
1438	8/50	11/57	1612	4/52	5/52	2090	8/50	7/51
			1619	2/53	4/63			

No.			No.			No.		
2107	8/50	12/52	3788	11/64	12/64	5165	8/50	7/57
2181			**28XX**			5167	8/50	6/55
2185	8/50	6/51	3816	4/60	5/61	5170	8/50	5/53
2186	8/50	6/51	3821	8/50	9/61	5176	4/57	1/61
2187	8/50	2/52	3825	1/55	10/62	5180	8/50	5/58
2189	8/50	10/50	3827	8/50	10/55	5186	6/56	5/58
2251			3831	4/59	3/61	5187	10/60	5/62
2209	10/52	5/53	3839	4/59	3/61	5189	8/50	7/59
2232	6/51	5/53	3846	6/59	6/60	5190	1/61	6/62
2246	8/50	5/53	3861	12/53	9/54	5191	8/50	11/57
2270	8/50	8/59	**51XX**			5193	8/50	10/52
2279	8/50	1/54	4104	8/50	6/62	5196	8/50	10/52
28XX			4110	9/59	9/61	5197	8/50	5/53
2804	11/52	7/55	4140	1/58	11/63	5199	8/50	9/61
	12/55	6/59	4146	8/50	1/57	**43XX**		
2823	1/59	4/59		5/57	9/59	5300	8/50	11/50
2829	1/56	5/58	4147	8/64	7/65	5309	5/52	6/52
2834	4/55	1/58	4150	8/50	5/53	5313	2/52	5/55
2841	6/57	9/58	4151	3/65	4/65	5371	9/51	5/58
2852	8/50	5/53	4153	8/64	11/64	5379	1/52	1/55
2853	1/59	9/59	4154	5/65	6/65	5381	10/57	9/58
2856	8/50	10/52	4161	4/59	8/62	**56XX**		
	4/59	4/61	4168	1/58	7/65	5606	11/50	9/58
2857	8/50	10/51	4172	12/51	3/52	5642	10/52	1/54
2865	12/52	5/53		6/63	1/65	5651	8/50	9/57
2868	11/52	5/53	4173	8/50	9/62	5658	8/50	9/58
2874	8/50	10/55		8/64	12/64	5659	4/65	9/65
2882	1/55	12/56	4175	8/64	9/65	5679	3/63	7/63
2885	8/50	5/58	4178	7/62	8/62	**57XX**		
	4/59	9/62	**43XX**			5719	8/50	10/57
2888	4/59	4/61	4326	4/53	2/57	5726	8/50	7/53
2897	4/59	4/61	4337	12/50	11/51	5754	8/50	6/60
ROD			4375	2/51	1/58	5794	8/50	11/54
3028	10/51	9/53	**57XX**			5795	8/50	4/60
2251			4602	5/60	4/64	**49XX**		
3206	5/53	1/54	4638	8/50	5/52	5912	4/60	9/61
3216	5/53	1/54	4646	6/51	7/66	5930	4/60	9/61
3217	5/53	1/54	4665	8/62	6/65	5944	10/60	9/61
3218	5/53	1/54	4687	8/50	4/64	5988	7/62	10/62
57XX			4696	8/50	7/66	**61XX**		
3601	8/64	10/64	**49XX**			6129	1/65	9/65
3605	6/61	10/62	4974	4/60	9/61	6137	11/63	11/64
3607	8/64	7/66	4986	5/59	12/59	**43XX**		
3619	8/64	7/66	**51XX**			6317	4/58	1/61
3649	8/50	1/61	5101	8/50	6/57	6324	3/53	4/53
3658	6/51	9/65	5105	8/50	10/57	6327	2/51	1/54
3667	8/50	9/51	5107	8/50	6/56	6332	8/50	7/51
	2/52	1/61		7/56	6/57		5/52	8/60
3710	9/50	8/60	5109	5/55	6/57	6340	6/57	1/61
3729	11/54	9/60	5122	8/50	9/50	6342	1/58	10/58
3740	8/50	5/52	5134	8/50	4/51	6349	10/57	11/60
3743	6/51	5/62	5136	8/50	10/51	6353	11/60	2/61
3745	4/54	10/62	5147	8/50	10/52	6354	12/50	4/53
3751	6/51	8/55	5155	8/50	4/53	6357	1/58	2/58
3782	11/64	1/65	5160	8/50	8/56	6364	8/64	11/64

6367	1/59	1/61	7418	3/63	8/64	9614	8/61	7/66
6391	12/50	4/55	7420	11/56	3/59	9624	11/55	1/65
6393	7/55	10/58	7424	3/64	9/64	9636	8/50	8/60
6395	8/64	11/64	7426	2/61	3/61	9641	11/64	7/66
64XX			7428	8/50	12/58	9646	4/62	5/65
6401	12/58	5/60	7429	8/50	2/61	9719	9/52	6/62
6403	1/58	1/60	7430	8/50	11/63	9724	8/64	1/66
	9/62	12/63	7432	8/50	10/50	9733	6/61	9/65
6418	7/62	1/63		2/51	3/62	9741	8/50	2/53
6424	11/62	8/64		4/62	8/64	9767	8/50	6/61
6428	1/58	3/59	7435	8/50	10/50	9782	7/51	10/64
6434	10/63	8/64		11/50	1/62	**5MT 4-6-0**		
56XX				6/62	11/63	44766	3/66	5/66
6604	3/59	9/61	7441	5/52	11/63	44875	3/66	5/66
6609	1/51	9/61	7442	5/52	7/52	45048	3/66	5/66
6617	8/50	6/51	7443	3/63	8/64	45064	3/66	5/66
6630	10/52	3/53	7447	7/56	4/59	**2MT 2-6-0**		
6644	5/61	4/62	7448	8/50	8/60	46427	3/66	7/66
6646	8/50	10/53	7449	8/50	5/63	46506	11/62	3/63
	11/53	6/63	**57XX**			46517	11/62	3/63
6656	7/63	9/65	7705	8/50	10/57	46526	12/62	3/63
6663	4/61	5/62	7722	3/60	9/60	46527	12/62	3/63
6667	8/50	6/64	7762	5/60	5/62	**8F 2-8-0**		
6674	8/50	5/53	7772	7/61	10/61	48121	9/65	7/66
	6/53	6/59	7788	3/62	6/62	48330	9/61	9/65
6677	8/50	1/63	**78XX**			48353	1/65	8/65
6678	8/50	11/64	7806	2/61	8/62	48402	3/61	12/65
6679	1/64	9/65	7816	9/61	9/62	48410	10/62	7/66
6681	12/53	4/57	7817	2/61	9/62	48412	2/65	7/66
6683	5/53	9/65	7824	2/61	7/62	48415	4/61	9/63
6692	12/53	9/65	**6959**			48417	3/61	7/66
6698	5/53	2/59	7922	8/62	11/62	48424	3/61	9/63
68XX			**94XX**				2/65	7/66
6803	7/51	9/62	8418	8/50	8/51	48430	3/61	11/63
6811	9/62	4/64	8419	8/50	9/55	48450	9/61	7/66
6823	5/53	9/55	8437	5/53	8/55	48459	9/61	7/66
6827	9/62	4/64	8438	5/53	9/55	48460	3/61	7/66
6828	8/50	6/57	**57XX**			48468	6/64	7/66
6834	4/63	4/64	8704	8/50	2/60	48474	9/62	3/63
6842	9/62	4/64	8718	8/64	7/66	48475	3/62	3/63
6855	11/59	4/60	8742	8/50	8/62	48478	8/62	9/64
6857	8/50	9/55	8767	4/66	7/66	48526	9/65	7/66
6858	7/60	9/62	8791	8/50	7/56	48531	9/65	7/66
6879	11/59	4/60	8792	8/50	2/62	48550	9/65	7/66
49XX			8797	8/50	4/62	48724	8/62	11/63
6904	9/60	9/61	**43XX**			48757	9/65	7/66
6930	9/58	12/59	9312	5/52	6/52	48762	11/64	6/65
6956	6/61	9/61	9318	9/54	1/55	**4MT 2-6-0**		
6959			**94XX**			76022	8/64	11/64
6986	8/62	11/62	9427	2/51	12/53	76036	11/65	4/66
6987	9/58	12/59	9450	7/51	12/53	76042	11/65	5/66
74XX			9477	7/52	10/55	76087	3/66	5/66
7402	8/50	5/53	**57XX**			**WD 2-8-0**		
7413	3/64	8/64	9608	11/64	7/66	90148	2/62	6/62
7414	3/63	8/64	9613	8/50	10/65	90261	2/62	6/62
						90268	2/62	6/62

Swansea East Dock
87D 8/50
Closed 7/64

TV 0-6-2T			4259	12/52	9/54		**56XX**		
308	8/50	6/54	4264	6/63	7/63	6602	7/61	12/63
309	8/50	1/53	4271	10/59	6/62	6613	8/50	7/58
SHT 0-4-0T			4295	7/63	12/63		9/59	2/63
1140	8/50	10/55	4296	8/50	3/52	6644	11/52	7/55
	3/56	5/58		**57XX**		6650	6/61	2/63
1144	8/50	7/55	4650	5/60	7/61	6662	8/50	4/63
	10/55	2/60	4658	12/63	7/64	6680	2/63	12/63
SHT 0-6-0T			4663	4/64	6/64	6688	6/61	8/61
1146	8/50	1/51	4699	1/64	7/64		**57XX**	
PM 0-4-0T				**42XX**		6700	8/59	6/61
1150	8/50	10/52	5210	8/50	5/59	6702	8/59	7/60
1151	11/59	8/63		10/59	12/63	6712	8/59	7/60
1152	8/50	12/61	5211	3/51	5/59	6714	8/50	4/54
MSWJ 2-4-0				10/59	12/63		8/59	12/63
1338	6/60	9/63	5221	8/50	1/58	6719	1/60	7/60
	16XX		5227	8/50	9/54	6720	8/59	6/61
1639	4/51	2/61	5230	10/59	12/63	6724	10/62	11/63
1640	10/52	6/53	5232	8/50	5/59	6738	8/59	9/62
1641	5/51	1/60		10/59	6/60	6741	3/61	11/63
1646	5/51	2/53	5240	4/55	8/59	6742	10/62	11/63
1652	12/54	2/60	5246	8/50	9/58	6749	8/59	9/62
BPGV 0-6-0T				10/59	6/60	6753	8/59	1/61
2166	8/50	5/55	5262	6/56	5/59	6754	5/60	10/60
	57XX			**43XX**			10/62	1/63
3603	4/64	6/64	5361	3/59	5/59	6755	7/60	6/62
3610	2/64	6/64		**56XX**		6757	7/60	1/63
3615	4/64	6/64	5602	7/63	11/63	6760	11/62	11/63
3633	8/50	8/56	5609	10/60	12/63	6762	10/59	3/63
3635	5/62	5/64	5616	8/50	5/59	6763	8/59	2/61
3641	8/50	7/62		10/59	9/63		11/62	12/63
3648	1/61	6/61	5623	10/60	12/63	6764	5/61	11/63
3661	9/59	6/61	5628	8/50	5/59	6765	7/60	7/64
3671	11/63	6/64		10/59	1/63	6767	8/59	1/63
3672	1/64	4/64	5631	6/61	8/62	6768	8/59	2/64
3679	8/50	8/56	5656	11/62	12/63	6770	8/59	1/60
3693	5/60	6/61	5675	9/59	6/63	6772	11/62	12/63
3694	8/59	11/59		**57XX**		6773	8/59	9/59
3721	12/63	4/64	5704	8/50	8/56	6774	8/59	12/59
3733	11/63	12/63		1/60	5/60	6776	8/59	1/61
3785	6/61	6/62	5731	6/53	1/56	6777	8/59	7/64
3797	6/61	6/64		3/56	9/56	6778	8/59	5/62
	42XX		5743	8/50	8/56		**72XX**	
4221	7/55	9/58	5783	5/60	3/62	7215	1/58	5/59
4227	10/63	12/63		**43XX**			10/59	6/63
4232	4/56	5/59	6355	5/51	10/52	7224	10/53	6/57
	9/59	10/63						

Shed by Shed

7225	1/58	5/59
	10/59	8/61
	11/61	1/63
7226	12/52	6/57
	1/58	5/59
	10/59	12/63
7244	5/62	11/62
7248	12/52	9/54
	1/58	5/59
	10/59	11/62
	2/63	12/63

74XX

7404	12/63	7/64
7408	8/59	1/61
7427	1/64	7/64

57XX

7704	8/50	12/60
7718	4/54	4/62
7756	8/50	1/57
	4/57	11/59

94XX

8408	8/56	8/59
8414	1/58	4/64
8418	6/59	11/59
8423	1/59	12/59
8431	1/53	6/64
8443	4/54	5/59
8475	8/56	6/64
8476	8/56	1/61
8483	8/56	2/62
8488	5/60	6/64

57XX

8714	1/63	7/64

8732	12/63	4/64
8739	12/63	5/64
8750	5/60	5/62
8774	5/60	6/61
8794	6/61	7/63
8798	5/60	6/61

94XX

9416	6/61	1/62
9431	1/59	4/64
9441	1/61	11/63
9446	4/64	6/64
9448	9/56	11/56
9472	4/64	6/64
9473	4/64	6/64
9480	4/64	6/64
9484	6/61	4/64
9485	9/56	9/59
9489	1/53	4/64
9491	8/56	5/59
9492	9/56	2/57

57XX

9606	7/63	7/64
9625	8/50	5/62
9645	8/50	11/57
9660	1/64	6/64
9675	4/64	6/64
9677	12/63	6/64
9678	4/64	6/64
9715	6/61	6/61
9732	11/63	3/64
9744	8/50	8/56
	1/60	5/61
	5/62	1/63

9746	11/62	3/64
9748	12/63	1/64
9749	9/60	10/60
9752	4/62	12/63
9761	6/61	9/62
9780	1/64	6/64

0F 0-4-0T

41535	9/63	6/64

4MT 2-6-4T Fairburn

42182	6/61	7/62

4MT 2-6-4T Fowler

42305	6/61	8/62
42307	6/61	6/61
42385	6/61	7/62
42387	6/61	3/62
42388	6/61	1/63
42394	6/61	7/62

0F 0-4-0T

47003	7/63	3/64

3F 0-6-0T

47478	8/59	9/59
47479	8/59	9/59

0F 0-4-0T

51218	11/62	6/64

4MT 2-6-4T

80069	7/62	8/64
80072	7/62	9/63
80097	7/62	7/63
80099	7/62	7/63
80133	7/62	3/63
80134	7/62	3/64

Swansea Victoria
87K 8/50
Closed 9/59

SHT 0-4-0T

1140	10/55	3/56
1144	7/55	10/55

PM 0-4-0T

1153	2/54	9/55

16XX

1622	9/50	5/52
1640	9/52	10/52
1651	12/54	4/55

2021

2082	1/51	3/51

2251

2272	3/51	4/51

57XX

3694	2/58	8/59
3768	7/54	7/54
4676	2/58	8/59
4684	1/55	3/55

56XX

5612	9/51	10/53
5646	8/51	1/52
5657	7/53	10/53
5673	9/52	10/52
5675	1/53	2/53

57XX

5703	9/54	10/54

5728	2/58	8/59
5731	1/56	3/56
5748	9/54	12/54
5761	2/52	8/59
5773	8/51	8/59
5778	1/52	2/52
5793	2/58	8/59

56XX

6644	8/51	11/52
6688	6/51	7/51

57XX

6700	4/57	8/59
6702	5/58	8/59

No.		
6712	10/57	8/59
6713	10/54	9/57
6714	4/55	8/59
6715	7/51	8/51
6717	5/57	1/59
6718	6/57	5/58
6720	7/53	8/59
6721	3/56	1/59
6723	6/57	1/59
6738	2/59	8/59
6749	5/57	8/59
6753	2/59	8/59
6761	6/53	7/53
6763	5/55	6/55
	6/56	8/59
6766	10/52	11/52
6767	2/59	8/59
6768	10/54	8/59
6770	2/59	8/59
6773	6/59	8/59
6774	7/57	8/59
6776	4/57	8/59
6777	4/57	8/59
6778	8/57	8/59
6779	6/56	5/59
74XX		
7400	4/51	5/51
7408	3/55	8/59
7439	8/50	4/51
	5/51	3/55
57XX		
7756	1/57	4/57
8706	11/53	8/59
8720	2/52	3/52
8738	11/53	1/54
8743	8/57	9/57
8787	8/57	9/57
9645	11/57	1/58
3MT 2-6-2T Stanier		
40097	5/55	3/57
40105	1/54	3/57
40141	6/54	3/57
2MT 2-6-2T		
41201	5/52	3/53
1F 0-6-0T		
41699	3/51	7/55
41769	8/50	6/57
41824	8/50	1/51
41852	8/50	4/51
41860	8/50	3/57
4MT 2-6-4T Fowler		
42305	8/50	8/59
42307	8/50	7/55
	10/55	8/59
42385	8/50	8/59

No.		
42387	8/50	8/59
42388	8/50	7/55
	8/55	8/59
42390	8/50	8/59
42394	8/50	8/59
1P 2-4-2T		
46616	2/53	8/55
46620	8/50	2/53
3F 0-6-0T		
47230	8/50	3/57
47232	8/50	4/55
47256	8/50	9/56
47258	8/50	3/57
47259	8/50	6/57
47477	8/50	7/57
47478	8/50	8/59
47479	8/50	8/59
47480	8/50	4/57
47481	8/50	3/59
47655	8/50	11/57
47681	8/50	11/57
8F 2-8-0		
48309	8/55	8/59
48330	11/50	8/59
48347	4/59	6/59
48400	4/57	8/59
48409	2/58	8/59
48419	2/58	8/59
48438	4/59	8/59
48452	2/58	8/59
48461	2/58	8/59
48463	2/58	8/59
48470	11/58	8/59
48524	12/50	1/58
	11/58	8/59
48525	11/50	8/59
48660	3/55	8/55
48706	12/50	8/59
48707	2/51	12/51
48724	11/50	8/55
48730	12/50	8/59
48732	12/50	8/59
48735	12/50	8/59
48737	11/50	8/59
48738	11/50	12/52
48739	12/50	12/51
48760	11/58	8/59
48761	11/50	8/59
48768	11/50	8/59
G1 & G2a 0-8-0		
48893	8/50	12/51
	3/53	6/53
49033	9/50	11/57
49035	9/50	1/57
49117	12/52	3/59

No.		
49146	4/57	2/58
49148	8/50	6/57
49177	8/50	1/59
49226	4/57	3/59
49260	8/50	12/51
49358	8/50	4/58
49376	8/50	3/58
2F 0-6-2T		
58880	8/52	4/54
58888	5/54	7/54
58889	2/53	7/53
58892	8/50	5/52
58899	7/53	6/54
58900	3/54	6/54
58910	8/50	7/52
58911	8/52	3/54
58915	3/54	7/54
58921	6/53	6/54
58924	5/54	7/54
4MT 4-6-0		
75022	6/57	7/57
3MT 2-6-2T		
82037	4/55	7/55
WD 2-8-0		
90102	8/50	11/50
90173	8/50	1/51
90186	8/50	11/50
90188	8/50	3/51
90205	8/50	12/50
90225	8/50	1/51
90297	8/50	12/50
90307	8/50	11/50
90359	8/50	11/50
90546	8/50	11/50
90568	8/50	12/50
90579	8/50	2/51
90712	8/50	12/50

Shed by Shed

Swindon
82C   8/50
Closed to Steam 10/64

Loco			Loco			Loco		
WCP			**1501**			2934	8/50	6/52
5	8/50	2/54	1542	8/50	2/51	2945	8/50	10/52
1901			**16XX**			2947	8/50	4/51
992	8/50	2/51	1621	8/60	1/63	2949	8/50	1/52
10XX			1630	9/55	11/55	2954	8/50	7/52
1000	1/64	7/64		3/62	10/62	**City**		
1004	3/54	12/60	1634	2/60	6/61	3440	9/58	8/61
1006	11/62	9/63	1640	2/60	6/61	**33XX**		
1008	9/63	10/63	1647	5/51	3/54	3444	8/50	6/51
1010	9/59	7/64	1648	5/51	3/54	3449	8/50	6/51
1011	11/63	11/64	1658	3/55	11/64	3451	8/50	4/51
1012	9/56	4/64	1664	12/61	11/64	3453	8/50	8/51
1013	9/63	7/64	**1901**			**57XX**		
1014	9/63	4/64	2014	8/50	11/51	3645	8/50	5/62
1015	9/59	8/61	2017	8/50	3/51	3666	8/50	6/62
1019	3/54	9/62	**2021**			3682	8/50	1/62
1020	10/63	3/64	2060	8/50	11/54	3684	8/50	5/62
1021	11/59	12/60	**BPGV**			3709	6/62	11/62
1023	3/61	9/62	2195	8/50	12/52	3711	1/59	9/62
1024	10/63	3/64	**2251**			3724	8/50	5/61
1027	9/63	10/63	2203	6/56	9/59	3737	8/50	3/56
1028	10/63	11/63	2214	9/54	10/54	3739	8/50	2/53
1029	7/61	1/63	2215	10/55	12/55		5/53	1/63
1361				9/59	11/59	3746	5/51	6/57
1364	2/60	2/61	2224	8/50	10/54	3748	8/50	5/51
1365	4/55	1/63	2230	7/59	3/60	3758	4/59	3/64
1366			2244	8/62	9/64	3763	3/56	5/62
1366	8/50	11/54	2250	8/50	10/52	3780	8/50	1/63
1367	3/53	9/53		10/59	7/62	**28XX**		
1369	8/50	3/60	2258	4/57	11/58	3818	2/61	5/61
1370	4/53	9/53	2262	12/54	9/55	3842	4/61	12/63
1371	8/50	10/60	2291	11/59	1/64	3854	7/52	10/52
14XX			2293	12/55	6/59	3865	5/51	4/53
1400	8/50	6/57	**2301**			**40XX**		
1403	8/50	6/51	2568	8/50	4/53	4015	8/50	2/51
	9/51	9/52	**28XX**			4022	8/50	2/52
1410	7/55	6/57	2818	8/52	8/59	4034	5/51	8/52
	6/57	6/61	2835	3/58	5/60	4036	8/50	3/52
1422	9/56	6/57	2852	5/53	11/62	4055	8/50	2/51
1426	5/60	7/60	2857	8/60	4/61	4057	8/50	2/52
1433	8/50	1/57	2865	5/53	3/60	4062	8/50	10/56
	2/57	2/60	2868	5/53	11/54	**4073**		
1436	8/50	10/55	2879	10/55	4/63	4074	11/60	1/62
1438	9/58	1/60	2890	11/59	9/63	4079	7/62	11/63
1446	8/50	7/55	**29XX**			4081	8/50	12/50
1462	10/55	3/59	2908	8/50	12/50	4086	4/57	9/59
1464	7/58	6/60	2927	8/50	12/51	4088	2/61	10/63

No.		
51XX		
4102	7/58	8/62
4129	2/59	6/59
42XX		
4254	8/52	12/54
43XX		
4381	8/50	8/52
45XX		
4502	8/50	10/51
4521	8/50	1/51
4536	12/50	4/51
4538	8/50	10/51
	1/52	7/55
	9/55	5/57
4544	8/50	5/51
4550	8/50	4/56
4551	8/50	5/51
4569	7/64	8/64
4573	9/53	6/56
4585	8/50	5/52
4590	8/50	5/51
4591	7/64	8/64
4592	8/50	8/51
57XX		
4612	8/50	5/61
	1/62	8/62
4644	2/61	5/61
	1/62	5/62
4651	8/50	5/62
4697	8/50	2/56
	6/56	6/64
49XX		
4907	2/53	5/53
4909	5/51	11/53
	3/62	8/62
4912	8/51	3/54
4916	8/51	10/53
	6/64	8/64
4919	1/63	1/64
4924	10/62	10/63
4925	8/50	11/56
4928	9/54	11/56
4930	9/62	11/63
4934	10/52	3/53
	4/61	6/61
4945	8/50	5/53
4947	9/61	11/61
4948	9/61	8/62
4950	7/63	1/64
4951	11/50	10/53
	1/63	1/64
4953	4/56	7/60
4956	8/50	12/50
4958	4/51	5/53
4959	11/56	1/58

No.		
4969	5/51	8/52
4972	1/54	6/62
4973	8/50	3/56
4978	9/61	10/61
4980	6/63	7/63
4983	8/50	3/51
	4/51	1/52
4991	6/63	12/63
4993	6/63	11/63
4073		
5000	11/55	10/63
5002	1/57	11/63
5005	9/58	5/59
	6/59	2/60
5007	2/59	3/61
5009	8/50	9/60
5018	11/50	1/51
5023	5/58	1/63
5025	6/56	10/63
5035	9/60	5/62
5058	9/59	11/59
5062	10/52	3/58
5064	3/58	9/61
5068	8/50	8/62
5083	8/50	6/56
5084	8/50	7/55
5091	8/50	5/53
42XX		
5226	7/52	10/55
5240	8/52	3/55
43XX		
5306	7/55	10/55
	9/58	9/59
5322	8/50	3/53
	8/59	9/59
5325	11/51	5/52
5327	11/51	1/54
5328	1/58	5/58
5350	7/55	6/56
5351	12/54	5/59
5367	8/50	12/52
5369	9/61	8/62
5371	8/50	9/51
5396	8/50	9/56
45XX		
5509	5/51	9/59
5510	8/50	9/60
5528	11/58	12/59
5532	11/58	5/59
5534	8/50	10/52
	3/53	9/53
5536	5/51	6/56
	12/59	12/60
5540	5/51	9/59
5547	6/57	2/62

No.		
5555	2/61	6/61
5563	8/50	10/52
5564	7/51	6/56
	1/63	11/63
5566	8/50	12/58
5568	8/61	9/61
5569	1/63	11/63
5570	8/61	11/63
57XX		
5784	5/54	5/59
58XX		
5800	8/50	5/58
5802	8/50	11/58
5804	8/50	5/59
5805	8/50	3/58
5815	4/58	4/61
49XX		
5922	8/50	10/61
5934	8/50	11/53
5939	9/62	2/63
5943	8/50	12/50
	9/61	6/63
5945	6/59	3/61
5949	9/60	5/61
5955	6/64	8/64
5964	8/58	6/62
5975	10/53	11/56
5978	8/58	2/63
5981	8/58	6/61
5983	8/58	7/60
5984	9/55	11/56
5986	8/57	9/61
5994	10/52	4/53
	5/53	11/56
5997	9/53	7/54
	8/58	7/60
	9/60	6/62
61XX		
6106	1/64	7/64
	8/64	11/64
6122	8/64	9/64
6130	1/64	7/64
6163	4/55	7/55
43XX		
6307	10/52	3/53
6309	10/54	6/57
	1/58	1/62
6314	10/52	9/54
6320	8/50	11/56
6322	8/50	11/51
6327	1/60	7/62
6334	11/57	4/59
6336	1/58	6/61
6348	10/52	9/54
6354	11/57	12/58

6355 10/56 3/58
6357 8/50 4/54
6358 8/50 5/53
6360 8/50 10/56
6366 2/58 2/60
6368 11/52 6/54
6374 8/50 11/51
6384 8/50 6/56
6387 8/50 10/55
6389 8/53 9/53
6391 2/59 5/61

56XX
6639 11/55 10/60
6699 3/55 5/58

57XX
6716 8/50 1/59
6736 3/58 1/59
6737 8/50 6/57
6739 8/50 1/55
6741 8/50 3/61
6758 2/59 9/60
6769 2/59 1/63

68XX
6805 10/52 1/58
6819 7/53 10/53
6823 2/53 5/53
6832 10/52 1/58
6850 10/52 1/58

49XX
6900 1/63 10/63
6902 9/56 5/61
6908 8/50 11/50
6912 9/55 6/57
6915 8/50 1/56
6935 12/55 6/56
6940 11/62 9/63
6945 12/52 4/53
6949 9/53 2/54

6959
6966 8/56 9/58
6967 9/53 12/56
     2/57 9/58
6986 9/60 8/62
6993 9/56 2/61

4073
7015 8/50 10/55
7031 9/59 3/62
7037 12/50 5/59
     6/59 2/63

43XX
7319 10/52 2/53
7321 8/50 6/56
7337 (ex 9315 5/59)
     9/55 9/64

74XX
7408 1/55 3/55
7413 4/54 8/61
7415 8/50 3/53
     9/53 9/57
     10/57 1/59
7418 8/50 5/51
     8/51 3/53
     9/53 7/59
7421 6/54 8/55
     11/55 10/61
7424 8/50 7/59
7427 3/59 6/61
7792 8/50 10/57
7794 8/50 7/59

78XX
7808 8/64 11/64
7813 8/64 11/64
7816 8/64 11/64
7829 8/64 11/64

6959
7907 9/61 11/61
7914 8/50 4/55
7916 8/50 9/50
     6/64 9/64
7923 10/50 9/58
7926 7/64 9/64

94XX
8433 11/55 2/63
8461 9/53 9/59
8465 12/58 7/62
8472 8/51 10/62
8497 11/52 12/52
8498 11/52 12/52
8499 11/52 12/52

57XX
8711 9/60 3/62
8733 8/50 1/52
8779 8/50 2/62
8783 1/52 5/62
8793 8/50 7/54
     9/54 2/63

90XX
9011 8/50 6/57
9018 8/50 11/52
9023 8/50 6/57

3252
9083 8/50 12/50
9089 8/50 1/51

93XX
9315 9/55
(renum 7337 5/59)

94XX
9400 8/50 11/55
9476 7/52 8/59

     11/59 6/62

57XX
9600 8/50 4/61
9604 3/55 1/63
9605 4/56 11/64
9672 6/56 8/64
9680 2/62 11/64
9720 8/50 10/61
9721 8/50 6/62
9740 6/56 2/62
9754 4/61 1/63
9772 8/50 12/58
9773 8/50 11/64
9790 8/50 11/64
9795 8/50 10/60

4MT 2-6-0
43094 4/51 11/51

V2
60845 4/52 9/52
     9/52 4/53

8P 4-6-2
71000 10/54 5/55

5MT 4-6-0
73001 11/56 1/64
73012 11/56 2/64
73017 11/56 9/58
73018 11/56 9/58
73020 11/56 9/58
73022 7/54 9/58
73027 7/54 2/64
73028 11/63 1/64
73029 9/57 9/58

4MT 4-6-0
75000 5/51 9/51
     12/53 8/59
75001 9/53 9/54
75002 9/53 9/56
     1/57 1/60
75003 12/53 2/58
75004 9/53 9/54
75006 10/51 4/52
75023 8/56 12/57
75024 3/59 8/59
75025 6/56 12/57
75026 6/56 1/57
75027 2/59 2/60
75029 2/59 11/60

2MT 2-6-0
78004 1/54 6/57

WD 2-8-0
90312 8/50 5/51
90324 8/50 12/50
90579 2/51 5/51
90589 8/50 9/50

Swindon Works

Taunton
83B 8/50
Closed to Steam 10/64

Car Rly		
1338	8/50	6/60
1361		
1361	12/53	1/54
	4/58	5/58
1362	9/52	11/57
	1/58	2/58
	7/58	5/61
1366		
1366	12/54	1/61
1368	4/53	12/54
14XX		
1442	12/63	9/64
1450	10/63	9/64
1466	10/63	12/63
16XX		
1608	1/56	3/56
1668	5/55	7/60
2021		
2038	8/50	2/52
2088	9/52	7/55
2127	8/50	8/52
BPGV		
2194	8/50	1/53
2251		
2208	3/53	7/55
2211	8/50	9/54
2212	8/50	5/58
2213	8/50	8/56
2214	8/50	9/54
2219	6/60	3/64
2229	8/53	10/53
2230	6/57	5/58
2235	9/58	7/59
2236	3/53	9/53
2240	6/61	9/61
2261	8/50	10/52
	6/61	9/61
2266	8/50	9/54
2267	8/50	4/56
2268	8/50	7/55

2275	8/50	4/56
2277	6/60	6/61
28XX		
2814	8/50	6/56
2822	8/57	9/64
2851	4/59	6/62
2871	9/61	5/63
2882	4/59	12/63
2887	12/63	7/64
57XX		
3669	8/50	11/63
3736	9/50	3/63
3787	12/61	10/62
28XX		
3802	4/64	9/64
3834	6/63	4/64
3863	6/64	9/64
4073		
4032	10/50	9/51
4079	?/60 [b]	1/61
4095	5/60	6/60
51XX		
4103	12/61	9/62
4109	7/55	9/55
4110	6/62	5/63
4113	8/50	10/53
4117	8/50	5/57
	6/57	9/57
	9/60	8/61
4128	5/58	9/62
4129	6/59	9/59
4136	8/50	8/58
4143	7/61	11/63
4150	9/55	10/56
4157	7/56	9/61
4159	6/56	11/60
4176	7/54	9/55
45XX		
4507	10/52	2/53
4521	10/52	8/53
4530	1/51	4/51

4538	7/55	9/55
4563	10/52	11/54
4581	1/51	8/53
4588	9/61	11/61
4593	8/61	8/63
57XX		
4604	8/50	7/62
4612	5/61	1/62
4622	1/62	1/64
4644	5/61	1/62
4655	10/61	2/63
4663	8/50	10/62
4673	3/62	6/62
49XX		
4902	6/63	9/63
4903	6/63	9/63
4904	12/59	12/63
4920	6/53	12/58
4924	6/59	5/60
	9/60	10/60
4928	2/57	7/57
4930	5/58	5/60
	9/60	10/60
4932	10/52	9/64
4934	6/62	8/62
4940	9/53	12/59
4946	1/60	4/60
4949	8/50	3/58
4955	11/59	1/63
4957	2/60	3/60
4970	8/50	4/51
	5/51	6/61
4971	8/50	9/60
4978	6/56	9/61
4985	9/53	1/63
4989	1/64	9/64
4991	2/56	9/62
4992	9/60	9/62
4993	6/62	9/62
4996	6/62	9/63

Shed by Shed

4073

5003	8/50	4/51
5020	5/60	6/60
5062	3/51	10/52
5073	?/60 [b]	9/61
5077	8/50	12/50
5096	?/60 [b]	9/61

51XX

5157	6/53	11/56
5172	8/50	9/58
5184	5/58	9/58
5185	5/58	3/60
5194	5/58	10/58
5198	12/60	6/61

43XX

5321	9/53	7/58
5325	9/54	7/55
5336	10/63	9/64
5344	9/56	8/58

54XX

5411	5/51	5/58
5412	8/50	10/54
5421	11/52	10/57

45XX

5501	8/50	5/58
5503	8/50	5/61
5504	8/50	9/60
5515	11/60	2/61
5516	10/60	7/61
5518	10/60	11/60
	?/62 [c]	9/63
5521	8/50	6/51
	8/58	11/61
5522	8/50	7/53
	8/53	3/59
5525	5/58	7/61
5531	?/62 [c]	9/63
5533	8/50	7/55
5536	6/56	9/56
5542	8/50	10/53
	7/55	9/57
5543	8/50	10/53
	7/55	7/60
5554	8/59	9/62
5558	5/51	7/55
5571	8/50	3/62

57XX

5721	9/53	7/59
5751	9/53	4/58
5760	10/54	9/57
5779	10/50	11/61
5780	5/58	9/61
5793	8/59	4/62
5798	4/51	8/62

49XX

5920	5/61	9/61
5946	1/60	3/60
5992	11/53	7/54
	9/54	9/64
5999	8/50	9/61

61XX

6113	7/61	11/63
6140	6/59	11/59
6146	5/62	8/62
6148	7/61	2/63
	6/64	9/64
6155	6/60	10/62
6157	6/61	5/62

43XX

6301	9/55	6/56
6305	8/50	10/52
6312	3/61	6/61
6317	8/50	12/53
6322	9/54	12/54
6323	8/50	3/58
	5/58	10/59
6326	12/63	9/64
6327	7/62	9/63
6328	8/50	6/56
6337	9/56	7/58
	10/58	10/59
	11/59	5/62
6340	4/61	6/62
6343	8/50	8/60
6345	12/63	9/64
6363	6/64	9/64
6364	8/50	10/59
6372	8/50	12/63
6375	6/56	9/60
6377	8/50	7/58
6390	9/53	5/62
6394	8/50	11/53
6398	8/50	9/60

68XX

6812	1/61	6/61
6815	8/50	6/61
6839	12/60	9/61
6848	3/55	1/56
6856	12/56	6/57
6860	11/60	6/61
6868	8/50	10/60
6871	1/60	7/60
6874	9/53	8/61
6875	8/50	1/58

49XX

6914	6/59	1/63
6936	6/63	11/63
6941	5/60	2/63
	6/63	3/64
6949	1/60	3/60

6959

6995	8/50	9/61
6996	7/54	3/58
6999	11/60	4/62

43XX

7303	11/63	9/64
7304	8/50	11/63
7305	11/60	8/62
7311	10/52	5/58
7317	9/63	12/63
7319	6/60	9/60
7320	8/64	9/64
7326	3/61	9/63
7332	9/63	3/64
7333	6/60	10/63

74XX

7421	8/50	3/53
7436	5/58	11/63

57XX

7713	8/59	7/62

78XX

7809	7/54	10/54

6959

7909	11/62	9/64
7924	11/59	1/62

57XX

8719	5/58	1/59
8783	5/62	1/63
9608	10/57	10/62
9635	3/63	7/64
9646	8/50	4/62
9647	5/51	9/64
9663	8/50	9/64
9670	8/50	9/64
9671	4/55	12/60
9707	8/64	9/64
9718	8/50	5/62
9757	8/50	7/62

3MT 2-6-2T

82001	12/63	6/64
82008	10/61	2/64
82030	10/61	6/64
82042	10/61	6/64
82043	1/62	2/62
82044	10/61	6/64

[b] After 1/60
[c] After 1/62

Templecombe
71H 8/50   82G 2/58
83G 10/63
Closed 3/66

2251

2204	6/62	12/63
2215	1/61	9/61
2217	12/63	11/64
2218	3/64	11/64
2223	?/?? [d]	5/62
2247	1/63	3/64
2251	11/63	12/63
2277	10/61	11/62
3200	12/63	1/65
3201	3/64	5/65
3205	5/65	5/65
3206	6/62	12/63
3210	10/60	11/64
3215	6/60	1/63
3216	9/60	11/63
3218	4/60	6/60
	12/63	5/65

57XX

3659	9/65	10/65
3720	9/59	12/63
3765	4/59	10/59
3795	2/61	4/61
	11/61	1/62
4631	12/63	6/65
4634	1/63	9/64
4673	5/65	6/65
4691	2/61	9/64
9647	5/65	6/65
9651	1/59	4/59
9670	9/64	5/65

G6

30274	8/50	2/59
30277	8/50	1/51

Z

30953	11/54	3/57
	7/57	2/59
30954	3/57	7/57

Stanier 3MT 2-6-2T

40098	12/60	4/61
40126	8/60	4/61
40161	10/60	12/60
40171	9/60	5/61

2P 4-4-0

40505	5/51	10/53
40509	9/50	6/55
40527	11/53	6/55
40537	3/62	7/62
40563	8/50	5/62
40564	8/50	2/62
40568	9/53	1/54
	9/55	2/59
40569	9/53	1/54
	6/55	10/61
40601	9/53	1/54
	6/55	9/55
40634	8/50	5/62
40652	5/59	5/60

3P 4-4-0

40741	8/50	11/50

2MT 2-6-2T

41206	5/65	3/66
41208	11/64	7/65
41214	8/64	7/65
41216	5/65	3/66
41223	5/65	3/66
41242	5/62	5/65
41243	7/62	7/65
41248	7/53	11/60
41249	7/53	1/59
	5/65	3/66
41283	6/65	3/66
41290	6/65	3/66
41291	5/65	2/66
41296	5/59	8/60
	9/65	3/66
41307	5/65	3/66

3F 0-6-0

43194	8/50	12/60
43204	8/50	10/56
43211	3/51	4/51
43216	8/50	7/62
43218	8/50	4/60
43228	8/50	11/52
43248	8/50	7/59
43356	8/50	5/58
43419	8/50	8/58

43427	10/58	3/60
	6/60	6/61
43436	11/52	7/61
43593	8/50	9/50
43682	6/59	7/62
43734	12/59	7/61
43792	8/50	5/53

4F 0-6-0

44102	8/50	10/63
44135	3/59	8/59
44146	8/50	7/57
44167	11/62	2/64
44272	7/62	6/63
44417	8/50	1/63
44422	11/60	11/64
44557	7/57	7/62
44560	4/60	11/64

3F 0-6-0T

47542	11/58	5/62
47552	10/59	1/60
	5/62	1/63

1P 0-4-4T

58046	8/50	12/51
58047	8/50	8/52
58086	8/50	7/60
58088	8/50	3/53

4MT 4-6-0

75002	9/61	6/62
75004	11/61	5/62
75007	3/63	9/64
75008	7/64	9/64
75009	9/61	11/62
75023	9/61	9/62
75027	2/60	11/62
75071	11/62	7/64
75072	10/62	12/65
75073	11/62	12/65

4MT 2-6-4T

80037	5/65	3/66
80039	6/65	2/66
80041	5/65	3/66
80043	9/64	3/66
80059	9/64	5/65
80067	9/64	5/65

3MT 2-6-2T

82001	4/61	8/62
82002	4/61	9/62
82039	1/59	8/60

[d] After 9/59

Tondu
86F 8/50   88H 1/61
Closed 4/64

1854		
1870	8/50	10/50
31XX		
3100	8/50	5/57
57XX		
3616	8/50	10/63
3627	8/50	1/60
3648	8/61	11/63
3652	8/50	7/54
3668	8/50	6/62
3674	8/50	12/55
3695	8/50	12/52
3699	8/50	1/53
3738	9/60	4/64
3756	2/61	3/63
3772	8/50	2/57
3781	11/59	5/62
51XX		
4108	9/60	7/63
4121	7/58	4/64
4144	8/57	11/62
42XX		
4213	10/62	2/64
4214	6/63	4/64
4215	2/51	12/52
4217	12/52	2/57
4218	8/50	9/62
4222	6/52	4/64
4224	10/55	1/59
4228	3/62	12/63
4233	11/63	4/64
4236	8/50	1/62
4241	8/50	8/59
4243	2/59	9/63
	11/63	4/64
4247	6/62	4/64
4251	8/50	6/63
4260	8/50	12/53
4262	8/62	4/64
4263	10/55	2/64

4269	4/57	1/63
4273	8/50	6/57
	5/62	4/64
4274	3/59	6/62
4276	8/50	4/57
4283	4/63	4/64
4295	12/63	4/64
44XX		
4404	8/50	3/52
4406	5/52	11/54
4408	8/50	12/52
45XX		
4557	8/50	9/53
4581	7/56	4/58
4589	5/58	9/58
57XX		
4634	8/50	10/55
4643	8/50	4/53
4652	11/62	4/64
4662	12/50	7/54
4663	10/62	4/64
4669	8/50	4/64
4675	8/50	4/64
4684	3/63	7/63
51XX		
5171	4/57	5/58
5179	7/58	9/58
42XX		
5202	8/50	11/51
5203	4/63	11/63
5208	11/53	4/64
5226	2/64	4/64
5236	11/51	11/53
5243	11/62	4/64
45XX		
5524	9/53	9/58
5529	7/59	9/59
	7/60	7/60
5534	3/59	1/60

5545	9/53	1/57
	6/57	9/60
5555	9/53	9/55
	10/55	9/60
5556	8/50	9/53
5560	9/53	9/57
	7/60	9/60
5574	9/53	12/55
	5/58	11/58
56XX		
5624	10/52	6/55
5629	10/57	12/62
5633	8/50	5/51
5690	5/60	8/63
5692	7/63	4/64
57XX		
5706	3/59	3/60
5707	8/50	3/59
5756	8/50	6/52
5789	4/53	9/53
5797	8/50	1/53
64XX		
6408	8/60	2/62
6419	8/60	4/64
6430	1/63	3/63
6431	2/62	1/63
6434	7/63	10/63
6435	7/62	11/63
6436	6/62	8/62
6438	8/61	9/61
56XX		
6601	1/62	1/63
6621	8/50	11/51
6638	10/52	1/53
6642	8/50	9/50
6649	8/50	9/53
6657	4/63	4/64
6672	6/56	7/56
6673	6/56	3/62
6675	8/50	11/51

6676	9/54	6/59	8448	7/54	7/59		**57XX**		
6679	9/50	3/55	8453	8/59	9/62	9609	2/57	4/64
	57XX		8497	1/53	6/60	9648	3/63	4/64
7725	8/50	7/60	8498	1/53	11/59	9649	8/50	10/63
7732	3/55	9/62	8499	1/53	9/53	9660	8/50	7/63
7746	8/50	9/59		**57XX**		9674	8/50	8/53
7752	8/50	12/59	8710	5/59	2/63	9678	9/62	11/63
7753	8/53	4/62	8712	8/50	1/63	9681	8/50	4/56
7770	8/50	4/59	8721	8/50	6/61	9711	7/61	5/62
7778	11/51	12/59	8740	8/50	2/61	9738	1/60	1/62
7798	8/50	5/61	8748	8/50	8/62	9780	1/63	1/64
	94XX		8777	8/50	9/53			
8437	?/?? [f]	11/64		**94XX**		[f] After 2/59		
8445	6/54	7/54	9466	6/62	7/63			
8446	7/54	10/55	9492	5/54	6/54			

Treherbert
88F 8/50
Closed 2/65

	TV 0-6-0T			**57XX**		5608	8/50	11/54
193	8/50	2/52	3737	7/63	8/63		7/55	8/63
194	8/50	10/53	3791	8/63	11/63	5610	8/50	11/54
195	8/50	11/51		**51XX**			7/55	1/60
	TV 0-6-2T		4101	7/56	8/56	5611	8/50	1/63
207	8/50	10/52	4162	8/50	12/53	5613	8/50	?/60 [g]
210	8/50	5/52	4177	8/50	10/50		1/61	5/65
	9/52	3/53		**45XX**		5615	8/50	11/54
211	9/52	3/53	4578	1/58	3/58	5632	2/56	3/63
215	8/50	3/53	4580	1/58	3/58	5636	3/56	4/56
216	8/50	4/53	4589	1/58	2/58	5646	9/55	8/62
217	5/52	8/52		**57XX**		5653	1/58	6/62
218	8/50	11/50	4621	8/63	3/65	5654	11/57	12/63
	10/51	11/52	4624	7/63	8/63	5659	4/64	6/64
236	10/51	8/52	4698	7/63	8/63	5663	8/50	10/53
278	8/50	5/51		**51XX**			1/58	1/59
279	8/50	3/53	5154	11/55	8/56	5665	9/55	3/65
285	8/50	3/53	5159	8/50	3/56	5668	8/50	6/61
290	8/50	3/53	5162	9/53	10/56	5669	9/58	10/58
299	8/50	6/51	5168	11/55	9/56		1/63	6/64
303	8/50	9/53	5183	10/50	7/53	5671	7/53	8/53
352	8/50	3/55	5195	12/53	9/56	5674	10/61	4/64
365	8/50	7/55		**42XX**		5676	8/50	6/64
366	8/50	9/55	5222	4/64	7/64	5678	10/56	1/64
368	8/50	2/56		**45XX**		5680	8/50	2/52
377	9/54	4/55	5511	9/53	10/53	5684	5/58	9/63
378	8/50	11/53	5572	9/53	10/53	5687	5/58	11/62
381	9/54	7/55		**56XX**		5688	8/50	4/63
384	1/54	9/55	5600	8/50	11/54	5691	8/50	2/63
385	9/54	3/56		7/55	6/62	5692	5/58	12/58
399	8/50	9/53	5607	8/50	12/63	5693	8/50	1/63

5694	6/56	3/64	8420	3/53	5/58		**3MT 2-6-2T**		
5695	8/50	1/63	8424	3/53	9/54	82000	9/53	11/55	
6619	8/56	9/56	8438	11/57	5/58	82001	9/56	3/58	
6621	6/63	6/64	8455	7/55	8/58	82002	9/56	5/58	
6633	9/55	10/62	8460	3/53	5/58	82005	8/56	5/58	
6648	8/50	10/56	8465	3/53	7/54	82007	7/55	11/55	
6654	11/62	6/64	8469	3/53	7/54	82032	9/56	3/58	
6655	8/50	9/53	8489	3/53	1/54	82033	9/56	3/58	
	7/63	9/63	8495	12/52	9/53	82034	9/56	3/58	
6681	7/63	6/64	9425	9/55	5/58				
6688	2/64	4/64	9470	12/52	9/53				
	57XX			**57XX**		[g] Before 12/60			
7722	11/50	3/52	9602	8/63	3/65				
	94XX		9666	8/63	3/65				
8419	9/55	5/58	9787	9/63	9/64				

Truro
83F 8/50   84C 9/63
Closed 10/65

	10XX		4567	1/62	4/62	5509	1/60	7/60
1006	7/55	9/55	4570	6/53	7/54		11/60	12/61
1007	12/54	9/59	4574	1/57	9/61	5515	8/50	11/60
1010	2/53	5/53	4587	7/54	7/60	5525	5/58	5/58
1013	8/50	9/51	4588	8/50	1/59	5526	8/50	3/59
1023	9/51	10/55	4589	8/50	9/53	5533	11/58	12/59
	11/55	9/59	4593	1/60	8/61	5537	8/50	1/62
	1501		4598	5/53	11/56	5538	1/60	6/61
1782	8/50	11/50		**57XX**		5544	7/60	7/61
	2021		4622	10/59	1/62	5546	6/59	7/60
2097	8/50	11/50	4673	7/60	3/62	5551	10/50	11/50
	57XX			**49XX**		5552	7/55	9/60
3702	10/55	12/61	4906	8/50	6/57	5559	9/58	2/60
3709	7/60	3/62	4924	9/57	10/57	5562	8/50	3/62
	4073		4928	9/57	5/58		**57XX**	
4032	9/50	10/50	4936	8/50	10/54	5744	7/60	3/62
	51XX		4952	2/52	3/52	5779	8/50	10/50
4106	6/56	7/56	4985	5/53	9/53		**49XX**	
4107	6/56	7/56		**51XX**		5972	7/54	9/55
4108	9/59	9/60	5102	6/56	7/56	5985	5/53	1/56
4134	6/56	7/56	5147	10/52	12/52		**61XX**	
4167	8/50	5/53	5150	11/50	12/50	6114	6/56	7/56
	45XX		5193	10/52	7/53		**43XX**	
4504	8/50	6/52	5196	10/52	12/52	6300	9/56	3/60
4508	9/56	5/58		**43XX**		6373	8/50	5/52
	5/58	9/59	5361	10/58	12/58		**57XX**	
4523	8/50	8/52	5376	4/52	10/52	6770	1/60	9/62
	7/55	9/55		10/57	1/60		**68XX**	
4549	8/60	6/61		**45XX**		6805	1/58	5/58
4554	8/50	5/58	5500	8/50	9/59		10/58	5/60
4561	8/50	11/58	5505	12/53	5/57	6823	10/58	9/61

6827	5/53	9/53		**74XX**			**94XX**	
6828	11/58	9/61	7422	8/50	1/57	8404	11/50	10/54
6848	2/54	4/54		**78XX**		8412	8/50	4/59
6849	12/55	8/56	7806	7/55	9/55	8485	7/52	1/59
6854	4/61	9/61	7812	9/59	9/60	8486	7/52	3/62
6855	11/58	6/59	7813	11/59	9/60		**93XX**	
6871	12/56	5/58	7814	6/54	9/54	9311	11/56	
6872	8/50	12/50	7820	11/59	6/60		(renum 7333 6/57)	
6879	12/58	6/59	7823	1/56	6/56		**94XX**	
6931	8/50	5/58		7/56	4/59	9434	2/51	6/56
	43XX			**81XX**			7/56	6/59
7333	(ex 9311 6/57)		8104	6/56	7/56	9476	8/59	11/59
	12/56	10/57						

Tyseley
84E 8/50   2A 9/63
Closed to Steam 11/66

	2251			**ROD**			**28XX**	
2203	8/50	1/52	3012	10/54	4/56	3802	10/62	3/63
	2/52	4/53	3016	8/50	12/52	3816	5/61	9/62
2206	1/51	3/51	3017	9/55	9/56	3829	7/52	9/54
2211	5/59	11/60	3023	10/54	9/55		10/62	3/63
2238	8/50	8/51	3044	6/56	9/56	3831	4/58	4/59
	11/51	5/59		**31XX**			3/61	9/61
2257	8/50	8/52	3101	8/50	10/52	3837	8/50	9/53
	10/52	11/60		11/52	8/57	3839	10/52	4/59
2267	2/59	11/60		**3151**			3/61	9/62
2279	1/54	12/58	3151	8/50	3/52	3865	10/62	3/63
2292	1/51	6/52	3180	8/50	3/53		**51XX**	
	9/52	11/52		**57XX**		4101	8/50	10/52
2296	8/50	6/56	3607	7/66	9/66	4103	10/53	11/53
	28XX		3619	7/66	8/66	4105	9/60	9/62
2809	1/58	5/58	3624	8/50	9/51	4106	8/50	10/52
2812	8/58	12/58	3625	8/50	7/66	4107	8/50	10/52
2826	7/52	9/54	3635	5/64	4/65	4110	8/50	12/56
2841	1/57	4/57	3650	8/50	10/53		9/61	6/62
2848	8/50	12/56	3653	8/50	9/53	4111	8/50	9/65
2849	8/50	11/59	3657	8/50	8/53	4116	8/50	8/58
2851	6/56	4/59	3658	8/50	5/51	4120	7/60	11/60
2856	10/52	4/59	3660	8/50	4/63		6/62	9/62
2857	7/55	5/58	3664	8/50	6/51	4125	4/57	10/57
2867	8/50	9/54	3673	8/50	4/64		5/58	7/58
2882	8/58	4/59	3689	8/50	1/59		7/61	1/62
2885	5/58	4/59	3693	8/50	5/60		3/65	6/65
2886	4/58	4/60	3694	9/53	11/53	4126	12/58	1/62
2897	11/56	4/59	3743	8/50	6/51	4127	4/57	10/57
2898	6/56	1/58	3751	8/50	6/51	4133	11/61	10/62
	29XX		3769	8/50	2/56	4146	1/57	5/57
2932	8/50	6/51	3770	4/63	4/65	4147	8/50	10/52
			3776	11/61	10/62		7/65	9/65

Shed by Shed

4155	5/55	9/65
4157	8/50	10/52
	9/61	6/62
4158	8/62	6/65
4159	8/50	10/52
4161	4/58	10/58
4162	4/58	10/58
4165	8/50	10/52
4166	8/50	7/52
4167	5/61	4/64
4168	7/65	9/65
4170	8/50	8/60
4171	5/54	9/54
4172	8/50	12/51
	3/52	6/63
4178	12/54	3/55
	10/64	6/65
4179	4/64	2/65

57XX

4605	8/50	5/51
4635	5/64	7/66
4646	7/66	11/66
4648	8/50	9/64
4683	8/50	2/51
4696	7/66	11/66

49XX

4902	12/59	2/60
4904	9/54	6/57
4910	7/60	9/60
4915	5/55	7/55
4924	8/50	11/52
4933	6/63	9/63
4934	5/53	11/53
4943	2/57	2/58
4954	9/61	7/64
4959	8/50	10/52
4964	8/50	11/55
4974	11/58	4/60
4980	8/50	12/50
4982	11/58	2/61
4988	9/55	5/58

4073

5014	6/64	2/65
5091	6/64	9/64

51XX

5102	8/50	10/52
5106	8/50	11/52
5112	2/53	7/53
5151	4/51	5/51
5152	8/50	9/55
5156	8/50	10/57
5163	2/53	12/59
5164	8/50	5/55
5166	8/50	10/57

5167	1/60	4/60
5171	8/50	10/52
5174	9/60	10/61
5175	8/50	10/52
5177	8/50	11/52
5181	9/53	10/57
5182	8/50	10/52
5187	8/50	7/52
5188	8/50	10/52
5190	8/50	10/52
5192	9/54	10/61
5195	8/53	9/53
5198	8/50	10/57

43XX

5317	4/56	10/56
5318	6/59	9/59
5322	5/53	10/54
	6/59	8/59
5325	7/56	7/57
5333	8/50	1/59
5341	9/57	6/59
5345	7/58	8/58
5346	8/50	5/51
5369	8/50	7/51
	11/51	10/60
5370	8/50	8/59
5378	8/57	4/59
5386	10/52	1/58
5391	9/52	11/52
	1/57	2/57

56XX

5605	4/65	12/65
5606	9/58	1/59
	3/64	11/65
5651	9/57	10/58
5658	9/58	11/62
5684	3/64	7/65

57XX

5700	8/50	9/51
5712	8/50	2/53
5724	9/53	11/53
5736	8/50	2/56
5738	8/50	8/52
	3/53	5/57
5745	8/50	6/53
5790	8/50	10/57

49XX

5900	3/53	11/55
5907	8/50	11/53
5909	8/50	12/54
5912	6/52	4/60
5916	8/50	7/52
5921	6/60	9/60
5926	9/61	4/62
5927	8/50	10/64

5931	11/59	8/62
5942	6/63	9/63
5950	8/50	9/52
5959	9/59	8/62
5972	10/51	10/52
5983	9/61	4/65
5984	2/57	9/57
5986	7/55	9/55
5988	6/63	9/65
5993	8/50	2/51
	10/51	5/52
5997	8/50	5/52

61XX

6101	12/60	3/62
6105	9/53	4/55
	5/55	11/59
6116	10/53	6/62
6118	9/53	7/58
6121	9/53	10/53
6134	9/53	11/57
6137	10/63	11/63
6139	9/53	11/59
6160	6/57	8/57
6166	9/53	10/57

43XX

6305	7/58	8/58
6307	3/53	4/59
6321	10/52	2/56
6327	1/54	1/55
6336	8/50	10/54
6337	7/58	10/58
6342	6/53	1/58
6357	5/58	4/59
6360	7/58	8/58
6364	1/60	10/60
6367	7/58	8/58
6377	7/58	9/58
6391	7/58	8/58
6394	11/53	3/55
6399	12/58	12/59

56XX

6604	9/61	8/62
6609	9/61	9/63
6611	8/50	6/51
6614	9/53	6/56
6618	3/61	7/61
6620	9/53	1/56
	7/56	9/56
6625	7/65	10/65
6630	8/50	10/52
6631	4/57	8/62
6633	12/63	6/65
6644	8/55	2/56
	6/65	7/65

No.				No.				No.		
6646	10/53	11/53		7426	3/61	6/63		**93XX**		
	6/63	4/64		7438	8/50	1/59		9303	11/53	9/56
6665	7/65	9/65		**57XX**				9305	7/58	9/58
6667	6/64	10/65		7713	8/50	8/59		9308	7/56	10/56
6668	9/53	11/62		7735	8/50	8/52		9319	11/53	7/56
6669	9/53	6/56			11/52	5/59		**94XX**		
6681	9/64	9/65		7758	8/50	5/57		9426	5/55	7/55
6697	10/65	11/65		7763	10/55	12/59		9432	12/50	12/59
68XX				**78XX**				9498	3/55	11/57
6834	4/64	7/64		7800	8/50	12/50		**57XX**		
6842	4/64	11/64			7/51	10/51		9608	8/50	10/57
6843	8/50	7/55			6/52	10/52		9610	8/50	10/53
6845	11/62	9/64		7802	11/62	9/63		9614	8/50	12/59
6847	8/50	10/52		7805	6/63	12/64			1/60	8/61
6851	6/65	8/65		7806	9/60	2/61		9635	8/50	3/62
6853	8/50	10/65		7808	1/61	9/62		9680	8/50	7/60
6854	6/65	9/65		7812	6/56	7/56		9682	8/50	7/60
6855	4/60	9/62		7813	6/56	7/56		9724	8/50	8/64
	5/65	10/65			10/60	10/62		9733	8/50	12/59
6857	5/65	9/65		7816	9/60	9/61			1/60	6/61
6858	8/50	9/54		7818	3/53	6/59		9748	8/50	8/53
	6/65	9/65		7821	12/53	6/59		9753	8/50	6/65
6861	11/55	10/65		7823	11/62	8/64		9774	8/64	11/66
6862	5/65	6/65		7824	8/59	2/61		9793	8/50	6/51
6864	5/65	9/65		**6959**				9798	8/50	7/52
6866	8/50	6/65		7908	9/55	9/65			11/52	12/62
6871	11/59	1/60		7912	8/50	5/55		**5MT 4-6-0**		
6879	4/60	10/65			7/55	4/62		44661	9/65	11/66
49XX				7913	8/50	5/55		44663	9/65	11/66
6904	8/50	8/59			7/55	5/58		44666	9/65	8/66
6922	11/64	6/65		7915	10/62	9/65		44760	9/65	1/66
6925	4/64	6/64		7918	8/50	2/65		44762	12/65	11/66
6926	9/61	5/65		7922	3/51	5/51		44774	9/65	8/66
6930	9/61	5/65		7929	12/50	7/55		44776	9/65	11/66
6933	4/64	6/64			6/62	8/65		44777	9/65	4/66
6938	1/53	11/53		**81XX**				44780	9/65	9/66
6942	8/50	11/50		8108	8/50	10/60		44859	10/65	9/66
6951	10/65	12/65		8109	11/60	7/65		44865	9/65	11/66
6952	9/62	11/62		**94XX**				44985	9/65	1/66
	10/65	12/65		8407	5/55	7/55		45038	9/65	1/66
6959				8410	8/50	8/51		45051	9/65	11/66
6964	11/64	5/65		8415	8/50	7/60		45052	9/65	11/66
6971	8/50	10/64		8452	8/50	6/51		45134	9/65	9/66
6980	5/55	7/55		8462	9/53	10/53		45264	11/65	4/66
4073				8463	2/51	9/53		45287	9/65	9/66
7013	6/64	2/65		8468	3/51	5/60		45292	9/65	11/66
7014	6/64	2/65		**57XX**				45302	9/65	1/66
7026	6/64	10/64		8700	8/50	2/62		45349	9/65	11/66
43XX				8713	2/56	9/59		**2MT 2-6-0**		
7309	3/53	5/53			11/59	3/62		46427	7/66	9/66
7317	8/50	11/60		8737	5/59	9/59		46428	6/65	10/66
74XX				8784	8/50	1/51		46442	6/65	9/66
7413	7/63	3/64		**90XX**				46457	6/65	10/66
7420	3/59	6/59		9008	8/50	6/52		46470	6/65	10/66
7424	7/59	3/64		9010	8/50	6/52		46509	12/65	9/66

Shed by Shed

46522	3/66	3/66	48477	2/66	8/66	82002	5/52	9/53
	3/66	7/66	48669	5/66	11/66	82003	5/52	9/53
8F 2-8-0			**5MT 4-6-0**			82004	5/52	9/53
48035	2/66	11/66	73026	6/65	4/66	82005	5/52	9/53
48061	2/66	11/66	73036	10/56	1/58	82006	6/52	9/53
48110	6/63	2/64	73037	10/56	1/58	82007	6/52	9/53
48402	4/59	3/61	73066	6/65	4/66	82008	6/52	9/53
48412	4/59	5/59	73069	6/65	4/66	82009	6/52	9/53
	3/63	2/65	73156	6/65	4/66	**9F 2-10-0**		
48415	4/59	2/61	**4MT 4-6-0**			92000	6/62	11/62
	9/63	6/65	75000	8/59	2/61	92001	11/62	10/66
48417	4/59	3/61	75003	7/60	10/63	92002	4/63	7/64
48418	4/59	12/60	75005	4/59	7/60		11/64	11/66
48424	4/59	3/61	75006	4/59	9/62	92085	11/63	9/64
	9/63	2/65		7/65	11/65	92087	9/65	11/66
48430	4/59	3/61	75014	6/64	9/64	92118	11/64	11/66
48444	4/59	7/60	75020	4/59	6/59	92150	5/64	6/64
48452	6/63	6/64	75024	8/59	11/62	92204	9/63	8/66
48460	2/60	3/61	75026	4/59	6/59	92212	6/62	11/66
48471	4/59	7/60	75029	1/61	11/62	92215	9/63	10/66
48474	3/63	6/65	**3MT 2-6-2T**			92217	9/63	7/66
48475	5/59	7/60	82000	5/52	7/53	92223	5/64	11/66
	3/63	11/64	82001	5/52	9/53	92234	7/62	9/64

Wadebridge
72F 8/50   84E 9/63
Closed 10/64

	1365		4666	12/59	1/63		**0298**	
1367	8/62	9/64	4694	12/59	1/63	30585	8/50	12/62
1368	4/62	9/64		**O2**		30586	8/50	12/62
1369	8/62	11/64	30192	9/51	3/53	30587	8/50	12/62
	57XX		30200	8/50	3/61		**2MT 2-6-2T**	
3633	11/59	12/59	30203	8/50	1/56	41275	1/63	6/64
3679	11/59	12/59	30236	12/55	1/60	41295	1/63	6/64

Wellington
84H 8/50   2M 9/63
Closed 8/64

	16XX			**57XX**		3760	8/50	11/58
1619	8/50	2/53	3613	8/50	7/55	3775	8/50	2/51
1663	3/55	10/58	3626	2/59	1/62	3776	10/62	8/64
	2021		3687	8/50	1/52	3782	1/52	2/52
2030	8/50	2/52	3732	8/50	5/62		**51XX**	
2061	2/53	4/55	3744	3/54	8/64	4110	12/56	9/59
			3749	8/50	10/58			

4120	4/57	7/60		5164	5/55	8/56	9741	6/57	10/60
	11/60	5/62		5167	6/55	9/59		11/60	7/62
4142	9/55	3/58		5178	8/50	8/56	9742	4/51	4/57
4154	8/50	6/53		**57XX**			9774	6/53	7/55
4155	9/53	5/55		5712	2/53	9/57		9/55	8/64
4158	12/52	8/62		5745	6/53	12/59	**2MT 2-6-2T**		
4178	2/53	12/54		5758	8/50	9/58	41201	10/59	1/64
	3/55	7/56		**64XX**				6/64	6/64
	9/60	7/62		6421	9/61	11/62	41204	1/60	11/60
44XX				6429	9/61	3/62		3/61	6/63
4400	8/50	4/51		**57XX**			41231	3/60	9/61
4401	8/50	2/52		7754	8/50	12/58	41232	2/60	2/64
4403	8/50	5/51		**94XX**			41241	10/59	1/64
4406	8/50	5/52		9435	10/53	11/53		6/64	6/64
57XX				**57XX**			**3MT 2-6-2T**		
4605	6/51	9/62		9621	12/59	1/61	82004	7/56	5/59
51XX				9624	8/50	11/55	82006	7/56	1/60
5109	8/50	5/55		9630	8/50	9/60	82007	5/58	7/58
5125	8/50	7/52			10/60	8/64	82009	8/56	5/59
5137	8/50	6/51		9636	8/60	10/63	82030	10/59	1/60
5138	8/50	10/52		9639	8/50	8/64	82034	8/56	9/56
5139	8/50	10/52					82038	9/59	1/60

Westbury
82D 8/50   83C 10/63
Closed to Steam 8/65

10XX				2846	7/60	10/60	**40XX**		
1027	8/50	12/50		2850	8/52	12/53	4028	8/50	11/51
14XX				2871	2/61	9/61	4034	12/50	5/51
1401	6/52	9/52		2875	7/60	11/62	4038	8/50	4/52
1442	10/62	11/62		2883	3/61	1/63	4045	8/50	11/50
1456	6/52	11/52		2886	11/62	7/64	**4073**		
2021				**2251**			4080	11/50	5/53
2023	8/50	1/52		3212	6/59	5/60	**51XX**		
2053	8/50	2/53			8/60	6/62	4133	10/53	3/55
2251				**57XX**				4/55	7/55
2200	9/60	8/62		3614	4/56	9/60	4150	6/62	7/62
2208	7/55	8/57			10/60	3/62	4157	6/62	4/63
2218	11/63	3/64		3629	9/58	1/63	4166	7/54	7/55
2268	7/55	6/64		3669	11/63	9/65	4174	1/62	4/63
2273	9/62	11/63		3675	5/61	10/61	**43XX**		
2301				3696	8/50	12/61	4377	8/50	7/55
2340	1/53	5/54		3735	8/50	9/65	**45XX**		
2426	8/50	9/50		3739	1/63	11/64	4508	8/50	4/51
	1/53	11/53		3746	2/63	7/64	4510	8/50	2/53
2444	8/50	10/52		3758	8/50	11/53	4536	4/51	4/59
2534	1/51	12/52		3787	10/62	1/63	4551	5/51	2/58
28XX				**28XX**			4555	9/57	8/59
2811	9/56	9/59		3819	8/58	9/61	4567	3/58	1/62
2827	10/56	7/58		3840	5/60	6/61	4569	4/63	11/63

Part		
4572	8/50	11/58
4573	8/50	2/53
57XX		
4607	11/53	9/65
4636	8/50	9/65
4647	8/50	3/52
	5/52	10/53
	11/53	9/62
4661	3/63	11/63
4673	11/63	5/65
4697	8/64	6/65
49XX		
4909	11/57	10/61
4917	4/54	8/62
4926	8/50	12/52
4927	8/50	9/56
4930	10/53	5/58
4933	12/50	8/52
	8/58	11/62
4941	9/61	9/62
4945	6/56	10/60
4949	6/62	9/62
4956	6/56	9/56
	9/62	7/63
4957	5/60	3/62
4961	5/60	1/63
4963	8/50	12/50
	5/61	10/61
4965	4/54	5/54
	7/54	7/54
4972	6/62	2/64
4978	6/64	8/64
4985	11/50	5/53
4989	7/63	1/64
4073		
5037	3/51	4/51
51XX		
5180	1/62	6/62
5182	9/55	4/56
43XX		
5306	8/50	10/52
5326	8/50	8/53
5327	1/54	7/56
5338	11/53	7/58
5356	6/53	7/53
5358	5/53	2/61
5368	5/53	9/53
5385	8/50	9/58
54XX		
5402	8/50	8/58
5403	8/50	1/57
	4/57	7/57
5406	8/50	8/57
5410	12/59	2/63
5414	8/57	9/59

Part		
5416	9/58	2/63
5419	8/50	2/58
5422	8/50	3/56
	6/56	7/56
	8/56	10/57
5423	8/50	5/59
45XX		
5508	8/50	5/51
	6/51	10/60
5509	8/50	5/51
5512	10/52	3/53
5526	3/59	6/62
5532	5/59	11/59
5542	9/57	12/61
5554	8/50	8/59
5573	4/63	12/63
56XX		
5689	8/50	1/63
57XX		
5701	12/53	1/58
5718	8/50	10/51
	12/51	5/58
5744	3/62	4/62
5757	8/50	1/53
	3/53	12/60
5767	11/53	8/58
5771	8/50	9/51
	10/51	8/52
	11/52	12/59
5781	8/50	8/52
5785	8/50	4/53
49XX		
5900	8/50	3/53
5904	5/59	11/60
5910	5/55	9/55
5920	9/61	1/62
5921	9/60	1/62
5924	8/50	11/50
5925	8/50	3/51
	9/62	9/62
5929	6/62	11/62
5932	4/64	8/64
5935	5/59	11/61
5945	9/58	6/59
5950	5/55	9/55
	5/61	10/61
5961	8/50	12/53
5963	2/56	1/63
5964	6/62	8/62
5967	3/60	10/60
	7/63	7/64
5971	8/50	12/50
5974	8/50	8/64
5975	12/50	10/53
	4/57	7/60

Part		
5978	8/52	8/52
5980	5/61	10/61
5982	4/57	12/58
5985	8/50	5/53
5986	9/62	9/63
5992	9/64	1/65
5999	9/61	8/62
61XX		
6147	10/63	1/64
43XX		
6314	8/50	10/52
6319	9/62	6/63
6320	11/56	9/61
6338	7/56	6/57
6339	5/53	9/53
6346	5/63	6/63
6353	11/62	5/63
6356	10/62	1/63
6358	5/53	9/59
6363	8/60	9/60
6365	8/50	2/54
6368	8/50	11/52
6369	8/50	11/53
6375	8/50	5/52
	7/53	10/53
6399	8/50	12/58
64XX		
6408	3/58	8/59
56XX		
6625	12/52	11/62
6690	8/50	10/52
6699	8/50	3/55
68XX		
6804	8/50	12/50
6822	9/55	3/58
6845	8/50	12/50
49XX		
6914	10/53	5/58
6915	1/56	9/56
6922	10/53	9/54
6935	8/50	12/55
6945	9/58	12/59
6951	5/59	10/61
6955	8/50	8/64
6957	5/61	10/61
6959		
6966	8/50	2/51
6968	5/60	2/62
	7/63	9/63
6973	5/59	8/59
6977	9/62	12/63
6978	8/50	12/53
6982	8/50	4/51
6988	9/63	9/64
6991	8/50	9/54

6994	4/54	10/61	**7917**	10/50	2/63	**9754**	1/63	3/65
6999	4/62	1/65	**7924**	10/50	11/59	**9762**	8/50	5/61
	43XX			**81XX**		**9764**	6/52	7/52
7300	8/50	2/60	**8102**	10/63	1/64	**9769**	9/60	3/63
7302	8/50	12/61		**94XX**		**9790**	11/64	9/65
7308	1/63	6/63	**8479**	7/52	11/61		**WD 2-8-0**	
7309	8/50	12/50	**8482**	1/58	1/61	**90225**	2/51	6/51
	2/51	3/53		**57XX**		**90343**	8/50	12/50
7332	(ex 9310 9/58)		**8714**	7/61	11/61	**90630**	8/50	4/51
	9/62	6/63	**8744**	8/50	2/53	**90701**	8/50	3/51
	57XX			9/53	9/62		**9F 2-10-0**	
7727	8/50	2/50	**9605**	11/64	9/65	**92205**	9/60	1/61
7728	9/57	11/57	**9612**	8/50	11/63	**92206**	9/60	1/61
7748	4/53	4/61	**9615**	8/50	12/61	**92211**	6/61	8/61
7784	8/50	3/62	**9628**	8/50	2/63	**92221**	8/60	9/60
	6959		**9668**	7/58	2/62	**92223**	8/60	3/61
7909	9/58	10/60	**9674**	10/62	3/64	**92239**	6/61	8/61
	9/64	11/64	**9729**	11/63	11/64			

Weymouth

82F 8/50   71G 2/58
70G 9/63
Closed 3/67

	1361			**29XX**		**4562**	8/50	7/54
1361	1/60	3/60	**2912**	8/50	2/51		11/54	12/54
	1365			**57XX**			1/55	3/60
1366	11/54	12/54	**3633**	11/62	9/63		**57XX**	
1367	8/50	3/53	**3643**	7/55	11/55	**4610**	6/63	9/63
	9/53	8/62	**3692**	9/53	2/56	**4616**	11/62	3/63
1368	8/50	4/53	**3737**	3/56	7/63	**4624**	3/54	7/63
	12/54	4/62	**3739**	2/53	5/53	**4647**	3/52	5/52
1369	3/60	8/62	**3746**	6/57	1/58	**4689**	2/59	9/63
1370	8/50	4/53	**3759**	7/59	9/63		**49XX**	
	9/53	1/60	**3764**	10/52	11/52	**4907**	1/52	2/53
	14XX			**4073**		**4930**	8/50	4/52
1403	6/51	9/51	**4080**	8/50	11/50	**4934**	7/52	10/52
	9/52	10/57		**51XX**		**4965**	5/54	7/54
1410	6/57	6/57	**4133**	7/55	10/61	**4988**	8/50	7/55
1418	6/57	9/58	**4150**	6/53	9/55		**4073**	
1453	8/50	3/60	**4166**	7/55	10/61	**5094**	6/51	7/51
1454	8/50	1/53		**45XX**			**51XX**	
	7/54	7/54	**4507**	8/50	10/52	**5190**	5/53	1/56
1459	11/57	8/58		2/53	9/53		**43XX**	
1467	8/50	3/59		6/56	3/60	**5305**	8/50	7/52
1472	9/58	3/59	**4520**	8/50	12/52	**5314**	8/50	6/57
1474	9/58	3/60	**4527**	8/50	2/53	**5328**	8/50	9/53
	1501		**4538**	10/51	1/52	**5337**	8/50	9/55
1789	8/50	10/50				**5338**	8/50	11/53
						5359	8/50	10/51

5384	8/50	9/60		**43XX**		**35019**	8/64	9/65
5392	4/57	5/58				**35020**	8/64	2/65
	54XX		**7303**	9/57	1/58	**35022**	8/64	6/66
5422	3/56	6/56		2/59	12/62	**35023**	10/66	4/67
	45XX			**74XX**		**35024**	8/64	2/65
5508	5/51	6/51	**7408**	8/50	1/55	**35026**	8/64	4/67
5548	3/56	6/56	**7415**	3/53	9/53	**35028**	8/64	4/67
	57XX			9/57	10/57	**35029**	8/64	9/66
5718	10/51	12/51	**7418**	5/51	8/51	**35030**	8/64	4/67
5757	1/53	3/53		3/53	9/53		**2MT 2-6-2T**	
5771	9/51	10/51	**7421**	3/53	6/54	**41261**	8/63	7/65
	8/52	11/52		8/55	11/55	**41284**	9/64	10/66
5781	8/52	3/56		**57XX**		**41293**	9/63	3/65
5784	6/53	10/53	**7726**	4/52	5/52	**41297**	9/63	9/63
	49XX		**7749**	7/54	10/54	**41298**	9/63	10/66
5932	6/52	7/52	**7780**	4/57	7/63	**41301**	5/65	9/66
5964	7/56	8/58	**7782**	7/56	9/63	**41305**	9/63	5/65
5968	8/50	2/51	**8744**	2/53	9/53	**41310**	9/63	11/64
5978	8/50	8/52	**8793**	7/54	9/54	**41311**	9/63	1/64
	8/52	8/58	**8799**	7/56	9/62	**41324**	9/63	10/65
5981	6/57	8/58	**9601**	3/56	4/57		**5MT 4-6-0**	
5997	7/54	8/58	**9620**	11/50	9/63	**73002**	9/63	3/67
	43XX		**9626**	4/57	5/57	**73016**	11/65	1/67
6309	6/57	1/58	**9642**	8/50	12/56	**73017**	9/58	9/64
6344	1/58	12/62	**9756**	4/60	9/62	**73018**	9/58	4/67
6375	5/52	7/53	**9764**	5/52	6/52	**73020**	9/58	4/67
6389	9/53	10/53		**N**		**73022**	9/58	9/64
	49XX		**31405**	5/61	6/64	**73029**	9/58	8/64
6902	8/50	9/56	**31406**	5/61	2/62	**73041**	11/59	3/61
6912	8/50	2/51	**31407**	5/61	7/63		4/61	8/64
6914	5/58	6/59	**31816**	7/63	6/64	**73042**	11/59	3/61
6919	4/54	1/58		**MN**			4/61	9/65
6945	8/50	12/52	**35003**	10/66	4/67	**73080**	11/59	3/61
	5/53	2/57	**35005**	8/64	10/65		4/61	1/67
	4/57	1/58	**35007**	1/65	4/67	**73083**	11/64	1/67
6967	12/56	2/57	**35008**	10/66	4/67	**73113**	10/65	1/67
6977	7/56	9/56	**35012**	8/64	4/67	**73114**	10/65	6/66
6988	8/50	1/54	**35013**	10/66	4/67		**4MT 2-6-4T**	
6993	8/50	9/56	**35014**	8/64	4/67	**80081**	7/63	8/63
			35016	8/64	9/65	**80147**	7/63	8/63
			35017	8/64	8/66			

Wolverhampton Stafford Road
84A 8/50
Closed 9/63

	10XX		**1019**	1/53	3/54	**1426**	7/51	9/51
1004	11/51	12/51	**1024**	8/50	11/50		**2021**	
	2/53	3/54	**1025**	8/50	11/50	**2061**	8/50	4/52
1016	8/50	10/52	**1029**	8/50	12/53		5/52	2/53
1017	8/50	12/51		**14XX**		**2095**	8/50	4/51
1018	1/53	9/54	**1410**	8/50	10/50	**2109**	8/50	2/51
				1/51	7/51			

2251		
2201	2/61	6/61
28XX		
2841	9/58	8/59
31XX		
3102	8/50	9/58
3104	8/50	6/57
3150		
3160	8/50	6/53
57XX		
3615	8/50	11/62
3658	5/51	6/51
3664	6/51	10/60
3715	2/60	5/62
3756	8/50	8/60
3769	2/56	10/58
3778	8/50	?/6? [h]
3792	5/53	9/63
3793	5/53	8/58
40XX/4073		
4000	8/50	10/54
	12/54	9/56
4018	8/50	4/51
4031	8/50	6/51
4049	8/50	6/53
4053	8/50	6/54
4058	8/50	4/51
4060	8/50	12/50
4061	11/50	2/57
4073		
4078	6/59	10/59
4079	10/52	6/57
4083	1/51	4/58
4090	8/53	12/55
4092	12/50	4/58
4094	7/54	6/57
51XX		
4103	8/50	10/53
	11/53	11/57
4105	8/50	5/53
4108	8/50	5/58
4115	8/50	6/53
4120	5/62	6/62
4140	9/54	1/58
4147	10/52	5/53
4148	9/62	6/63
4161	10/58	4/59
4165	6/62	6/63
4179	4/61	6/63
43XX		
4337	8/50	12/50
57XX		
4605	5/51	6/51
49XX		
4901	9/57	7/60

4912	3/54	11/58
4918	8/52	5/53
	5/59	11/61
4923	7/60	9/61
4926	7/54	2/58
4938	12/59	8/61
4954	12/59	9/61
4960	8/50	12/50
	8/52	10/52
4964	6/62	9/62
4986	6/56	5/59
	12/59	12/60
4990	5/57	8/59
4991	8/52	11/53
4997	12/53	9/55
4073		
5008	8/50	11/56
5010	8/50	4/58
5015	8/50	4/58
5019	4/58	8/62
5022	8/50	2/56
	3/56	6/63
5026	4/58	9/63
5027	12/51	6/54
5031	8/50	11/54
	3/55	9/63
5032	12/51	4/58
5045	12/50	8/62
5046	4/58	8/62
5047	11/54	8/62
5053	8/50	12/54
5059	4/58	5/59
5061	2/51	7/51
5063	5/58	9/63
5070	8/50	11/62
5072	4/58	9/60
	10/60	9/62
5075	6/56	4/58
5088	8/50	8/62
5089	5/58	9/63
51XX		
5106	11/52	10/57
5112	7/53	9/55
5143	8/50	12/51
5151	8/50	4/51
	5/51	10/60
5152	9/61	11/62
5183	4/61	5/62
5187	7/52	10/60
5188	10/52	7/55
	9/55	7/57
5190	10/52	5/53
5199	9/61	2/63
43XX		
5391	6/54	10/55

56XX		
5634	2/54	6/55
57XX		
5701	8/50	10/53
5738	8/52	3/53
5739	8/50	11/54
5780	8/50	5/58
49XX		
5926	5/57	9/61
5942	8/50	11/50
5944	8/50	12/50
	8/52	1/53
5983	7/60	9/61
5995	8/50	11/50
60XX		
6001	9/54	8/62
6002	6/62	8/62
6004	8/50	3/54
6005	8/50	9/62
6006	8/50	2/62
6007	9/59	8/62
6008	8/50	7/52
	1/59	6/62
6011	8/50	9/62
6012	4/62	8/62
6013	5/61	6/62
6014	3/54	8/62
6015	6/62	8/62
6016	7/52	12/54
	12/58	1/59
	6/62	8/62
6017	2/59	6/62
6019	3/62	8/62
6020	8/50	6/62
6022	6/59	8/62
6027	12/58	1/59
	1/60	8/62
43XX		
6321	8/50	10/52
6391	8/50	12/50
64XX		
6404	11/54	1/55
6418	7/51	7/62
68XX		
6812	8/50	6/51
6848	8/50	2/52
6867	3/58	5/58
49XX		
6901	8/50	12/50
6924	8/50	12/50
6926	5/58	11/58
	5/59	9/61
6930	12/59	9/61
6931	7/60	9/62
6933	3/60	9/61

Shed by Shed

6934	7/60	4/61
6940	10/51	2/52
6942	11/50	12/50
6945	3/60	9/62
6949	2/54	9/58
6956	12/50	1/53
	3/54	11/58
6959		
6964	8/50	10/53
	11/53	6/57
6966	10/51	12/51
6975	7/54	9/55
	12/58	5/59
6987	12/59	9/62
4073		
7001	8/61	9/63
7012	6/61	9/63
7014	6/62	9/63
7015	5/59	11/59
7019	5/61	9/63
7024	8/61	9/63
7026	8/50	9/62
	11/62	9/63
7036	6/62	9/62

72XX		
7220	3/54	9/54
43XX		
7309	5/53	3/54
7315	8/50	10/52
57XX		
7735	8/52	11/52
6959		
7915	8/50	5/51
94XX		
8411	8/50	6/60
8423	1/51	2/51
8425	10/58	7/60
8426	10/58	9/60
	6/61	12/62
8452	5/60	11/62
8461	9/59	9/60
8462	8/50	9/53
	10/53	9/58
	10/58	1/59
8498	5/60	7/63
57XX		
8705	8/50	3/56
8726	8/50	7/60

8734	8/50	10/58
8796	9/58	4/61
8798	5/53	5/60
93XX		
9312	7/54	1/56
94XX		
9428	1/51	6/60
9435	2/51	10/53
	11/53	7/63
9470	7/60	7/63
9496	10/54	12/59
57XX		
9621	8/50	12/58
9640	7/63	7/63
9658	7/63	7/63
9661	7/63	7/63
9798	7/52	11/52
2MT 2-6-0		
78008	3/62	11/62

[h] Before 3/64

Worcester
85A 8/50
Closed to Steam 12/65

14XX		
1408	8/50	5/55
1418	8/50	6/57
1461	8/53	9/57
16XX		
1605	9/53	10/57
1629	8/53	6/60
1630	10/61	11/61
1639	2/61	11/64
1647	4/60	4/61
1661	10/57	7/64
1662	3/55	10/56
1901		
2001	8/50	8/52
2016	8/50	1/52
2021		
2034	5/51	4/54
2040	9/52	3/54
	4/54	7/54
2093	8/50	1/52
2100	8/50	6/52

2101	8/50	9/51
	5/53	9/53
2109	4/51	2/52
2115	9/50	6/52
2144	1/53	5/53
	4/54	5/55
2251		
2201	12/53	1/54
2205	8/50	7/55
	9/55	6/57
2206	7/55	9/55
	8/57	12/59
2207	8/50	5/53
2209	10/57	7/60
2222	6/62	5/65
2232	3/63	9/64
2234	3/60	5/62
2237	8/50	9/55
2241	8/50	5/58
2242	8/50	6/57
2243	11/58	7/60
2244	9/64	5/65

2246	10/60	12/63
2247	8/50	5/53
	9/57	3/60
2253	12/53	9/55
	12/58	2/59
	12/63	3/65
2258	12/53	4/56
	9/56	4/57
2262	10/51	11/54
2263	8/50	8/55
2267	1/58	2/59
2273	11/59	6/61
2274	8/50	10/52
2277	8/50	2/59
2278	8/50	11/55
2289	1/60	12/60
2290	8/50	6/55
2291	1/64	9/64
2294	8/50	6/55
2295	10/51	12/51
	9/54	6/55
2296	10/57	2/59

	2301	
2339	12/50	3/52
2458	8/50	1/54
2551	8/50	8/53
	2721	
2743	8/50	10/50
	28XX	
2807	7/51	9/57
2811	6/56	9/56
2813	6/56	9/57
2825	12/52	9/57
2841	4/57	6/57
2855	10/52	9/57
	ROD	
3022	8/50	2/53
3029	8/50	8/53
3031	10/52	2/53
3048	8/50	2/53
	2251	
3204	9/54	5/58
	3/60	7/61
3205	6/55	8/55
	9/55	7/60
3207	9/60	1/63
3209	6/55	5/58
3213	10/54	7/60
	11/62	9/63
3214	8/50	9/60
3216	6/55	9/60
3217	1/54	4/54
	6/55	3/60
3218	1/54	4/60
3219	8/50	11/53
	33XX	
3377	8/50	3/51
3447	8/50	4/51
	57XX	
3605	4/57	6/61
3607	8/50	6/61
3615	1/65	10/65
3682	6/64	12/65
3725	8/50	1/65
3775	2/51	3/61
	29XX	
3839	8/50	8/52
3848	9/51	6/57
	40XX	
4007	8/50	9/51
4051	8/50	10/50
	4073	
4082	8/50	9/63
4085	4/58	5/58
	3/60	8/60
4086	8/50	10/52
4088	4/58	2/61

4089	12/58	7/60
4092	8/50	12/50
4093	12/50	10/52
	51XX	
4104	6/62	3/63
4109	3/59	9/61
4113	11/53	12/65
4114	8/50	9/54
4124	8/58	10/63
	12/63	8/64
4138	1/58	4/58
4139	8/50	2/53
4140	8/50	10/50
4142	3/58	7/60
4143	11/51	12/51
4148	7/55	6/56
	7/56	11/57
4152	8/58	3/60
4154	11/53	1/60
4155	2/51	9/53
4167	9/60	5/61
	45XX	
4546	8/50	10/52
4553	7/55	6/56
4567	6/51	4/57
4571	2/53	2/59
4573	2/53	9/53
4594	3/52	12/55
4596	8/50	5/51
	4/57	8/57
4599	6/51	9/53
	57XX	
4613	8/50	1/65
4614	8/50	12/53
	10/55	1/56
	7/56	7/61
4625	4/52	5/58
	7/58	7/61
4628	12/60	7/64
4629	8/50	5/59
4641	8/50	5/51
	9/60	10/60
4664	8/50	7/52
	8/52	11/57
	5/58	7/65
4680	7/57	12/65
	49XX	
4900	8/52	6/56
4903	9/64	9/64
4907	11/59	4/62
4919	9/64	11/64
4926	2/58	5/58
4933	9/57	1/58
4952	5/57	5/59
4963	10/61	6/62

4976	2/56	6/56
4993	8/50	7/51
	4/52	7/52
	12/59	6/61
4996	11/59	7/61
	4073	
5017	8/50	11/51
5018	1/51	3/51
	7/51	8/51
5023	1/58	4/58
5029	4/58	5/59
5037	6/54	6/60
5042	3/59	4/60
5054	3/64	9/64
5063	8/50	6/54
5071	2/59	4/59
	6/59	9/60
5081	12/54	8/60
5083	6/56	12/58
5086	12/50	3/58
	4/58	10/58
5090	12/52	4/58
5091	3/64	6/64
5092	8/50	3/55
5096	3/64	7/64
5099	2/62	9/62
	51XX	
5110	11/59	12/60
5152	11/62	11/63
5156	5/58	7/58
5173	8/50	10/52
5179	9/58	7/60
	42XX	
5200	11/63	1/64
5205	1/62	11/63
5226	4/60	1/64
5245	3/60	1/64
	43XX	
5303	8/50	5/51
5312	4/54	5/54
5326	4/54	5/54
5334	5/53	12/53
5337	9/56	5/58
5350	8/56	2/58
5358	2/61	6/62
5375	8/58	2/59
5379	1/55	2/56
5392	5/58	7/58
5396	9/56	10/57
	2/58	11/58
	12/58	3/59
	5/59	5/60
	45XX	
5573	8/50	9/53

	56XX	
5614	9/61	8/62
	58XX	
5815	8/50	4/57
5816	8/50	6/57
5818	11/56	6/57
	49XX	
5909	9/55	5/58
5913	1/61	6/61
5914	8/50	7/52
	8/52	1/58
5917	8/50	12/60
5930	9/61	8/62
5943	12/50	6/56
5944	9/61	3/63
5951	11/51	11/52
5952	9/55	8/59
5962	6/64	1/65
5971	12/50	7/59
	1/65	7/65
5979	9/64	11/64
5980	11/58	6/59
	10/61	3/62
5981	4/57	6/57
5984	11/56	2/57
	9/57	6/59
5988	4/52	5/53
5994	11/56	7/61
5996	11/59	7/61
	10/61	12/61
	61XX	
6106	7/64	8/64
6140	1/64	7/64
6144	11/63	12/63
6147	1/64	12/65
6155	10/62	10/65
6165	10/65	12/65
6169	6/64	10/65
	43XX	
6306	8/50	7/54
6314	9/54	10/54
6324	8/50	3/53
	4/53	2/54
6334	7/55	9/55
	6/56	11/57
6335	5/51	6/56
	7/60	9/61
6340	4/57	5/57
6348	9/54	6/57
6354	4/53	11/57
6357	4/54	6/57
6359	11/53	10/55
6367	1/58	7/58
	9/58	1/59

6368	6/59	12/59
	7/60	6/62
6375	9/60	3/62
6378	8/50	2/56
6382	9/53	9/55
	7/60	10/60
6387	12/60	6/62
6388	10/53	5/58
6389	10/53	6/56
6393	5/53	12/53
6395	9/56	6/57
	8/60	11/60
6396	8/50	2/53
	5/53	6/56
	56XX	
6604	10/58	3/59
6618	9/60	3/61
6670	9/61	8/62
6671	9/61	2/62
6681	10/58	3/59
6696	9/60	2/61
	68XX	
6802	9/57	10/57
6806	6/61	11/64
6807	8/50	12/63
6813	6/64	9/65
6816	6/65	7/65
6817	6/61	5/65
6819	6/64	12/65
6820	9/57	4/61
6829	6/65	12/65
6836	6/64	3/65
	4/65	7/65
6838	7/65	12/65
6847	10/65	12/65
6848	1/64	12/65
6851	8/50	7/60
6856	9/57	12/65
6872	7/65	12/65
6876	10/65	12/65
6877	8/50	3/65
6878	6/64	1/65
	49XX	
6930	8/50	9/58
6938	8/50	1/53
6940	6/62	9/62
6947	8/50	9/62
6948	5/58	9/62
6950	8/50	6/61
6951	8/51	4/53
	10/61	3/63
6958	11/64	6/65
	6959	
6984	5/58	2/63
6987	5/52	9/58

6989	3/56	5/57
	7/59	9/62
6992	9/59	7/64
6995	9/64	4/65
	4073	
7000	2/63	12/63
7002	12/59	3/64
7004	7/60	9/63
7005	8/50	9/64
7006	8/60	3/62
7007	8/50	1/63
7009	2/62	10/62
7011	1/61	6/64
7013	5/60	3/64
7022	3/64	9/64
7023	7/60	6/64
7025	9/62	9/64
7027	5/60	8/63
7031	3/62	7/63
7037	9/50	12/50
	72XX	
7222	8/50	4/51
7235	4/58	11/58
7236	8/50	4/51
7238	10/61	1/62
7240	8/50	4/51
7248	8/50	4/51
7250	9/57	5/58
	43XX	
7301	8/50	3/52
	4/53	5/53
7315	12/60	7/62
7319	12/58	12/59
7321	8/56	5/58
7338	**(ex 9316 3/58)**	
	1/55	12/59
	8/60	4/62
	74XX	
7437	8/50	1/53
	57XX	
7707	6/55	10/60
7750	8/50	5/58
7777	1/56	5/58
	10/58	10/60
	78XX	
7813	9/60	10/60
7815	9/55	5/58
7824	1/51	2/51
	6959	
7904	1/65	7/65
7909	11/64	6/65
7919	1/65	6/65
7920	3/51	5/65
7926	9/62	4/64
7928	11/50	5/65

Top section

No.			No.			No.		
81XX			8796	1/58	9/58	75008	5/65	12/65
8102	1/64	7/64	**93XX**			75009	5/58	9/58
8104	9/62	1/65	9316	1/55		75022	5/65	12/65
8105	12/51	6/57	(renum 7338 3/58)			75023	12/57	9/58
8106	8/50	11/63	9318	1/55	2/56	75025	12/57	7/60
8107	7/61	5/62	**94XX**				11/60	1/64
94XX			9401	10/57	11/62		5/65	12/65
8412	4/59	6/59	9429	11/50	8/61	**2MT 2-6-0**		
8415	7/60	2/65		9/61	3/62	78001	5/54	1/64
	5/65	6/65	9455	1/57	2/58	78003	3/58	5/58
8426	9/60	6/61		5/58	2/61	78008	6/53	3/62
8427	3/51	3/58	9466	3/52	1/61	78009	6/53	3/63
	5/58	8/60	9480	8/52	10/52	**3MT 2-6-2T**		
8452	4/57	6/57		12/52	1/60	82007	9/58	9/58
8458	9/53	1/56	9486	1/57	6/62	82008	8/57	12/57
8460	9/59	1/61	9490	3/60	1/65		1/58	6/61
8480	5/52	8/61	**57XX**			82030	12/55	4/59
	9/61	9/62	9626	9/65	12/65		5/59	5/59
8492	4/57	6/57	9630	9/60	10/60		6/59	10/59
8496	10/52	1/61	9680	11/64	2/65	82038	11/55	9/59
57XX			9741	4/57	6/57	**WD 2-8-0**		
8722	7/57	7/58	**8F 2-8-0**			90179	4/51	5/52
8731	1/51	3/51	48436	8/55	9/55		6/57	6/60
8737	3/59	5/59	**4MT 4-6-0**			90284	8/50	8/51
8743	7/57	8/57	75000	6/65	12/65		9/51	5/52
	9/57	10/58	75003	2/58	7/60	90485	6/57	3/58
8787	7/57	8/57		6/65	10/65	90524	5/51	9/51
	9/57	7/58	75005	7/60	1/64	90691	10/50	9/51
8793	2/63	1/65		6/65	12/65	90715	8/50	9/50

Wrexham LNW
6E 9/50   84K 2/58
Closed 1/60

No.			No.			No.		
16XX			4683	11/58	1/60	40070	5/56	10/56
1618	10/58	1/60	4693	10/58	1/59	**Stanier 3MT 2-6-2T**		
1663	10/58	1/60	**56XX**			40073	7/56	10/58
1669	10/58	1/60	5606	1/59	1/60	40080	10/51	12/51
2251			5651	12/58	1/60	40085	9/50	10/50
2236	10/58	11/58	6610	2/59	1/60		10/56	1/60
2294	10/58	11/58	**43XX**			40086	6/56	2/60
3201	11/58	6/59	7323	(ex 9301 9/56)		40088	4/51	11/52
3204	10/58	2/60		11/58	12/58	40103	9/50	10/50
3207	11/58	6/59	**57XX**				4/51	11/52
57XX			8725	12/58	1/59	40106	10/56	10/58
3600	10/58	2/59	8734	10/58	1/60	40110	7/56	1/60
3626	12/58	2/59	9610	10/58	1/60	40126	4/51	11/52
3742	12/58	1/59	9651	12/58	1/59		7/56	1/60
3749	10/58	1/60	**Fowler 3MT 2-6-2T**			40127	9/50	10/50
3760	11/58	1/60	40008	11/58	1/59	40128	4/51	11/52
3769	10/58	1/59	40058	8/58	11/58		8/56	1/59

Shed by Shed

40156	9/50	10/50	67414	6/54	6/55	68714	2/57	10/58
40205	5/56	1/60	67428	8/50	11/57	68727	7/54	10/58
2MT 2-6-2T			67429	8/50	1/55	**N5**		
41223	2/55	4/55	67430	8/50	6/56	69254	10/55	5/56
41231	10/56	3/60	67432	8/50	1/55	69267	8/50	9/57
41232	10/56	2/60	67435	8/50	1/53	69281	7/55	7/58
41234	9/55	8/56	**C14**			69288	10/50	4/55
41235	9/55	7/57	67442	8/50	11/57	69289	9/52	2/54
41236	5/57	10/58	67449	8/50	12/57	69290	8/50	9/57
41237	10/56	10/58	**J94**			69329	8/50	9/57
41244	4/55	7/55	68063	8/50	12/50	69330	8/50	3/55
	10/56	10/58	**Y3**			69335	5/55	9/57
41285	7/59	1/60	68162	7/51	2/56	69340	8/50	6/56
41324	10/56	2/57	68163	8/50	5/51	69343	10/55	11/56
4F 0-6-0			68164	8/50	10/56	69346	8/50	9/57
43877	11/54	10/58		8/57	9/57	69349	8/50	7/58
43981	11/52	11/54	**J62**			69352	8/50	6/55
44058	11/52	10/58	68200	8/50	11/52	69362	8/50	7/58
44307	11/55	10/58	**J63**			69366	8/50	8/56
44364	11/57	11/58	68209	1/52	3/55	**3MT 2-6-2T**		
2F 0-6-0T			**J67/J69**			82000	1/59	2/60
47160	3/57	5/57	68531	8/50	10/55	82007	7/58	9/58
47184	9/50	2/51	68553	4/57	10/58	82020	10/56	1/60
3F 0-6-0T			68559	10/51	3/52	82021	10/56	1/60
47284	10/56	10/58		12/54	1/55	82031	1/59	1/60
47491	11/56	10/58		4/56	6/56	82037	1/59	1/60
2F 0-6-0T			68584	11/51	7/55	**2MT 2-6-2T**		
51397	1/57	2/57	68585	4/56	8/58	84000	3/54	7/56
J11			68595	8/54	10/54	84001	3/54	9/55
64338	8/50	10/52		12/54	1/57	84002	3/54	9/55
64381	8/50	10/52	68598	1/57	5/57	84003	3/54	7/56
C13			**J72**			84004	9/54	7/56
67400	10/55	1/57	68671	12/50	10/58			
67412	12/52	6/54						

Yeovil GW
82E 8/50   71H 2/58
Closed 1/59

57XX			**55XX**			5784	2/53	6/53
3671	8/50	2/59	5529	8/50	9/53	8745	8/50	2/59
3733	8/50	2/59	5548	6/56	2/59	9601	8/50	3/56
45XX			5563	10/52	2/59	9732	8/50	2/59
4507	9/53	6/56	5565	8/50	2/53	9764	4/51	5/52
57XX			**57XX**				7/52	2/59
4647	10/53	11/53	5767	8/50	11/53	9771	8/50	5/51
4689	8/50	2/59	5781	3/56	1/59			

Yeovil SR
72C 8/50   83E 9/63
Closed 7/65

14XX		
1442	10/63	12/63
	9/64	2/65
1450	9/64	2/65
1451	9/63	11/63
57XX		
3671	2/59	11/63
3733	2/59	11/63
45XX		
4507	3/60	10/63
4569	11/63	7/64
4591	5/63	7/64
4593	8/63	9/64
57XX		
4631	7/62	12/63
4656	2/59	9/62
54XX		
5410	2/63	10/63
5416	2/63	8/63
5420	8/63	9/63
55XX		
5548	2/59	5/63
5563	2/59	9/64
64XX		
6400	11/63	4/64
6412	11/63	8/64
6419	4/64	1/65
6430	11/63	9/64
6435	11/63	9/64
57XX		
8745	2/59	11/63
9670	5/65	6/65
9732	2/59	11/63
9754	3/65	6/65
9764	2/59	7/63
M7		
30052	10/62	3/63
30058	8/50	9/51
T9		
30117	8/50	1/51
30122	1/51	4/51

M7		
30128	9/51	11/51
30129	8/50	3/53
	6/56	3/63
30131	9/51	12/62
L11		
30134	8/50	3/51
O2		
30182	3/53	9/58
T9		
30336	1/51	11/51
30337	8/50	11/51
30338	4/51	11/51
K10		
30384	4/51	6/51
30389	8/50	7/51
L11		
30407	8/50	10/50
30412	8/50	11/50
30414	3/51	5/51
30438	7/51	9/51
T9		
30704	8/50	1/51
30706	11/51	11/54
30707	11/51	6/52
	1/53	10/54
	11/54	2/55
30714	8/50	9/50
U		
31610	10/54	6/55
31613	2/59	2/60
31614	2/60	11/63
31622	4/54	10/54
31623	7/53	2/60
31626	2/55	9/58
	2/59	2/60
31632	2/60	9/64
31633	2/59	2/60
31634	8/50	1/51
31636	8/50	1/51
31637	2/60	8/63

31639	6/52	1/53
31790	8/50	9/58
	5/59	2/60
31791	8/50	9/58
	5/59	2/60
31792	8/50	9/58
	2/60	9/64
31793	11/50	9/58
31794	1/51	9/58
31795	11/51	9/58
31796	11/51	9/58
31798	2/60	9/64
31802	2/60	9/64
31805	2/60	7/63
N		
31837	11/52	1/53
2MT 2-6-2T		
41283	9/64	6/65
41290	9/64	6/65
41295	6/64	9/64
5MT 4-6-0		
73166	9/64	6/65
4MT 4-6-0		
75000	9/63	6/65
75001	9/63	1/65
75003	10/63	6/65
75005	5/65	6/65
75007	9/64	4/65
4MT 2-6-0		
76009	9/58	2/59
76010	9/58	2/59
76011	9/58	2/59
4MT 2-6-4T		
80035	2/65	4/65
80038	7/63	9/63
80039	5/65	6/65
3MT 2-6-2T		
82035	9/64	7/65

BR Shed Code List

Code	Name	From	To
1A	Willesden	9/50	9/65
1B	Camden	9/50	9/63
1C	Watford Junction	9/50	3/65
1D	Devons Road	9/50	9/63
1E	Bletchley	3/52	7/65
1F	Rugby	9/63	5/65
1G	Woodford Halse	9/63	6/65
1H	Northampton	9/63	9/65
2A	Rugby	9/50	9/63
2A	Tyseley	9/63	11/66
2B	Nuneaton	9/50	9/63
2B	Oxley	9/63	3/67
2C	Warwick	9/50	11/58
2C	Stourbridge	9/63	7/66
2D	Coventry	9/50	11/58
2D	Banbury	9/63	10/66
2E	Northampton	3/52	9/63
2E	Saltley	9/63	3/67
2F	Market Harborough	10/55	4/58
2F	Woodford Halse	4/58	6/63
2F	Bescot	9/63	3/66
2G	Woodford Halse	2/58	4/58
2G	Walsall	9/63	4/67
2H	Monument Lane	9/63	4/67
2J	Aston	9/63	10/65
2K	Bushbury	9/63	4/65
2L	Leamington	9/63	6/65
2M	Wellington	9/63	8/64
2P	Kidderminster	9/63	8/64
3A	Bescot	9/50	6/60
3B	Bushbury	9/50	6/60
3C	Walsall	9/50	6/60
3D	Aston	9/50	6/60
3E	Monument Lane	9/50	6/60
4A	Bletchley	9/50	3/52
4B	Northampton	9/50	3/52
5A	Crewe North	9/50	5/65
5B	Crewe South	9/50	11/67
5C	Stafford	9/50	7/65
5D	Stoke on Trent	9/50	8/67

Code	Name	From	To
5E	Alsager	9/50	6/62
5E	Nuneaton	9/63	6/66
5F	Uttoxeter	9/50	11/64
6A	Chester LNW	9/50	6/67
6B	Mold Junction	9/50	4/66
6C	Birkenhead	9/50	9/63
6C	Croes Newydd	9/63	6/67
6D	Chester Northgate	9/50	1/60
6D	Shrewsbury	9/63	3/67
6E	Wrexham LNW	9/50	2/58
6E	Chester GW	2/58	4/60
6E	Oswestry	9/63	1/65
6F	Bidston	9/50	2/63
6F	Machynlleth	9/63	12/66
6G	Llandudno Junction	4/52	10/66
6H	Bangor	4/52	6/65
6J	Holyhead	4/52	12/66
6K	Rhyl	4/52	2/63
7A	Llandudno Junction	9/50	4/52
7B	Bangor	9/50	4/52
7C	Holyhead	9/50	4/52
7D	Rhyl	9/50	4/52
8A	Edge Hill	9/50	5/68
8B	Warrington Dallam	9/50	10/67
8C	Speke Junction	9/50	5/68
8D	Widnes	9/50	4/64
8E	Brunswick	9/50	4/58
8E	Northwich	4/58	3/68
8F	Wigan Springs Branch	2/58	12/67
8G	Sutton Oak	2/58	6/67
8H	Birkenhead	9/63	11/67
8K	Bank Hall	9/63	10/66
8L	Aintree	9/63	6/67
8M	Southport	9/63	6/66
8P	Wigan Central L&Y	9/63	4/64

Code	Name	From	To
8R	Walton	9/63	1/64
9A	Longsight	9/50	2/65
9B	Edgeley	9/50	5/68
9C	Macclesfield	9/50	6/61
9D	Buxton	9/50	9/63
9D	Newton Heath	9/63	7/68
9E	Trafford Park	9/50	12/56
9E	Trafford Park	4/58	3/68
9F	Heaton Mersey	9/50	12/56
9F	Heaton Mersey	4/58	5/68
9G	Northwich	9/50	4/58
9G	Gorton	4/58	6/65
9H	Gorton	2/58	4/58
9H	Patricroft	9/63	7/68
9J	Agecroft	9/63	10/66
9K	Bolton .	9/63	7/68
9L	Buxton	9/63	3/68
9M	Bury	9/63	4/65
9P	Lees	9/63	4/64
10A	Wigan Springs Branch		
		9/50	2/58
10A	Carnforth	9/63	8/68
10B	Preston	9/50	2/58
10B	Blackpool	9/63	9/64
10C	Patricroft	9/50	2/58
10C	Fleetwood	9/63	2/66
10D	Plodder Lane	9/50	10/54
10D	Sutton Oak	10/55	2/58
10D	Lostock Hall	9/63	8/68
10E	Sutton Oak	9/50	10/55
10F	Wigan GC	9/50	3/52
10F	Rose Grove	9/63	8/68
10G	Skipton	9/63	4/67
10H	Lower Darwen	9/63	2/66
10J	Lancaster	9/63	4/66
11A	Carnforth	9/50	4/58
11A	Barrow in Furness		
		4/58	6/60
11B	Barrow in Furness		
		9/50	4/58
11B	Workington	4/58	6/60
11C	Oxenholme	9/50	6/60
11D	Tebay	9/50	6/60
11E	Lancaster	10/51	3/57
12A	Carlisle Upperby	9/50	2/58
12A	Carlisle Kingmoor	2/58	1/68
12B	Carlisle Canal	9/50	10/51

Code	Name	From	To
12B	Penrith	10/55	12/55
12B	Carlisle Upperby	2/58	12/66
12C	Penrith	9/50	10/55
12C	Workington	10/55	4/58
12C	Carlisle Canal	4/58	6/63
12C	Barrow in Furness		
		9/63	12/66
12D	Workington	9/50	10/55
12D	Carlisle Canal	2/58	4/58
12D	Kirkby Stephen	4/58	11/61
12D	Workington	9/63	1/68
12E	Moor Row	9/50	7/54
12E	Kirkby Stephen	2/58	4/58
12E	Barrow in Furness		
		9/60	9/63
12E	Tebay	9/63	1/68
12F	Workington	9/60	9/63
12G	Oxenholme	6/60	6/62
12H	Tebay	6/60	9/63
14A	Cricklewood	9/50	9/63
14A	Cricklewood	11/64	12/64
14B	Kentish Town	9/50	4/63
14B	Cricklewood	9/63	11/64
14C	St. Albans	9/50	2/60
14C	Bedford	9/63	9/63
14D	Neasden	2/58	6/62
14E	Bedford	4/58	9/63
15A	Wellingborough	9/50	9/63
15A	Leicester MR	9/63	7/66
15B	Kettering	9/50	9/63
15B	Wellingborough	9/63	6/65
15C	Leicester MR	9/50	9/63
15C	Kettering	9/63	3/65
15D	Bedford	9/50	4/58
15D	Coalville	4/58	6/63
15D	Leicester GC	9/63	7/64
15E	Leicester GC	2/58	9/63
15E	Coalville	9/63	12/65
15F	Market Harborough		
		4/58	5/65
16A	Nottingham	9/50	9/63
16A	Toton	9/63	11/66
16B	Kirkby in Ashfield		
		10/55	9/63
16B	Annesley	9/63	12/65
16B	Colwick	1/66	7/67

Code	Name	From	To
16C	Kirkby in Ashfield		
		9/50	10/55
16C	Mansfield	10/55	4/60
16D	Annesley	2/58	9/63
16D	Nottingham	9/63	7/65
16E	Kirkby in Ashfield		
		9/63	2/67
16F	Burton on Trent	9/63	9/66
16G	Westhouses	9/63	10/67
16H	Hasland	9/63	11/64
16J	Rowsley	9/63	5/64
17A	Derby	9/50	9/63
17B	Burton on Trent	9/50	9/63
17C	Coalville	9/50	4/58
17C	Rowsley	4/58	9/63
17D	Rowsley	9/50	4/58
17E	Heaton Mersey	12/56	4/58
17F	Trafford Park	12/56	4/58
18A	Toton	9/50	9/63
18B	Westhouses	9/50	9/63
18C	Hasland	9/50	9/63
18D	Staveley Barrow Hill		
		9/50	2/58
19A	Sheffield Grimesthorpe		
		9/50	2/58
19B	Sheffield Millhouses		
		9/50	2/58
19C	Canklow	9/50	2/58
20A	Holbeck	9/50	9/56
20B	Stourton	9/50	9/56
20C	Royston Yorks	9/50	9/56
20D	Normanton	9/50	9/56
20E	Manningham	9/50	9/56
20F	Skipton	10/51	3/57
20G	Hellifield	10/51	3/57
21A	Saltley	9/50	9/63
21B	Bourneville	9/50	2/60
21B	Bescot	6/60	9/63
21C	Bromsgrove	9/50	2/58
21C	Bushbury	6/60	9/63
21D	Stratford upon Avon		
		9/50	2/53
21D	Aston	6/60	9/63
21E	Monument Lane	6/60	9/63
21F	Walsall	6/60	9/63
22A	Bristol Barrow Road		
		9/50	2/58

Code	Name	From	To
22B	Gloucester Barnwood		
		9/50	2/58
23A	Skipton	9/50	10/51
23B	Hellifield	9/50	10/51
23C	Lancaster	9/50	10/51
24A	Accrington	9/50	?/61
24B	Rose Grove	9/50	9/63
24C	Lostock Hall	9/50	9/63
24D	Lower Darwen	9/50	9/63
24E	Blackpool	4/52	9/63
24F	Fleetwood	4/52	9/63
24G	Skipton	3/57	9/63
24H	Hellifield	3/57	6/63
24J	Lancaster	3/57	9/63
24K	Preston	2/58	9/61
24L	Carnforth	4/58	9/63
25A	Wakefield	9/50	9/56
25B	Huddersfield	9/50	9/56
25C	Goole	9/50	9/56
25D	Mirfield	9/50	9/56
25E	Sowerby Bridge	9/50	9/56
25F	Low Moor	9/50	9/56
25G	Farnley Junction	9/50	9/56
26A	Newton Heath	9/50	9/63
26B	Agecroft	9/50	9/63
26C	Bolton	9/50	9/63
26D	Bury	9/50	9/63
26E	Bacup	9/50	10/54
26E	Lees	10/55	9/63
26F	Lees	9/50	10/55
26F	Belle Vue	10/55	4/56
26F	Patricroft	2/58	9/63
26G	Belle Vue	9/50	10/55
27A	Bank Hall	9/50	9/63
27B	Aintree	9/50	9/63
27C	Southport	9/50	9/63
27D	Wigan Central L&Y		
		9/50	9/63
27E	Walton	9/50	9/63
27F	Brunswick	4/58	9/61
28A	Blackpool	9/50	4/52
28B	Fleetwood	9/50	4/52
30A	Stratford	8/50	9/62
30B	Hertford East	8/50	11/60
30C	Bishops Stortford	8/50	11/60
30D	Southend Victoria	8/50	2/59
30E	Colchester	8/50	11/59

Code	Name	From	To
30F	Parkeston Quay	8/50	1/61
31A	Cambridge	8/50	6/62
31B	March	8/50	12/63
31C	Kings Lynn	8/50	7/62
31D	South Lynn	8/50	3/59
31E	Bury St Edmunds	8/50	1/59
31F	Peterboro Spital Bdge	4/58	1/60
32A	Norwich	8/50	4/62
32B	Ipswich	8/50	5/68
32C	Lowestoft	8/50	7/62
32D	Yarmouth South Town	8/50	7/62
32E	Yarmouth Vauxhall	8/50	1/59
32F	Yarmouth Beach	8/50	3/59
32G	Melton Constable	8/50	3/59
33A	Plaistow	8/50	10/59
33B	Tilbury	8/50	9/62
33C	Shoeburyness	8/50	6/62
34A	Kings Cross	8/50	6/63
34B	Hornsey	8/50	7/61
34C	Hatfield	8/50	1/61
34D	Hitchin	8/50	
34E	Neasden	8/50	2/58
34E	Peterboro N. England	4/58	1/65
34F	Grantham	4/58	9/63
35A	Peterboro N. England	8/50	4/58
35B	Grantham	8/50	4/58
35C	Peterboro Spital Bdg	8/50	4/58
36A	Doncaster	8/50	4/66
36B	Mexborough	8/50	4/58
36C	Frodingham	8/50	2/66
36D	Barnsley	8/50	4/58
36E	Retford	8/50	6/65
37A	Ardsley	8/50	9/56
37B	Copley Hill	8/50	9/56
37C	Hammerton Street	8/50	9/56
38A	Colwick	8/50	4/58
38B	Annesley	8/50	2/58
38C	Leicester GC	8/50	2/58
38D	Staveley GC	8/50	4/58
38E	Woodford Halse	8/50	2/58

Code	Name	From	To
39A	Gorton	8/50	2/58
39B	Sheffield Darnall	8/50	12/55
40A	Lincoln	8/50	1/64
40B	Immingham	8/50	2/66
40C	Louth	8/50	12/56
40D	Tuxford	8/50	4/58
40E	Langwith Junction	8/50	4/58
40E	Colwick	4/58	1/66
40F	Boston	8/50	1/64
41A	Sheffield Darnall	12/55	4/64
41B	Sheffield Grimesthorpe	2/58	9/61
41B	Sheffield Darnall	4/64	10/65
41C	Sheffield Millhouses	2/58	12/61
41D	Canklow	2/58	6/65
41E	Staveley Barrow Hill	2/58	10/65
41F	Mexborough	4/58	2/64
41G	Barnsley	4/58	1/60
41H	Staveley GC	4/58	6/65
41J	Langwith Junction	4/58	12/66
41K	Tuxford	4/58	2/59
50A	York	8/50	6/67
50B	Neville Hill	8/50	1/60
50B	Hull Dairycoates	1/60	6/67
50C	Selby	8/50	9/59
50C	Hull Botanic Gardens	1/60	11/67
50D	Starbeck	8/50	9/59
50D	Goole	1/60	6/67
50E	Scarborough	8/50	4/63
50F	Malton	8/50	4/63
50G	Whitby	8/50	4/59
51A	Darlington	8/50	3/66
51B	Newport NER	8/50	6/58
51C	West Hartlepool	8/50	9/67
51D	Middlesborough	8/50	6/58
51E	Stockton	8/50	6/59
51F	West Auckland	8/50	2/64
51G	Haverton Hill	8/50	6/59
51H	Kirkby Stephen	8/50	2/58
51J	Northallerton	8/50	3/63
51K	Saltburn	8/50	1/58
51L	Thornaby	6/58	11/64

Code	Name	From	To
52A	Gateshead	8/50	10/65
52B	Heaton	8/50	6/63
52C	Blaydon	8/50	6/63
52D	Tweedmouth	8/50	6/66
52E	Percy Main	8/50	2/65
52F	Blyth	8/50	9/67
52G	Sunderland	10/58	9/67
52H	Tyne Dock	10/58	9/67
52J	Borough Gardens	10/58	6/59
52K	Consett	10/58	5/65
53A	Hull Dairycoates	8/50	1/60
53B	Hull Botanic Gardens		
		8/50	1/60
53C	Hull Springhead	8/50	11/58
53C	Alexander Dock	11/58	1/60
53D	Bridlington	8/50	6/58
53E	Cudworth	8/50	7/51
53E	Goole	9/56	1/60
54A	Sunderland	8/50	10/58
54B	Tyne Dock	8/50	10/58
54C	Borough Gardens	8/50	10/58
54D	Consett	8/50	10/58
55A	Holbeck	9/56	12/67
55B	Stourton	9/56	1/67
55C	Farnley Junction	9/56	11/66
55D	Royston Yorks	9/56	11/67
55E	Normanton	9/56	9/67
55F	Manningham	9/56	4/67
55G	Huddersfield	9/56	1/67
55H	Neville Hill	1/60	6/66
56A	Wakefield	9/56	6/67
56B	Ardsley	9/56	10/65
56C	Copley Hill	9/56	9/64
56D	Mirfield	9/56	4/67
56E	Sowerby Bridge	9/56	1/64
56F	Low Moor	9/56	10/67
56G	Hammerton Street		
		9/56	3/68
60A	Inverness	8/50	12/62
60B	Aviemore	8/50	7/62
60C	Helmsdale	8/50	12/62
60D	Wick	8/50	8/62
60E	Forres	8/50	1/64
61A	Kittybrewster	8/50	6/61
61B	Aberdeen Ferryhill		
		8/50	3/67
61C	Keith	8/50	6/61

Code	Name	From	To
62A	Thornton	8/50	6/67
62B	Dundee	8/50	5/67
62C	Dunfermline	8/50	6/67
63A	Perth	8/50	5/67
63B	Stirling	8/50	6/60
63B	Fort William	6/60	5/63
63C	Forfar	8/50	11/59
63C	Oban	11/59	5/63
63D	Fort William	8/50	5/55
63D	Oban	5/55	11/59
63E	Oban	8/50	5/55
64A	St Margarets	8/50	4/6
64B	Haymarket	8/50	9/63
64C	Dalry Road	8/50	10/65
64D	Carstairs	8/50	6/60
64E	Polmont	8/50	6/60
64F	Bathgate	8/50	12/66
64G	Hawick	8/50	1/66
64H	Leith Central	12/59	11/63
65A	Eastfield	8/50	11/66
65B	St Rollox	8/50	11/66
65C	Parkhead	8/50	10/65
65D	Dawsholme	8/50	10/64
65E	Kipps	8/50	12/62
65F	Grangemouth	8/50	11/65
65G	Yoker	8/50	1/64
65H	Helensburgh	8/50	11/60
65I	Balloch	8/50	?/63
65J	Fort William	5/55	6/60
65J	Stirling	6/60	12/66
65K	Polmont	6/60	5/64
66A	Polmadie	8/50	5/67
66B	Motherwell	8/50	5/67
66C	Hamilton	8/50	12/62
66D	Greenock	8/50	12/66
66E	Carstairs	6/60	2/67
66F	Beattock	9/62	5/67
67A	Corkerhill	8/50	5/67
67B	Hurlford	8/50	12/66
67C	Ayr	8/50	12/66
67D	Ardrossan	8/50	2/65
67E	Dumfries	9/62	8/66
67F	Stranraer	9/62	11/66
68A	Carlisle Kingmoor	8/50	2/58
68B	Dumfries	8/50	9/62
68C	Stranraer	8/50	9/62
68D	Beattock	8/50	9/62

Code	Name	From	To
68E	Carlisle Canal	10/51	2/58
70A	Nine Elms	8/50	7/67
70B	Feltham	8/50	10/66
70C	Guildford	8/50	7/67
70D	Basingstoke	8/50	3/63
70D	Eastleigh	9/63	7/67
70E	Reading SR	8/50	12/62
70E	Salisbury	12/62	7/67
70F	Fratton	10/54	11/59
70F	Bournemouth	9/63	7/67
70G	Newport IoW	10/54	11/57
70G	Weymouth	9/63	3/67
70H	Ryde	10/54	3/67
70I	Southampton Docks	9/63	1/66
71A	Eastleigh	8/50	9/63
71B	Bournemouth	8/50	9/63
71C	Dorchester	8/50	11/56
71D	Fratton	8/50	10/54
71E	Newport IoW	8/50	10/54
71F	Ryde	8/50	10/54
71G	Bath Green Park	8/50	2/58
71G	Weymouth	2/58	9/63
71H	Templecombe	8/50	2/58
71H	Yeovil GW	2/58	1/59
71I	Southampton Docks	8/50	9/63
71J	Highbridge	?/5?	2/58
72A	Exmouth Junction	8/50	9/63
72B	Salisbury	8/50	12/62
72C	Yeovil SR	8/50	9/63
72D	Plymouth Friary	8/50	2/58
72E	Barnstaple	8/50	9/63
72F	Wadebridge	8/50	9/63
73A	Stewarts Lane	8/50	6/62
73B	Bricklayers Arms	8/50	6/62
73C	Hither Green	8/50	10/61
73D	Gillingham	8/50	6/59
73D	St Leonards	7/63	10/67
73E	Faversham	8/50	6/59
73F	Ashford	10/58	6/62
73G	Ramsgate	10/58	6/59
73H	Dover	10/58	10/61
73J	Tonbridge	10/58	6/62
74A	Ashford	8/50	10/58
74B	Ramsgate	8/50	10/58

Code	Name	From	To
74C	Dover	8/50	10/58
74D	Tonbridge	8/50	10/58
74E	St Leonards	8/50	6/58
75A	Brighton	8/50	6/64
75B	Redhill	8/50	6/65
75C	Norwood Junction	8/50	1/64
75D	Horsham	8/50	7/59
75D	Stewarts Lane	6/62	9/63
75E	Three Bridges	8/50	1/64
75F	Tunbridge Wells West	8/50	9/63
75G	Eastbourne	8/50	10/52
81A	Old Oak Common	8/50	3/65
81B	Slough	8/50	5/64
81C	Southall	8/50	8/65
81D	Reading GW	8/50	1/65
81E	Didcot	8/50	7/65
81F	Oxford	8/50	12/65
82A	Bristol Bath Road	8/50	9/60
82B	Bristol St Phillips Marsh	8/50	5/64
82C	Swindon	8/50	10/64
82D	Westbury	8/50	10/63
82E	Yeovil GW	8/50	2/58
82E	Bristol Barrow Road	2/58	11/65
82F	Weymouth	8/50	2/58
82F	Bath Green Park	2/58	3/66
82G	Templecombe	2/58	10/63
83A	Newton Abbot	8/50	6/62
83B	Taunton	8/50	10/64
83C	Exeter St Davids	8/50	10/63
83C	Westbury	10/63	8/65
83D	Laira	8/50	9/63
83D	Exmouth Junction	9/63	6/65
83E	St Blazey	8/50	4/62
83E	Yeovil SR	9/63	7/65
83F	Truro	8/50	9/63
83F	Barnstaple	9/63	9/64
83G	Penzance	8/50	9/62
83G	Templecombe	10/63	3/66
83H	Plymouth Friary	2/58	5/63
84A	Wolverhampton Stafford Road	8/50	9/63
84A	Laira	9/63	5/64

Code	Name	From	To		Code	Name	From	To
84B	Oxley	8/50	9/63		87J	Goodwick	8/50	9/63
84C	Banbury	8/50	9/63		87K	Swansea Victoria	8/50	9/59
84C	Truro	9/63	10/65		88A	Cardiff Cathays	8/50	12/57
84D	Leamington	8/50	9/63		88A	Cardiff Radyr	12/57	1/61
84E	Tyseley	8/50	9/63		88A	Cardiff Canton	1/61	9/63
84E	Wadebridge	9/63	10/64		88A	Cardiff East Dock	9/63	7/65
84F	Stourbridge	8/50	9/63		88B	Cardiff East Dock	8/50	1/61
84G	Shrewsbury	8/50	1/61		88B	Cardiff Radyr	1/61	3/62
84G	Kidderminster	1/61	9/63		88C	Barry	8/50	10/64
84H	Wellington	8/50	9/63		88D	Merthyr	8/50	10/64
84J	Croes Newydd	8/50	1/61		88D	Rhymney	11/64	4/65
84K	Chester GW	8/50	2/58		88E	Abercynon	8/50	10/64
84K	Wrexham LNW	2/58	1/60		88F	Treherbert	8/50	2/65
85A	Worcester	8/50	12/65		88G	Llantrisant	1/61	10/64
85B	Gloucester GW	8/50	12/65		88H	Tondu	1/61	4/64
85C	Hereford	8/50	1/61		88J	Aberdare	1/61	3/65
85C	Gloucester Barnwood				88K	Brecon	1/61	12/62
		1/61	4/64		88L	Cardiff East Dock	1/61	9/63
85D	Kidderminster	8/50	1/61		88M	Cardiff Cathays	3/62	11/64
85D	Bromsgrove	1/61	9/64		89A	Oswestry	8/50	1/61
85E	Gloucester Barnwood				89A	Shrewsbury	1/61	9/63
		2/58	1/61		89B	Brecon	8/50	11/59
85F	Bromsgrove	2/58	1/61		89B	Croes Newydd	1/61	9/63
86A	Ebbw Junction	8/50	9/63		89C	Machynlleth	8/50	9/63
86B	Newport Pill	8/50	6/63		89D	Oswestry	1/61	9/63
86B	Ebbw Junction	9/63	10/65					
86C	Cardiff Canton	8/50	1/61					
86C	Hereford	1/61	10/64					
86D	Llantrisant	8/50	1/61					
86E	Severn Tunnel Jct							
		8/50	11/65					
86F	Tondu	8/50	1/61					
86F	Aberbeeg	1/61	12/64					
86G	Pontypool Road	8/50	5/65					
86H	Aberbeeg	8/50	1/61					
86J	Aberdare	8/50	1/61					
86K	Abergavenny	8/50	?/58					
87A	Neath	8/50	7/65					
87B	Duffryn Yard	8/50	3/64					
87C	Danycraig	8/50	3/64					
87D	Swansea East Dock							
		8/50	7/64					
87E	Landore	8/50	6/61					
87F	Llanelly	8/50	10/65					
87G	Carmarthen	8/50	4/64					
87H	Neyland	8/50	9/63					
87H	Whitland	10/63	1/66					